Global Justice and Transnational Politics

Studies in Contemporary German Social Thought (partial listing)
Thomas McCarthy, general editor

Global Justice and Transnational Politics

Essays on the Moral and Political Challenges
of Globalization

edited by Pablo De Greiff and Ciaran Cronin

The MIT Press
Cambridge, Massachusetts
London, England

#47297695

This book was set in New Baskerville by SNP Best-set Typesetter Limited and printed and bound in the United States of America.

Library of Congress Cataloging-in-Publication Data

Global justice and transnational politics : essays on the moral and political challenges of globalization / edited by Pablo De Greiff and Ciaran Cronin.
   p.   cm.—(Studies in contemporary German social thought)
   Includes bibliographical references and index.
   ISBN 0-262-04205-3 (hc. : alk. paper)—ISBN 0-262-54133-5 (pbk. : alk. paper)
   1. Political science—Philosophy. 2. Justice. 3. World politics. 4. Globalization.
I. De Greiff, Pablo. II. Cronin, Ciaran. III. Series.
JA71 .G58   2002
172'.4—dc21   2001045270

Contents

Introduction: Normative Responses to Current Challenges of Global Governance

Ciaran Cronin and Pablo De Greiff

1 The Challenge of Globalization and the Task of Normative Theory

The essays in this volume offer a variety of responses to a crisis in global governance reflected in the failure of existing international institutions to deal in a timely manner with human rights violations and to address the economic, environmental, health, and security challenges posed by accelerating globalization. The essays address normative rather than empirical aspects of the crisis, though these dimensions cannot be rigorously separated. They are less concerned with how developmental processes that are threatening to run out of control can be stabilized than with promoting recognition of the fact that the current global order is also a political order, and that those who are in a position to influence its design and operation have a responsibility to ensure that it satisfies basic requirements of justice. They challenge the traditional view that the international order is a normatively neutral domain whose rules lie beyond the competence of individuals, nations, or international actors to alter—a view supported by the "realist" model of international relations as a struggle for power, which tends to encourage an abdication of responsible politics at the international level. All of the contributors to this volume agree that the citizens of the developed countries and their governments share some degree of moral responsibility for the misery, insecurity, and injustice to which a large proportion of the world's population is currently exposed, and that this responsibility is far from being discharged in the global order as it is presently constituted.

Viewed from a normative standpoint, globalization is an ambiguous phenomenon whose implications for transnational governance point in different directions.[1] Even economic globalization, which has been the focus of much normative criticism for aggravating problems of global inequality, arguably has the potential to stimulate economic development and political stability in poorer countries, provided that investment policies are subject to appropriate democratic political controls.[2] And other aspects of globalization may be creating favorable conditions for transnational political initiatives to address unequal development and the injustices associated with it. Most importantly, the increasing power and global reach of telecommunications and news-gathering networks mean that economic, environmental, health, and security crises as well as human rights violations can gain almost instantaneous international publicity and generate pressure on international actors to make appropriate responses, such as withdrawing support from repressive regimes. In the long run these developments may contribute to the emergence of a global civil society of nongovernmental organizations, transnational networks, movements, and the like, and a corresponding global public opinion that could generate pressure for transnational political initiatives to address structural inequalities in the global political order.[3]

The essays address in a variety of ways the issue of what normative resources we can draw on to clarify the nature and extent of our common responsibility concerning issues of global governance and to provide orientation for political initiatives intended to promote toward a more just global political order. Before examining the individual contributions, we must address a likely objection to the idea of seeking norms and values in Western traditions to provide orientation for global political initiatives. Might this project be doomed from the start by the provinciality of its outlook—by the fact that, regardless of what principles and orientations it might yield, they could not expect to meet with the agreement of cultural traditions that reject some core Western political values? The moral force of such an objection rests on the undeniable fact that a disproportionate share of the responsibility for the injustices of the current global political order must be laid at the door of the West. One form of this objection might be that an analysis of the global political order through the phenomenon of globalization already tacitly presupposes the dominance of Western values, in that globalization represents an intensification and universalization of processes of modernization emanating from the West that have led to the global spread of aggressive individualism and the exploitation and destruction of nature, to the detriment of the values, traditions, and conceptions of community of other cultures. This objection should alert us to the danger of ideological uses of the concept of globalization that equate capitalist development and the liberalization of trade with the promotion of political freedom and democracy, while ignoring the grossly unequal competitive advantages and negotiation power currently enjoyed by developed countries and multinational corporations.[4] However, such well-founded suspicions do not apply to the normative perspectives developed by the contributors to this volume, who fully acknowledge the injustices of the current global political order and ask how it might be subjected to forms of political regulation that could command legitimacy in the eyes of a wide global public. Moreover, global interconnection has already reached such a level that no country or people, however remote, can escape the pressure to modernize their social institutions and integrate them into global markets and networks, though it remains an open question whether modernization must be accompanied by increasing social atomism and the destruction of communal political traditions. Globalization has already advanced so far that opting out of modernization is not a realistic option and the pursuit of isolationist policies would effectively mean self-imposed exclusion from the process of politically shaping an increasingly pervasive global order. As Thomas Pogge succinctly puts the dilemma, there is only one global order, and the challenge is to develop principles and institutions for governing it that are capable of winning a broad international consensus.

A more radical version of the provinciality objection, by contrast, might question the tenability of moral and political universalism as

such. Advocates of cultural pluralism and postmodernist critics of
Western rationalism have in recent decades argued that claims concerning the universal validity of moral or political norms are expressions of cultural imperialism or masks for illegitimate forms of power.
Critiques of universalist models of reason gain considerable credibility from the fact that Western countries have committed gross
injustices against non-Western peoples in the name of allegedly universal ideals of reason and progress. Yet if we look at the history of
the idea of human rights in the West, we find that it can also be interpreted as one of an internal rational critique through which groups
previously denied the status of "human beings" have gradually won
emancipation from oppression.[5] Moreover, arguments against universalist moral ideas that appeal to the distinctive ethical conceptions
of other cultures can be turned against their proponents, for moral
universalism is by no means the exclusive preserve of the West. All
of the major world religions give expression to universalist moral
visions, and it can be argued, as does David Luban in his contribution, that analogues of certain fundamental values are to be found
in all human societies and cultures. A more plausible and hopeful
alternative to cultural relativism in an increasingly interconnected
world, therefore, would be a universalism that is sensitive to cultural
differences and seeks a basis of agreement in dialogue among cultures rather than in a priori philosophical prescriptions.

In contrasting ways, many of the essays in this volume can be read
as contributions to the articulation of such context-sensitive universalism. Luban, for example, argues that a distinction between
civilization and barbarism based on a conception of fundamental
human needs and the evil involved in their violation provides a basis
for moral argument in all cultures, while recognizing that the distinction can be drawn differently by different cultures and even in
the same culture over time. In a similar spirit, Martha Nussbaum
seeks a basis for meaningful cross-cultural comparisons of quality of
life in a list of basic human capabilities that are essential to living a
fulfilled human life and embody norms by which we can evaluate the
justice of different social and constitutional orders. Their shared
concern with standards of evaluation that can claim validity across
cultures addresses the problem of how, in the absence of such stan-

dards, it would even be possible to *perceive* problems of global injustice, let alone mobilize political initiatives to address them.

Advocates of strong, universalistic conceptions of human rights such as Jürgen Habermas and Thomas Pogge, by contrast, must confront criticisms of non-Western intellectuals to the effect that the interpretations of rights originating in the West are at odds with the values embodied in non-Western cultural traditions.[6] In response to such criticisms, Habermas offers a justification of human rights that he believes can counter criticisms of the provinciality of a political conception of human rights that gives priority to the autonomy of the individual. Pogge, by contrast, takes the concept of human rights that has become entrenched in existing international declarations and argues that a suitable institutional interpretation of this concept is both global in scope and broadly sharable across cultures. Thus while he defends a stronger universalistic conception of human rights than Habermas's, Pogge hopes to secure a broader basis for cross-cultural consensus around this conception by drawing on less controversial philosophical premises. An alternative approach is also possible, however, one that defends a weaker conception of human rights, which therefore might lead to less ambitious principles of international justice but that could nonetheless form the basis for a more just organization of the existing international political order. John Rawls has recently developed such a weak universalist approach, which forms the point of departure for the essays of Amartya Sen and Leif Wenar that open this volume.

2 Weak Universalism: John Rawls's "Law of Peoples"

In *A Theory of Justice*, John Rawls reinvigorated liberal political philosophy through a novel adaptation of the theory of the social contract.[7] Beginning with the question of what principles of justice should govern the "basic structure" or major social and political institutions of a liberal democratic society, Rawls argued that the appropriate principles are those that would be chosen by representatives of the citizens in a counterfactual choice situation, the "original position," in which the parties would be ignorant of the social position, whether relatively privileged or disadvantaged, of those they represent. By placing the parties behind a "veil of ignorance," the original position device ensures that the principles of justice chosen will be impartial between the basic interests of different groups within society, and hence that the resulting basic structure will not confer unfair advantages on members of one group over another. The resulting conception of justice, "justice as fairness," accords priority to a principle guaranteeing certain basic individual rights and liberties to all citizens equally and, once these have been secured, supports an egalitarian principle of distributive justice, which states that social and economic inequalities are (a) to be attached to positions and offices open to all on the basis of fair equality of opportunity and (b) to be to the greatest benefit of the least advantaged members of society.[8]

Though Rawls had little to say about international justice in *A Theory of Justice*,[9] advocates of a Rawlsian approach argued that its egalitarian conception of justice and contractualist methodology could also be applied at the global level to generate powerful redistributive principles governing relations between individuals, states, and international associations. Assuming that the world can be viewed as a system of social cooperation in which transnational economic relations and other international institutions influence the fates of individuals everywhere, it seemed natural to inquire into the principles of justice that should govern this global basic structure by imagining which principles the parties to a global original position would choose, though now as representatives of individual human beings everywhere.[10]

When Rawls finally published his views on international justice, however, he defended a much more restrictive and, to some at least, a disappointingly conservative approach.[11] In the intervening decades he had revised his theory of justice to give greater emphasis to the question of how a liberal polity might justify its basic constitutional principles to its citizens in view of the pluralism of religions and world-views that a liberal political culture inevitably fosters.[12] Although this did not entail substantial changes to his conception of justice, it did involve a shift to a more contextualist methodology and a consequent modesty concerning the scope of validity of the theory. Given the fact of pluralism, Rawls argued, a theory of justice cannot expect to meet with the agreement of all reasonable citizens if it draws on philosophical theories or religious belief systems that they do not share. Instead, a liberal theory that is committed to tolerating all reasonable comprehensive doctrines must be "freestanding" in drawing exclusively on principles and ideals implicit in the political culture of liberal democratic societies. The hope is that these may form the basis of an "overlapping consensus" on shared principles of justice in which the adherents of different reasonable philosophical and religious world-views affirm the same principles on the basis of their respective commitments and thereby foster a stable social and political order.

With his recent account of the "law of peoples," Rawls extends this approach to the international domain by asking what principles a liberal polity could reasonably propose to govern its relations with other peoples. In light of the even greater cultural and religious pluralism at the international level, he argues that a liberal theory must seek a basis of agreement in the widely recognized principles of traditional international law, such as those mandating respect for the freedom and independence of peoples, the honoring of treaties, and the restriction of war to cases of self-defense.[13] The parties to the second, global original position through which these and related principles can be justified are to be thought of as representatives of peoples, not of individual world citizens; for to insist on a cosmopolitan application of the original position argument would be to imply that only liberal democratic societies should be regarded as responsible members of the community of peoples, and this contradicts both liberal toleration and the well-established principles of international justice. A liberal approach must allow for the existence of *decent* though nonliberal peoples who respect the basic human rights of their members (though not their equal individual liberties), grant all social groups a consultative role in the political process, and do not seek to impose their religious views or social system on other peoples but are willing to coexist with them on peaceful terms.[14] The Law of Peoples, therefore, does not support a cosmopolitan regime operating on a global scale to redistribute wealth from wealthy to poorer nations in line with a global difference principle, but only a voluntary confederation of liberal and decent peoples that recognizes a duty to assist the inhabitants of societies burdened by unfavorable conditions to reach a sufficient level of economic development to enable them to establish liberal or decent social institutions. "Outlaw states" that refuse to accept the principles of a reasonable law of peoples may be opposed with force if they threaten the peace of liberal and decent peoples, and the latter also have a limited duty to intervene in the domestic affairs of outlaw states to prevent egregious violations of human rights.[15]

The law of peoples deserves close attention in the context of debates concerning potentially universal principles of justice, for one of its major motivations is to avoid ethnocentrically projecting the values of liberal democracies onto nations and peoples that cannot be reasonably expected to accept them. Since a shared liberal political culture does not exist at the international level, Rawls argues that a theory of international justice must instead build on established principles of international law that have demonstrated their ability to foster peaceful relations among liberal peoples, in the hope that they will also be acceptable to peaceful nonliberal peoples.[16] Rawls's approach also has the advantage that it does not require as radical a departure from the current global political system of nation-states as would cosmopolitan adaptations of his theory.

However, the theory as currently formulated leaves unanswered some fundamental questions concerning its scope and its adequacy as a response to the challenges posed by the existing global order. Perhaps most troubling is its failure to specify clearly which groups constitute peoples in the relevant sense. Rawls does not regard states as appropriate subjects of the Law of Peoples because the interests of states as they have been interpreted in traditional international law are inimical to peaceful international relations. One possible candidate for the role of peoples is *nations*, understood roughly as culturally and historically distinct groups who have an aspiration to political self-determination. But there are many more national groups who do or might come to aspire to political self-determination than there are states, and such aspirations have been a major source of political conflicts for more than two centuries. For the purposes of ideal theory Rawls appears to assume that peoples should be understood as groups that already have a state, but his discussion of nonideal theory—that is, the application of ideal principles under real conditions—provides no guidance concerning how we could get from the existing world of nationalist conflicts to one of peoples satisfied with international divisions of territory and sovereignty.[17]

In his essay "Justice Across Borders," Amartya Sen criticizes Rawls's exclusive focus on peoples and argues that a normative treatment of transnational justice must take account of a variety of commitments and obligations grounded in memberships in groups other than the peoples or nations. He shares Rawls's skepticism about the application of the contractualist approach to all human beings everywhere, regardless of their group memberships, on the grounds that, for the present at least, we lack the global political institutions that would be required to implement the fully universal principles such an approach would generate.[18] On the other hand, he also rejects the particularism of the law of peoples, which restricts its purview to relations between whole societies (whether these are conceived as peoples, nations, or states). For this is to privilege issues of justice that arise from relations between whole societies, while ignoring those that involve features of individuals' identities other than their national memberships or practical relations across borders that are not mediated by states. Commitments and obligations to other human beings across borders may be rooted in one's professional identity or membership in a professional group, in one's gender or commitment to gender-based issues, or simply in solidarity with the poor grounded in one's sense of shared identity as a human being. What is required, then, is a theory of *global* justice that takes account of the full scope of our multiple identities and the full range of interconnections across borders, and hence is more comprehensive than a theory of *international* justice.

Sen seems to allow that Rawlsian contractualism could be modified to take account of some of these additional dimensions of global justice, perhaps through a series of original position arguments in which the parties are imagined as representing groups of different scope. But he clearly thinks that the contractualist methodology runs up against definitive limits when it comes to policy questions that would have an impact on the composition of the population. If we imagine a policy issue that, if decided in one way, would mean that a large number of people would not exist who would exist if it were decided in another way, it is difficult to conceive how this group of people could coherently be represented in an original position construction. As Sen writes: "People who would not be born under some social arrangement cannot be seen to be evaluating that arrangement—a 'non-being' cannot assess a society from the position of never having existed" (p. 45). This limitation is arguably endemic to all contractarian approaches since they require "the congruence of the set of judges and the set of lives being judged" (p. 46). What is required instead is a form of impartial moral reasoning that is not subject to these kinds of perspectival anomalies, and Sen suggests that a suitable model can be found in Adam Smith's concept of an "impartial spectator." The impartial spectator can be imagined as weighing the interests of all individuals and groups that might be affected by a particular institution or policy. This model does not succumb to the paradox of varying populations, since it does not require the impartial spectators to put themselves in the actual position of groups that might not exist as a result of one of the policies or institutional orders being evaluated.

In "The Legitimacy of Peoples" Leif Wenar takes a more sympathetic view of the law of peoples, though he too thinks that it needs to be supplemented if it is to take account of some important dimensions of international justice. On Wenar's reading, Rawls's reasons for rejecting the cosmopolitan approach and opting for peoples as the appropriate subjects of a theory of international justice can be traced back to the recent focus of his work on questions of political legitimacy. Legitimacy is a weaker normative standard than justice: a social order is legitimate if the coercion exercised by its basic institutions is acceptable to its members on reasonable or responsible grounds. To count as legitimate a society must respect certain core human rights (though not necessarily the full complement of liberal basic rights), it must enforce the rule of law, and it must be responsive to citizen dissent. This conception of legitimacy has far-reaching implications if taken as a point of orientation for a theory of international justice, for it implies that outside agencies have no legitimate grounds for intervening in the internal affairs of any society that satisfies its requirements. And indeed Rawls's distaste for cosmopolitanism appears to be based on his conviction that cosmopolitan institutions are inconsistent with the right of societies that satisfy the requirements of legitimacy to realize their own conceptions of justice free from undue external interference.[19]

A more specific reason for Rawls's rejection of cosmopolitanism, however, Wenar argues, is that there is no shared normative framework within which an application of the social contract construction to individuals viewed as world citizens could be justified to all reasonable peoples. Just as, in the domestic case, political liberalism, as a freestanding political theory, must restrict itself to ideas latent in the political culture of liberal democratic societies, at the international level it must draw exclusively on the normative contents of global political culture to which all liberal and decent peoples can be assumed to give their assent. The contents of global political culture are to be found in the basic documents of international law, such as human rights declarations, and these have been overwhelmingly interpreted as applying to the relations between individuals and their governments. Thus, rather than representing individuals as free and equal citizens of a single global system of social cooperation, the parties to a global original position must be thought of as representing free and equal peoples. But why then does Rawls not support a global difference principle according to which economic inequalities between peoples should be regulated so as to benefit the least well-off among them? The reason for the asymmetry between the domestic and international cases, Wenar argues, is that there is an important difference between the interests of individuals and those of peoples as Rawls conceives them: whereas domestic citizens are assumed to want more income and wealth as necessary means to pursuing their visions of the good life, peoples as such do not have a vision of the good life and should not be assumed to have an interest in increasing their level of economic well-being above the minimum required to support just basic institutions.[20]

Although Wenar accepts the seriousness of Rawls's reasons for restricting the scope of his theory, like Sen he thinks that there are important aspects of transnational justice that the law of peoples fails to address. In particular, its focus on relations between peoples blinds it to the economic interests of individuals. But there are many ways in which the economic interests of individuals are affected by the international economic order that principles governing trade between peoples do not address. In reality a global basic structure exists comprised of economic institutions whose operation influences the well-being of individuals everywhere but that is excluded from the purview of Rawls's theory by its focus on relations between peoples. For this reason Wenar proposes that the law of peoples be supplemented by a corporatist application of the original position argument to global economic relations in which the parties would be thought of as representative of producers, consumers, and owners. In this way principles of justice could be grounded that would regulate the international economic order while respecting the methodological constraints placed on the contractualist approach by its orientation to problems of legitimacy. Thus Wenar's and Sen's proposals can be seen as contrasting attempts to enrich Rawls's weak universalist approach to questions of international justice by taking account of plural group memberships.

3 Strong Universalism and Transnational Commitments

One of the problems posed by the weakness of existing global governance institutions concerns the source and nature of transnational commitments in an increasingly interconnected world. The essays in the second part of this volume address the question of normative sources and possible types of cross-border commitments from different theoretical perspectives. We speak of "transnational commitments" rather than "cosmopolitan obligations" because the latter expression, while increasingly common, begs some crucial questions. As the essays make clear, there are normative commitments that cut across national borders but do not necessarily amount to obligations; and some of these commitments are not necessarily cosmopolitan despite their transnational character.

In the first essay in this part, David Luban addresses the fraught question of the possible moral basis for a commitment to intervene militarily in defense of human rights; the two following essays discuss the normative grounds of a transnational distributive commitment

(Nussbaum and Pogge); and in the final essay Habermas explores the basis of a commitment to transnational democracy. The authors find the normative source of the various commitments they defend in different places. Two appeal to explicitly moral conceptions, although quite different ones: while Nussbaum anchors transnational commitments in "a thick and vague concept of the good" that is intended to give flesh to the idea of our common humanity, Luban anchors them in a distinction between civilization and barbarism. Pogge and Habermas look to the concept of human rights to ground commitments to transnational justice, though they disagree as to whether rights should be conceived primarily in moral or in legal terms. The diversity and ambition of the arguments developed in these essays provide a good illustration of the kinds of orientation that normative theory can provide when faced with the political challenges posed by the current global order.

Luban approaches the task of clarifying the normative source of a transnational commitment to humanitarian intervention by appealing to the moral distinction between civilization and barbarism. The notion of human rights by itself does not ground a moral obligation to intervene abroad but at most a negative duty not to violate the rights of others. What is required, according to Luban, is a substantive moral argument that is not best framed in terms of the vocabulary of rights, where this leads to an overly hasty focus on obligations (taking one's orientation from the correlativity of rights and duties). This focus deflects attention from the bearers of rights to the subjects of obligations, thereby obscuring the fact "that others are obligated not to violate us because of something about *us*—because we are valuable, and that value demands respect" (p. 95). In addition to the obligation not to violate rights, the commitment to the substantive principle that every human being has intrinsic worth gives us moral reasons for helping other people in hard times, for trying to forestall or impede violations of human rights, and for supporting institutions that promote human rights.

This argument has the advantage that it avoids making humanitarian interventions morally *required*. The question is whether it offers any guidance concerning when and for what specific reasons interventions would be justified. Ultimately Luban offers, in his own words, "a very old-fashioned answer to the question 'which human rights are worth going to war over?' The answer is: those human rights the violation of which is uncivilized, so that standing idly by while they are violated calls into question our very commitment to civilization over barbarism" (p. 101). But if the distinction between civilization and barbarism is old-fashioned, Luban's understanding of it is not. Although he takes the distinction to be "a kind of anthropological primitive" (p. 102), he freely acknowledges that different cultures draw the line in different places and that the issue of where the line should be drawn is not a matter of philosophical principle. Yet despite these cultural differences over which of the "great evils"[21] it is "civilized" to impose on whom, the recognition that they are evils, and the commitment to the ideal of human worth that stands centrally behind the notion of civilization, provide moral reasons, however contingent and historically variable, for intervening to protect victims and frustrate perpetrators. This commitment to civilization is doubly contingent—it is not forced upon us by reason alone, and its meaning is historically and contextually open—and yet Luban finds in it the only—perhaps brittle, but nevertheless sufficient—ground for transnational commitments.[22]

Nussbaum's work also makes an important contribution to discussions of transnational commitments, though she is more concerned with issues of international development and distribution. Nussbaum's reflections focus on a complementary notion to that of rights, namely, the concept of capabilities, and in her essay she explicitly ties her account of capabilities to an interest in distributive justice that is supposed to cut across national borders.[23] Initially, it makes sense to think about the notion of capabilities as part of an answer to questions concerning the quality of life or of living standards, and hence as an independent notion whose relationship to rights or to a broader theory of justice remains to be specified. The guiding idea behind this approach is the attempt to measure what people can actually do or be, rather than simply their subjective level of satisfaction or the resources they possess, as a basis for transnational assessments of quality of life.

The merits of this approach become apparent when it is contrasted with alternative measures of quality of life, such as gross national product (GNP) per capita, utility, or (following Rawls) access to a predefined list of "basic goods." These three measures share a common difficulty, namely, how to deal with severe inequalities. GNP per capita simply has nothing to say about distributive issues. Utilitarians tend to focus on aggregate utility, which allows for the possibility of highly unequal distributions. Furthermore, because it understands utility in terms of satisfaction and takes preferences as given, utilitarianism falls foul of the well-established phenomenon of adaptive preferences—the tendency of agents to adjust their expectations in light of what they consider feasible. If utility means nothing more than the satisfaction of preferences that may have been lowered in the face of adversity, this may serve to entrench the very inequalities that lead agents to lower their expectations in the first place. Finally, while Nussbaum is sympathetic to Rawls's approach,[24] she shares Sen's reservation that Rawls's list of basic goods is loaded with resources (or of things thought of as resources), whereas individuals vary in their need for resources and in their ability to convert them into improvements in their quality of life. The appropriate index of quality of life, Nussbaum argues, is not primarily command over resources (no matter of which kind or how evenly distributed) or level of satisfaction, but what individuals are capable of doing or becoming. Hence her focus on capabilities.

The argument up to this point merely identifies the appropriate objects of measurement if one wants to talk sensibly about the quality of life. If the approach is to be of value for discussions concerning distribution and rights, the next step must be to determine some capabilities of central importance to human life. Nussbaum defends "a thick and vague conception of the good" containing those capabilities that can be convincingly held to be of central importance in any human life, whatever else the person pursues or chooses. Rather than being the result of philosophical reflection on what makes life good after the fashion of Rawls's "thin theory of the good," the list is an attempt to summarize the findings of a broad and ongoing cross-cultural inquiry (this is the sense in which it is a "thick" conception of the good); therefore it does not claim to be exhaustive, and it is open to revision. In one sense the list calls for revisions: it is self-consciously formulated at a high level of generality to allow for the fact that different cultures will specify its elements differently to reflect local beliefs and circumstances (and in this sense it is part of a "vague" conception of the good).

The articulation of the list of central capabilities still makes this approach largely, though no longer completely, independent of a theory of justice or of rights. First, to the extent that it includes elements of central importance to any human life, it provides reasons for individuals to care about the acquisition of these goods; more importantly, it provides a criterion for assessing the legitimacy of an institutional order, namely the degree to which it enables members to achieve the relevant goods.[25] Second, the list has been revised over time to include rights; for instance, Nussbaum argues that the capability to use one's practical reason can only be fully secured in a context where "legal guarantees of freedom of expression . . . and freedom of religious exercise" are operative.[26] One task of Nussbaum's paper is, accordingly, to clarify the relationship between capabilities and rights. She does not propose the notion of capability as a substitute for that of rights, for she acknowledges that rights talk plays important roles in public discourse. Nevertheless, Nussbaum thinks that analyzing rights in terms of capabilities allows us to see more perspicuously what is involved in *securing* a right rather than merely declaring it. Equal rights are not enjoyed simply in virtue of setting such equality on paper; only by asking whether people are in fact equally capable of doing certain things will we become aware of complexities to which the discourse of rights does not, by itself, call attention. The question may even provide a rationale for differential investments for the sake of guaranteeing equal rights.

Although Pogge shares Nussbaum's concern with issues of distributive justice across borders, he takes his orientation more directly from a universalistic conception of human rights.[27] The reason for this focus is his view, eloquently documented in his essay, that most underfulfillment of human rights is more or less directly connected to poverty. Pogge investigates the concept of human rights with the aim of clarifying the nature of our transnational distributive obligations, though in contrast to much recent work on cosmopolitanism, he understands rights in the first instance in moral rather than political terms.[28]

In his essay Pogge defends his preferred conception of rights by way of a dialectical survey of the weaknesses of three widely supported alternatives. The first, U_1, defended by Luban among others, conceives human rights as moral rights that every human being has against every other human agent. Despite its popularity, this conception is vulnerable to a number of challenges. We usually distinguish between violations of rights in general and violations of *human* rights, for the latter have an official, or at least an institutional, dimension; that is, in most international documents, human rights make demands on institutions rather than on individuals, and these same documents limit the scope of most rights territorially and thereby impose few duties upon foreigners. A second conception, U_2, addresses these problems by narrowing the understanding of human rights to moral rights that human beings have against governments in particular. But while U_1 was too prodigal, U_2 is too parsimonious, for it unburdens private individuals of any concern for, or commitment to, rights.

A third understanding of human rights, U_3, according to which human rights are basic or constitutional rights that every state ought to enshrine in its legal system and give effect through appropriate institutions and policies, overcomes this problem. To say that there is a human right to X is to say that every state ought to enshrine a right to X in its constitution or comparable basic legal documents. This moral right to effective legal rights to X imposes on all citizens of a state a moral duty to help ensure that an effectively enforced and suitably broad right to X exists within the state, and it imposes on each government and its officials a duty to ensure that the right to X is enforced. But U_3 is too demanding in insisting on the juridification of all rights, for, according to Pogge, what matters most in the idea of human rights is *secure access* to the relevant goods, and legal rights are just one means of guaranteeing such access. And yet U_3 is not demanding enough, first, in that even a fully juridified right may fail to guarantee secure access to the objects of human rights and, second, in unburdening agents of obligations for human rights fulfillment abroad, since our task as citizens or government officials is to ensure that human rights are juridified and observed within our own society.

In contrast with the foregoing conceptions, Pogge defends an understanding of human rights, U_4, according to which human rights are moral claims on any coercively imposed institutional order. Given his conviction that what matters most in talking about rights is secure access to certain goods, to postulate a human right to X is, according to U_4, to declare that every society and comparable social system ought to be so organized that all its members enjoy secure access to X as far as possible. One notable feature of this understanding of rights is that it can provide substantive guidance concerning transnational commitments without undermining the distinction between positive and negative rights.[29]

For Pogge, when the institutional order of a society fails to realize human rights, then those of its members who significantly collaborate in the imposition of this order are violating a negative duty of justice. This negative duty is understood as a duty not to contribute to the coercive imposition of any institutional order that avoidably fails to realize human rights, unless one also compensates for doing so by working toward appropriate institutional reforms or toward shielding the victims of injustice from the harm one helps produce. According to U_4, therefore, a person's human rights are not only moral claims *on* any institutional order imposed upon that person, but also moral claims *against* those—especially, the more influential and privileged—who collaborate in its imposition. Since human rights-based responsibilities arise from collaboration in the coercive imposition of any institutional order in which some persons avoidably lack secure access to the objects of their human rights, it follows that there are transnational obligations that fall primarily on the more influential and privileged agents (individual and collective) who collaborate in the imposition of the current international order since it satisfies this condition.

Habermas also grounds transnational commitments in a conception of human rights, but, in contrast with Pogge, he conceives of these commitments in *political* rather than moral terms (along the lines of Pogge's U_3). One reason for taking this approach is to forestall objections that question the universality of moral understandings of human rights. According to Habermas, while rights can be justified by appealing to moral reasons, human rights are not moral but legal in character; and as actionable claims, rights are conceptually tailored to their implementation in legal orders.[30] Although this conception of rights does not specify which rights people should have, this question can be answered from a discourse-theoretic perspective as part of a response to the prior, more general, question of which rights people must grant one another if they want to regulate their life in common legitimately by means of positive law.[31] And since, as Habermas argues, complex societies have no substitute for law as a mechanism for coordinating social relationships—not just within but, in an increasingly interconnected world, also across their borders—the rights that follow from this analysis can be shown to be universal in scope.

This approach to the notion of rights is just one of the distinctive features of Habermas's contribution to the discussion of transnational commitments. Another is the emphasis he places on transnational democracy. Consistent with the focus of his project on discursive procedures, Habermas argues that in answering the question of which rights persons must grant one another if they want to regulate their life in common legitimately by means of positive law, nothing must be presupposed other than a discursive principle of normative validity and the notion of law involved in the formulation of the question itself.[32] Each of these elements is pregnant with consequences. Of particular importance in the present context is that the form of law itself presupposes some rights. Laws are addressed to individuals as legal subjects, and the status of legal subject is constituted, in turn, through the attribution of certain rights. As Habermas puts it, "there is no law without the private autonomy of legal persons in general." This private autonomy is secured by means of rights that ensure the greatest possible measure of equal individual liberty, rights that secure membership in an association under the rule of law, and rights that guarantee legal protection.[33]

The legitimacy of law, however, is not guaranteed simply by securing the right to private autonomy or liberty rights. First, limiting rights to liberty rights fails to do justice to the self-understanding of citizens as the authors of their own laws; in the absence of political rights, no matter how liberal a regime of liberty rights might be, citizens would at best enjoy a paternalistically imposed set of rights.

Second, without the ability to participate in the political processes through which rights are interpreted, equal enjoyment of rights cannot be secured for all. Consequently, in addition to liberty rights, citizens must also be accorded political rights. But formal political rights are not sufficient of themselves for the exercise of popular sovereignty either. The correct way to think about the relationship between legal legitimacy and democracy, Habermas maintains, involves a realization that citizens participate in the political process as legal subjects, which presupposes the right to private autonomy. As he summarizes his position,

[t]he internal relation between democracy and the rule of law consists in this: on the one hand, citizens can make appropriate use of their public autonomy only if, on the basis of their equally protected private autonomy, they are sufficiently independent; on the other hand, they can realize equality in their enjoyment of private autonomy only if they make appropriate use of their political autonomy as citizens. (p. 202)

The broader aim of Habermas's approach is to establish that human rights and democracy presuppose one another. Although the theory is originally framed in terms of the rights that members of the same nation-state ought to grant one another, the hypothetical procedure of a mutual conferring of rights does not predetermine the scope of the political unit for which the answer is valid. Rather, it can be conceived as being performed at different levels of political organization beyond that of particular nation-states, where it would require the institutionalization of all the relevant rights across national borders. Any community, whether local, national, regional, or global, whose members want to regulate their interactions by means of legitimate positive law ought to institutionalize the same set of rights. Although the basic human rights are essentially the same in each case, the political institutions required for their implementation would have to reflect the different scope of the practical matters to be regulated and the different composition of the populations subject to the laws enacted. Thus Habermas's general theory of human rights provides a powerful normative rationale for a global democratic political order in which sovereignty, which in the modern state system resides more or less exclusively in the nation-state, would be divided among local, national, and regional regimes, with a global regime taking responsibility for the implementation of human rights at the transnational level.

4 Transnational Politics and National Identities

In the latter part of his essay "On Legitimation through Human Rights," Habermas turns from the political interpretation of human rights and how they can be institutionalized at different levels of political organization to criticisms that challenge their viability as a basis for a cosmopolitan political order. Specifically he addresses the concerns raised in recent debates in which Asian intellectuals have argued that liberal interpretations of human rights foster an individualistic social and political culture at odds with the priority accorded the community by indigenous Asian traditions, in particular those shaped by Confucianism.

Although he accepts that human rights principles that claim cross-cultural validity must not be implemented in ways that privilege the provincial outlook of any particular culture, he is unimpressed by the contrast between the community-based political ethos of Asian countries and the individualistic ethos of the West invoked in this debate. In his view, this contrast deflects attention away from the real predicament these countries face once they embrace economic modernization. Modern economies are structured around markets that empower individuals to make independent decisions within an increasingly globalized system of market relations. But decentralized decision-making structures require legal and political institutions that exact a high price on traditional forms of community, for modern legal systems necessarily equip individuals with rights that enable them to pursue their own conceptions of the good and to make choices governed by their own preferences free from collective moral scrutiny. Thus the priority of rights over duties to which the proponents of Asian values object is built into the logic of the legal institutions required by the modernized economies they nevertheless embrace. Something similar holds for the priority of individual rights over collective rights to development and culture. Freedom of speech, for example, cannot be legitimately restricted for the sake of economic development, as the leaders of some Asian governments have argued, since such collective goals as economic development have no normative justification unless they operate to the benefit of all members of society.[34]

Finally, from this perspective, critiques of the atomizing effects of an individualistic legal culture on communal forms of life cannot be sustained. It is true that a constitutional order that equips individuals with actionable legal rights tends to undermine forms of community based on inherited authority (for example, patriarchal authority); but far from presupposing an atomistic ontology that views the individual as existing prior to society, Habermas insists that basic rights must be understood as grounded in the intersubjective relations of recognition of a legal community. This implies a more abstract form of collective identity than those characteristic of traditional societies, but one that can nevertheless form the basis of substantive forms of community.

The debate over the possible forms of transnational political community is brought closer to home in Habermas's essay on "The European Nation-State and the Pressures of Globalization," in which he discusses the possibility of a democratic political order developing within the institutional framework of the European Union. Against the objection that democracy is impossible at the European level because a culturally unified European people does not exist, Habermas previously argued that a shared ethnocultural identity is no more a precondition of European democracy than ethnically homogeneous nations were a precondition of the emergence of democratic nation-states in early modern Europe.[35] Here he examines the process of European political integration from the perspective of the political challenges posed by the erosion of the prerogatives of the nation-state and the interstate order due to globalization. The political challenge posed by globalization derives from the fact that it is eroding the traditional functions of the nation-state, most important its role in securing social justice through welfare programs, and is thereby undermining the legitimacy of democratic decision-making within the nation-state; at the same time it is giving rise to global interdependencies in which there is an increasing mismatch between the set of agents who make economic decisions and those

who must live with their ecological, social, and cultural consequences. Faced with this challenge, Habermas advocates a domestication of global social and economic interdependencies by
transforming the current dysfunctional system of international relations into a world "domestic politics."

But while the call for the democratization of transnational social
and economic relations may represent a cogent normative response
to the postnational constellation, it is far from clear how this might
be translated into a practical political program. Rejecting both the
politics of globalization embraced by adherents of neoliberal economic theory—because the gains in individual freedom that it
promises would not counterbalance the drastic increase in social
inequalities and the decrease in democratic control it would entail—
and the protectionist and even isolationist politics of the opponents
of globalization—who frequently find themselves allied with reac-
tionary political movements that oppose cultural diversity, immigration, and modernization and whose politics fly in the face of the
legitimacy that international economic institutions can claim as
the products of negotiated agreements between governments[36]—
Habermas defends an "offensive" variant of the "third way" proposed
by the New Left. Where the defensive variant seeks a political accommodation with the globalized economic order by modifying national
social policy to empower citizens to cope with the demands of the
globalized economy, the offensive variant advocates the construction
of supranational political institutions with the power and legitimacy
to shape the environment in which global markets operate in accordance with democratic political imperatives.

Habermas's proposal for cosmopolitan democracy raises a number
of difficult questions. Perhaps the most urgent is how political
institutions operating outside the framework of the nation-state
could function in a genuinely democratic way. The requirement
that Habermas emphasizes is that transnational democratic regimes
would have to foster relations of solidarity across the national divides
that have traditionally defined the limits of citizens' primary political loyalties. If individuals are to participate in such regimes, they will
have to develop a sense of themselves as Europeans, and ultimately

as world citizens, and this new sensibility would have to take precedence over their national allegiances at least for certain purposes.

In "On Reconciling Cosmopolitan Unity and National Diversity," Thomas McCarthy addresses the issue of how cosmopolitanism could be reconciled with the legacy of nationalism, given that national diversity is likely to remain an important feature of any future global political order. The fact that identification with the nation played an important role in the consolidation of republican forms of government in the modern period accentuates both the importance and the difficulty of this question. National identification fostered the solidarity that was necessary for democratic institutions to gain a foothold in mass societies coming to terms with the upheavals of modernization; and nationality also appeared to provide a ready answer to the question of which groups have a right to establish independent political communities. At the same time, national sentiment often proved to be intolerant of cultural differences and to be easily manipulable by authoritarian political movements of different ideological stripes. The horrendous crimes of genocide and ethnic cleansing that have been committed in the name of nationalism serve as a reminder that forms of nationalism that tie the political community to communities of origin, however conceived, can be a source of instability and injustice in a culturally diverse and religiously pluralistic world. But, as McCarthy emphasizes, ethnonationalism does not constitute the whole of the nationalist heritage. It is now widely accepted that nations and national identities are political constructs and that nationalist traditions exist that take their orientation from constitutional principles rather than from a mythic common ancestry or shared historical memories. It is in the tradition of civic nationalism that McCarthy hopes to find a basis for mediation between the claims of the nation and those of cosmopolitan justice.

McCarthy looks to Kant for orientation in his project of reconciling cosmopolitanism and nationalism, which come as a surprise to those who think of Kant as an advocate of abstract reason who was insensitive to cultural diversity. In his later political writings, however, Kant developed a powerful, and in many ways prescient, theory of cosmopolitan justice that, McCarthy argues, was centrally concerned with accommodating diversity among peoples and cultures. Kant's theory of "right" or of justice in the external relations among human beings is the prototype of juridical theories of human rights that tie the legitimacy of the state to its securing equal individual rights through a positive legal order, and that affirm an essential interconnection between the problem of securing rights within states and that of securing rights at the levels of interstate relations and of relations between human beings everywhere. In his first published political essays, Kant argued that a republican form of constitution is necessary to achieve legitimacy and justice at the level of the state and that, in view of the ever-increasing interconnections between states, the rights of individuals would only be fully secured when states came together to form a world republic under an international rule of law.

Although Kant never abandoned the ideal of a cosmopolitan world republic in which individuals and states would be subject to a higher governmental authority, he gradually distanced himself from this ideal as impracticable and proposed instead the weaker model of a voluntary league of sovereign nations as an acceptable substitute. This retreat was motivated in part by his belief that the forcible subordination of all states and peoples to a single world government would destroy the distinctive identities of nations, in contravention of the right of nations that have already constituted themselves as states to preserve their distinct identities.

Although McCarthy argues that Kant's less ambitious model of a voluntary league still contains some strong provisions that are relevant to our current global predicament—in particular, the requirement that the constitutions of all states should be republican—he traces its deficiencies to the fact that Kant's model of republican government did not include equal political rights for all citizens and the fact that he understood nations in quasi-naturalistic terms as founded on racial, ethnic, and cultural commonalities. If Kantian cosmopolitanism is to remain a viable project, therefore, we must abandon Kant's essentialistic conception of the nation in favor of a conception of nations as the products of processes of political construction, thereby opening national identities to criticism in response to rights-based claims, such as the demand of cultural minorities that their distinctive identities be respected. In addition, Kant's republicanism must be given positive democratic content, so that his cosmopolitan ideal can be reconceptualized in terms of a transnational democratic political order.

In "Constitutional Patriotism and the Public Sphere: Interests, Identity, and Solidarity in the Integration of Europe" Craig Calhoun also addresses the problem of the social and cultural conditions of a transnational political order. Like Habermas and McCarthy, he holds that its capacity to generate legitimate decisions is contingent on its successfully institutionalizing democracy beyond the limits of the nation-state. But Calhoun shares McCarthy's concern that the bonds of solidarity across national borders presupposed by a transnational democratic political culture will also have to accommodate national cultural differences. And although he shares the intention informing the idea of "constitutional patriotism" as a form of shared political identification grounded in democratic constitutional principles, he thinks that Habermas's understanding of constitutional patriotism relies too heavily on a contrast with nationalism that tends to assimilate nationalism as such to ethnic nationalism. Calhoun wants to retrieve a positive moment of the tradition of nationalism, namely that it provides large populations with a powerful way of imagining political community across space and time.[37]

The lesson to be drawn from the history of the nation-state, Calhoun suggests, is that the viability of transnational political institutions depends on the emergence of a corresponding transnational "social imaginary," since social reality is shaped in part by how it is represented in the culture of the society in question and thereby comes to be collectively imagined. Considering the example of the European Union, Calhoun notes that European integration was historically imagined primarily in economic terms and that if the process of political integration is to develop in a democratic direction it will have to be based on a solidarity-generating European political imaginary.[38] Democratic states depend on a strong sense of "peoplehood"—stronger than that implied by Habermas's account of constitutional patriotism—for they are founded on the idea of government of *all* the people and their legitimacy is predicated on the promise of inclusion. A key issue for the project of transnational democracy then becomes that of identifying a social practice or space of practices in which solidarity-generating representations of political community can be produced. Drawing on Hannah Arendt's conception of the public as the space in which what is authentically human is created, Calhoun argues that the network of discourses of the public sphere should be seen as a potential source of democratic solidarity.

This is not to say, however, that social solidarity is, or even could be, wholly constituted through discourse. In addition to publics, Calhoun identifies three major sources of social cohesion in modern society: functional integration through anonymous social systems such as markets, unification through categorical identities such as class or nationality, and interconnection through networks of direct social relations. But it is preeminently in the discursive practices of the public sphere that society can act upon itself to transform *ascribed* identities into *achieved* identities and invest social relations with new meaning. Discursive practices facilitate the production of public representations through which individuals and groups can imagine new relations of community and solidarity, both within and across existing social boundaries. Drawing on his differentiated analysis of the public sphere, Calhoun argues that the prospects of democracy at the European level depend crucially on the constitution of a European-wide public sphere through which bonds of solidarity can be forged between the citizens of the different members states. He interprets the resurgence of chauvinistic nationalism as a response to the pressures of globalization in the absence of substantive political communication at the European level. At the same time the question of the legitimacy of the EU has been primarily discussed in terms of the concept of national sovereignty, that is, in terms of the erosion of the sovereign rights of national institutions by the institutions of the union. If nationalism is no longer identified with its ethnic forms, however, it ceases to represent a fundamental barrier to European political integration, since the national imaginary was from the beginning closely allied with the projects of republicanism and democracy.

5 Conclusion

The essays in this volume can be seen collectively as a response to the fact that normative reflection on transnational commitments has lagged behind the reality of transnational social and economic integration. This situation urgently requires redress, for although the key issue that must be addressed in developing proposals about the scope and design of global political institutions is ultimately the same as at the national level—namely, how can the exercise of power be subordinated to the imperatives of justice and political legitimacy?—this question is particularly urgent at a time when globalization is generating new power potentials and unexpected interdependencies.

Closing the gap between normative reflection and the reality of transnational integration will require overcoming familiar divisions of labor such as those between morality and politics and between political theory and sociology. In the absence of well-established institutions to promote justice across national borders, for the present, progress in this area is largely dependent on the persuasive force of moral reasons. Yet given the complexity of the problems of justice proliferating at the global level, this is a task that can ultimately be accomplished only with the aid of institutions that allocate responsibilities, coordinate actions, adjudicate conflicts, and enforce obligations.

In line with the increasing and welcome appeal to democratic criteria for assessing the legitimacy of public institutions, one of the uncompleted tasks of theories of transnational politics is the elaboration of accounts of transnational democracy. Indeed, given the increasing functional interdependencies between systems and networks, it may turn out that the relationship between national and transnational democracy is one of mutual interdependence. As defenders of cosmopolitan democracy are keen to point out, if democracy is understood to involve at the minimum self-governance, then unless democracy is institutionalized transnationally, cross-border forces that escape domestic democratic controls might effectively undermine a people's capacity to govern themselves. Conversely, the controversies over whether human rights as interpreted in certain international treaties and declarations are compatible with Asian or African values suggest that the question of legitimacy at the transnational level cannot be uncoupled from the legitimacy of social and political orders at the national level. For these controversies invite the question: who can claim to speak authoritatively about Asian or African values? Whether or not a leader or political party can legitimately speak for a whole people is ultimately a question of democracy, of whether the political institutions that invest their speech with authority are responsive to the interests of those they claim to represent. A world characterized by increasing interdependence, therefore, is one in which theorizing about politics and justice cannot be pursued exclusively in the traditional state-centric fashion. Rather, it calls for deliberation about the appropriate interpretation and institutional realization of democracy and justice at the transnational level.

Notes

1. We employ the term "globalization" to refer to a range of trends toward increasing interconnection in a number of different dimensions—including financial, production, and labor markets, telecommunications, information, and transportation networks, security systems, and culture and lifestyles—that result in unforeseen causal interdependencies between actions and events in distant parts of the globe. See Anthony Giddens, *The Consequences of Modernity* (Stanford, CA: Stanford University Press, 1990), 70–78, David Held, *Democracy and the Global Order* (Stanford: Stanford University Press, 1995), 20–21, 121–136, and, for an in-depth analysis, Ulrich Beck, *What is Globalization?* trans. Patrick Camiller (Cambridge: Polity Press, 2000).

2. Wholesale criticisms of the evils of globalization tend to overlook the fact that the governments and populations of underdeveloped countries have a clear and urgent interest in promoting economic development, provided that it does not give rise to one-sided dependencies and is consistent with basic principles of social justice.

3. See, for instance, Margaret E. Keck and Kathryn Sikkink, *Activists Beyond Borders: Advocacy Networks In International Politics* (Ithaca, NY: Cornell University Press, 1998). It is important, however, not to overestimate the scope of international civil society and its current potential for democratizing the international potential order. As Craig Calhoun argues in his contribution, both national and transnational civil society depend on news media that are vulnerable to subversion by commercial interests. In addition, there is the problem of the representativeness of groups that are all too willing to arrogate to themselves the right to speak for *all* of civil society.

4. For a critique of ideological misuses of the concept of globalization by neoliberals see Pierre Bourdieu, *Acts of Resistance*, trans. Richard Nice (Cambridge: Polity Press, 1998), 29–44.

5. As Jürgen Habermas argues in his first contribution to this volume. See also Jack Donnelly, "Human Rights and Asian Values: A Defense of 'Western' Universalism," in Joanne R. Bauer and Daniel A. Bell., eds., *The East Asian Challenge for Human Rights* (Cambridge: Cambridge University Press, 1999), 60–87.

6. It is a measure of the power of human rights discourse that such critics do not generally reject the concept of human rights as such but challenge Western interpretations of human rights, in particular, what they see as an excessive importance accorded the autonomy of the individual at the expense of the community. Indeed the recent debates about Asian values have if anything confirmed the transcultural appeal of the idea of human rights; see the essays in Bauer and Bell, eds., *The East Asian Challenge For Human Rights*.

7. See John Rawls, *A Theory of Justice*, rev. ed. (Cambridge, Mass.: Harvard University Press, [1971] 1999).

8. The latter provision is known as the "difference principle." See *Theory of Justice*, pp. 52ff.; for the more recent formulation followed here, see Rawls, *Political Liberalism* (New York: Columbia University Press, 1993) (expanded paperback ed., 1996), 6.

9. His brief treatment of how justice as fairness could be extended to the law of nations was restricted to issues in traditional just war theory; see *Theory of Justice*, §58, 331–335.

10. Two well-known examples of this general approach to a Rawlsian theory of cosmopolitan justice are Charles R. Beitz, *Political Theory and International Relations* (Princeton, NJ: Princeton University Press, [1979] 1999) and Thomas W. Pogge, *Realizing Rawls* (Ithaca, NY: Cornell University Press, 1989).

11. See Rawls, "The Law of Peoples," in Stephen Shute and Susan Hurley, eds., *On Human Rights: The Oxford Amnesty Lectures, 1993* (New York: Basic Books, 1993), and, much extended, *The Law of Peoples* (Cambridge, Mass.: Harvard University Press, 1999).

12. See Rawls, *Political Liberalism*. In his contribution to this volume Leif Wenar argues that *Political Liberalism* and the essays that led up to it represent a shift in Rawls's thought from a theory of justice to a theory of political legitimacy.

13. See *The Law of Peoples*, 37. In accordance with his policy of avoiding any controversial philosophical assumptions, Rawls does not attempt to justify these principles, for example by grounding them in principles of practical reason in a Kantian fashion, but simply lists them. Thus, in contrast with the domestic original position argument, the parties to the global original position do not weigh arguments for and against alternative principles of international justice but only consider alternative interpretations of the same principles.

14. Rawls refers to such peoples as "decent hierarchical peoples" or "decent hierarchical societies." Like his category of liberal peoples, this represents an ideal type to which existing states may approximate to a greater or lesser degree.

15. On interventions to prevent human rights violations, see *Law of Peoples*, 93–94, n. 6. While Rawls takes a relatively conservative view of defensible changes to the

current international order, he does not regard the status quo in international rela-tions as just. On progressive aspects of his theory, see Beitz, "Rawls's Law of Peoples," *Ethics* 110 (July 2000): 669–696, 672.

16. A key claim of the law of peoples is that honoring these principles will foster rela-tions of trust and mutual respect among peoples and thereby gradually promote international peace. While the thesis that the future peaceful society of peoples which the law of peoples anticipates is a "realistic utopia" is a matter of conjecture, Rawls argues that it is supported by the well-known, though controversial, hypothesis of a "democratic peace," i.e., the alleged historical fact that liberal democratic states do not go to war with one another; see *Law of Peoples*, 44–54.

17. On this and related criticisms of the law of peoples, see Allen Buchanan, "Rawls's Law of Peoples: Rules for a Vanished Westphalian World," *Ethics* 110 (July 2000): 697–721.

18. While Sen's reservations about global governmental institutions appear to be more a matter of political realism than principled objections, Rawls emphatically rejects the idea of a global political regime with state-like powers. See *Law of Peoples*, 36, where he follows Kant in arguing that a world government would either be despotic or would rule over a fragile empire riven by conflicts among its component regions and peoples.

19. This reading is supported by Rawls's claim that a people's self-determination is an important political good, even if their political system does not guarantee equal individual rights, because it fosters members' attachment to their political culture and their participation in the public and civic life of their society; see *Law of Peoples*, 111–112.

20. It should be noted that these claims about the interests of citizens and of peoples are claims in ideal theory. Thus Rawls does not claim that peoples as a matter of fact are indifferent to their levels of material well-being, but rather that they have no legit-imate interest in increasing their level of wealth above a decent minimum, and hence that wealthy peoples do not have an obligation to participate with poorer peoples in an ongoing scheme to redistribute some of their wealth to the latter.

21. Luban borrows the term "great evils" from Stuart Hampshire, who includes under this rubric "murder and the destruction of life, imprisonment, enslavement, starvation, poverty, physical pain and torture, homelessness, friendlessness." See his *Innocence and Experience* (Cambridge: Harvard University Press, 1991), 90.

22. An important source on the notion of civilization and the education of sense that the civilizing process involves is the work of Norbert Elias. See his *The Civilizing Process: The History of Manners and State-Formation and Civilization*, trans., Edmund Jephcott (Oxford: Blackwell, 1994), and *The Germans: Power Struggles and the Develop-ment of Habitus in the Nineteenth and Twentieth Centuries*, ed. Michael Schroter, trans. Eric Dunning and Stephen Mennell (Cambridge: Polity Press, 1996).

23. In her recent work she has also been a strong advocate of a cosmopolitan view that she traces back to the Stoics. See Martha Nussbaum, "Patriotism and Cos-mopolitanism," in *For Love of Country*, ed. Joshua Cohen (Boston: Beacon Press, 1996), and "Cosmopolitanism Duties of Justice, Duties of Material Aid," *Journal of Political Philosophy* 8, 2 (2000): 176–206.

24. On recent convergences of her views with Rawls, see Nussbaum, "Aristotle, Politics, and Human Capabilities: A Response to Anthony, Arneson, Charlesworth, and Mulgan," *Ethics* 111 (October 2000): 102–140.

25. See Martha Nussbaum, "Aristotelian Social Democracy," in *Liberalism and the Good*, ed. R. B. Douglass, et al. (New York: Routledge, 1990), 203–252.

26. Martha Nussbaum, "Human Capabilities, Female Human Beings," in Martha Nussbaum and Jonathan Glover, eds., *Women, Culture, and Development* (Oxford: Clarendon Press, 1995), 61–104, here at 84–85.

27. See Pogge's "A Global Resource Dividend," in David A. Crocker and Toby Linden, eds., *Ethics of Consumption: The Good Life, Justice, and Global Stewardship* (Lanham, MD: Rowman & Littlefield, 1998), 501–536. However, the emphasis on distributive justice in Pogge's work does not signal indifference to matters of procedural, democratic justice at the transnational level; see his "Cosmopolitanism and Sovereignty," *Ethics* 103 (1992): 48–75.

28. See David Held, *Democracy and the Global Order* and the essays in Daniele Archibugi, David Held, and Martin Köhler, eds., *Re-imagining Political Community. Studies in Cosmopolitan Democracy* (Stanford: Stanford University Press, 1998).

29. As is done, for example, by Henry Shue in his now classic *Basic Rights* (Princeton: Princeton University Press, 1980; second revised ed., 1996).

30. See Jürgen Habermas, "Kant's Idea of Perpetual Peace: With the Benefit of Two Hundred Years' Hindsight," in *The Inclusion of the Other*, Ciaran Cronin and Pablo De Greiff, eds., (Cambridge, Mass.: MIT Press, 1998), 189–193, and *Between Facts and Norms*, trans. William Rehg (Cambridge, Mass.: MIT Press, 1996), §3.3.

31. This question forms part of a theory of political legitimacy that reformulates the social contract model of voluntary submission to a higher authority in terms of the idea of a democratic polity as involving the mutual conferring of rights by its citizens; see Habermas, *Between Facts and Norms*, 118, 122, 126, 129.

32. The discourse principle, which Habermas argues is implicit in the presuppositions of communicative speech, states that "Just those action norms are valid to which all possible affected persons could agree as participants in rational discourses." See *Between Facts and Norms*, 107; on the legal medium, see ibid., 127–128, and 129.

33. See Habermas, *Between Facts and Norms*, 122.

34. That is, they can only be justified on the grounds that they are necessary to secure the conditions for the equal opportunity to exercise individual rights. For a similar argument see Inoue, "Liberal Democracy and Asian Orientalism," in Bauer and Bell, eds., *The East Asian Challenge for Human Rights*, 34–35.

35. See Habermas, *The Inclusion of the Other*, 158–161.

36. Habermas's claim that existing transnational economic regulatory regimes, such as the WTO and GATT, possess a degree of legitimacy because they are based on negotiated agreements represents an important corrective to accounts of globalization as an impersonal process that escapes political control. Such agreements are

nevertheless often problematic from the perspective of democracy since the negotiation stances of the governments involved do not always reflect the interests of their citizens as a whole and the more powerful states are able to use their bargaining power to impose terms favorable to their own multinational corporations.

37. See Benedict Anderson, *Imagined Communities* (London: Verso, 1983; second ed. 1991) and Calhoun's own important study, *Nationalism* (Minneapolis: University of Minnesota Press, 1997).

38. The public symbolism of names already indicates a shift from an economic to a political imaginary, for the European Union was formerly called the Common Market, the European Economic Community, and the European Community.

I

Weak Universalism

1

Justice across Borders

Amartya Sen

Major progress has occurred in the theory of justice over the last three or four decades, to a great extent initiated by John Rawls's path-breaking work on "justice as fairness."[1] This has involved the use of the "contractarian" method of analysis used in moral and political philosophy. The contractarian approach has strongly Kantian antecedents, and the works of Immanuel Kant have been deeply influential in analyzing how rational social arrangements and reasonable social behavior can be derived. In the Rawlsian theory of justice the contractarian method has been put to elegant and powerful use.

In the Rawlsian version of this approach, a central concept is that of an "original position"—a hypothetical state of primordial equality in which the persons involved do not yet know who they are going to be. The guiding principles for the basic structure of society are chosen in this state of postulated ignorance, which helps to make the deliberations in the original position disinterested. Indeed, this is how the requirement of "fairness" is incorporated into the analysis of justice. Since the process is taken to be *fair* (people are not guided by their respective vested interests), the rules for the basic structure of the society that are chosen—by this exercise of social contract—are taken to be *just*. Rawls's well-known theory of "justice as fairness" is thus grounded, and this analytical structure is used to derive the implications of justice, thus characterized.

Rawlsian principles of justice include the priority of liberty (the "first principle"), giving precedence to maximal liberty for each person subject to similar liberty for all. The "second principle" deals with other matters, including equity and efficiency in the distribution of opportunities. In particular, it invokes the "difference principle" involving the allocational criterion of "lexicographic maximin" in the space of holdings of "primary goods" (or general-purpose resources) of the different individuals, giving priority to the worst-off people, respectively, in each conglomeration. Questions can be raised about the plausibility of the specific principles of justice that Rawls derives from his general principles of fairness, and it can, in particular, be asked whether the device of the original position must point inescapably to these principles of justice.[2] Furthermore, the adequacy of Rawlsian focus on primary goods, which makes his "difference principle" resource-oriented rather than freedom-oriented, can also be questioned.[3] I am not directly concerned with those specific debates in this essay, though they will have to be examined and reassessed once the basic format of the original position has been subjected to critical scrutiny.

My concentration in this essay is on the more fundamental issue of the composition of the "original position" and also on the viability of the notion as a response to the challenging problems we face.[4] That question has significant relevance for our understanding of fairness and justice as well as in the derivation of their practical implications. There is substantial room for ambivalence as to who the parties are who are assumed to be undertaking this contract. Are they all the people in the world—is it a global social contract? Or is it a contract that is worked out for each nation or each polity on its own? Does the coverage admit all of humanity—irrespective of nationality and citizenship of the persons involved—or is the "original position" to be limited instead to the citizenry of each nation acting separately? Does each country have an original position of its own?

When Rawls's book *A Theory of Justice* first appeared, I interpreted the argument to be available for application to all the people taken together. But as subsequent writings of Rawls have made clear, he intends to apply the device to each nation—each people—taken separately. There is an additional exercise in which an international contractual undertaking may be considered for obtaining some guidance regarding national policies toward other nations. But this is clearly a subsequent and subsidiary exercise, following the basic operation of distinct original positions for each nation—or each people—taken separately.

These two different conceptions can be identified, respectively, as "universalist" in a grand and comprehensive sense, and "particularist" in its nation-based orientation. Their respective implications for the scope of the theory of justice may be stated as follows:

Grand universalism: The domain of the exercise of fairness is all people everywhere taken together, and the device of the original position is applied to a hypothetical exercise in the selection of rules and principles of justice for all, seen without distinction of nationality and other classifications.

National particularism: The domain of the exercise of fairness involves each nation taken separately, to which the device of the original position is correspondingly applied, though the relations between the different nations may be influenced by supplementary international negotiations.

Even though the original position is no more than a figment of our constructive imagination, the contrast between these rival conceptions can have far-reaching implications for the way we see global justice. The formulation of the demands of global justice as well as the identification of the agencies charged with meeting these demands are influenced by the choice of the appropriate conception of the original position and the corresponding characterization of the domain of justice as fairness.

Grand Universalism

Even though I am attracted to grand universalism, I shall presently argue that neither of these two conceptions—grand universalism and national particularism—can give us an adequate understanding of the demands of global justice. There is a need for a third conception with an adequate recognition of the plurality of relations involved across the globe. But let me, first, elaborate briefly on the claims of each of these two classic conceptions.

Grand universalism has an ethical stature that draws on its comprehensive coverage and nonsectarian openness. It rivals the universalism of classical utilitarianism and that of a generalized interpretation of the Kantian conception of reasoned ethics. It can speak in the name of the whole of humanity in a way that the separatism of national particularist conceptions would not allow.

And yet grand universalism is hard to adopt in working out the institutional implications of Rawlsian justice as fairness. The explication of fairness through a device like the original position is used, in Rawlsian analysis, to yield principles that should govern the choice of the basic political and social structure for each society considered as a political unit in which the principles of justice find their application. There are great difficulties in trying to apply this mode of reasoning to the whole of humanity, without an adequately comprehensive institutional base that can serve to implement the rules hypothetically arrived at in the original position for the entire world. Obviously, the United Nations cannot play this role (even if the United States were to come round to paying the money it owes to this international organization). Indeed, even the very conception of the United Nations—as its name indicates—is thoroughly dependent on drawing on the basic political and social organizations prevalent in the respective national states.

Particularist Conceptions and the Law of the Peoples

All this may forcefully suggest that we should opt for the tractability and coherence of the particularist—ultimately nationalist—conception of Rawlsian justice. That is, in fact, the direction in which Rawls himself has proceeded, considering separately the application of justice as fairness in each political society, but then supplementing this exercise through linkages between societies and nations by the use of intersocietal norms. We can even work out a different hypothetical exercise—an international "original position"—in which the representatives of the nations contract together and work out what they might reasonably owe to each other—one "people" to another.

How that reasoning should work has recently been explored by Rawls himself in the form of a theory of what he calls the "law of peoples."[5] The "peoples"—as collectivities—in distinct political formations consider their concern for each other and the imperatives that follow from such linkages. The principles of justice as fairness can in this way be used to illuminate the relation between these political communities (and not just between individuals, as in the original Rawlsian conception).

It must be noted, however, that in this particularist conception, the demands of global justice—in so far as they emerge—operate primarily through *inter-societal* relations rather than through *person-to-person* relations, which some may see as central to an adequate understanding of the nature and content of global justice. This effectively nation-based characterization of justice identifies the domain of *international* justice, broadly defined, but the basic work of the inter-individual original position is done within each nation, acting separately. The imperatives that follow, despite the limits of the formulation, have far-reaching moral content, which has been analyzed with characteristic lucidity by Rawls.[6] However, the restrictions of an "international"—as opposed to a more directly "global"—approach set narrow limits to the reach of the Rawlsian "law of peoples."

How should we take account of the role of direct relations between different peoples across borders whose identities include, inter alia, solidarities based on classifications *other than* those of nationality or political unit, such as class, gender, or social convictions? How do we account for professional identities (such as being a doctor or an educator) and the imperatives they generate across frontiers? These concerns, responsibilities, and obligations may not only not be parasitic on national identities and international relations, they may often run in contrary directions to international relations. Even the identity of being a human being—perhaps our most basic identity—may have the effect, when fully seized, of broadening our viewpoint, and the imperatives that we may associate with our shared humanity may not be mediated by our membership of collectivities such as "nations" or "peoples."

Aside from this basic issue of different identities, our practical interactions across the borders often involve norms and rules that are not derived *through* relations between nations. This applies powerfully to economic and social relations across borders, with their own conventions and mores. Obviously, when the need for legal enforcement arises, the national laws must still be important in giving force to some of these relations. And yet so much of global commerce, global culture, even global protests (like those on the streets of Seattle, Washington, or Prague) draw on direct relations between human beings—with their own ethics and priorities. These ethics can, of course, be supported or scrutinized or criticized in terms of intergroup relations, but the inter-group relations need not be confined to international relations only. They may involve very many diverse groups, with identities that vary from seeing oneself as a businessman or a worker, as a woman or a man, as being poor (or being committed to the poor) or rich, or as a member of one professional group or another (such as, say, doctors or lawyers). Thus collectivities of many different types may be invoked as bases of commitments and obligations that reach across national borders.

Plural Affiliations

We need a different conception of global justice that is neither as ambitious and uninstitutionalized as the grand universalism of *one* comprehensive "original position" encompassing the whole world (despite its obvious ethical interest and possible relevance at the level of some very general principles), nor as separatist and restrictive as national particularism (even when supplemented by international relations). The starting point of an alternative approach, drawing on plural affiliations, can be the recognition of the fact that we all have multiple identities, and that each of these identities can yield concerns and demands that can significantly supplement, or seriously compete with, other concerns and demands arising from other identities. The implications of this approach for the theory of justice can be stated as follows:

Plural affiliation: The exercise of fairness can be applied to different groups (including, but not uniquely, the nations), and the respective demands related to our multiple identities can all be taken seriously (there may be different ways in which their conflicting claims are ultimately resolved).

The exercise of "fairness," which can be illustrated with the device of the original position, need not look for a unique application. The original position is a rich way of characterizing the discipline of reciprocity and within-group universalization, and it can be used to provide insights and inspirations for different group identities and affiliations. Nor is it entirely necessary, to benefit from Rawls's foundational characterization of fairness, to work out an elaborate system—as in Rawls's own theory—through a detailed specification of a stage-by-stage emergence of basic structures, legislation, and administration. The device of the original position can be employed in less grand, less unique, and less fully structured forms, without giving complete priority to one canonical formulation involving national particularism.

For example, a doctor could well ask what kind of commitments she may have in a community of doctors and patients, where the parties involved do not necessarily belong to the same nation. It is well to remember that the Hippocratic oath was not mediated—explicitly or by implication—by any national or international contract. Similarly, a feminist activist could well consider what her commitments should be to address the special deprivation of women in general—not necessarily only in her own country. There may well be conflicting demands arising from different identities and affiliations, and these respective demands cannot all be victorious. The exercise of assessing the relative strength of divergent demands arising from competing affiliations is not trivial, but it would beg a very large question if we were to deny our multiple identities and affiliations just to avoid having to face this problem. The alternative of subjugating all affiliations to one overarching identity—that of membership of a national polity—misses the force and far-reaching relevance of the diverse relations that operate between persons. The political conception of a person as a citizen of a nation—important as it is—cannot override all other conceptions and the behavioral consequences of other forms of group association.[7]

Contractarianism versus the Impartial Spectator

Pursuing the idea of plural affiliation is both possible and important within the general contractarian approach involving different groups and plural pluralities. But one might still ask whether this is the most sensible way of going about incorporating the demands of justice and of impersonality in these relations? Is the original position the right framework?

Here I want to suggest a possible departure, which can be seen, to some extent, as a move from Immanuel Kant to Adam Smith. Like Kant, Smith was convinced of the need for impersonality in ethical reasoning in working out the demands of justice, but he invoked a different notion—that of the "impartial spectator"—to do this job rather than using the contractarian method.[8]

Although Smith argued that "the general rules of morality" were "ultimately founded upon experience of what, in particular instances, our moral faculties, our natural sense of merit and propriety, approve, or disapprove of," he emphasized the importance of moral reasoning in an adequately broad framework. Indeed, he argued that it is "from reason . . . we are very properly said to derive all those general maxims and ideas." Smith went on to emphasize the role of reasoning in the process of systematizing our ideas of what is or is not acceptable, drawing on observations "in a great variety of particular cases" of "what pleases or displeases our moral faculties, what these approve or disapprove of," and using reasoned induction to "establish those general rules."[9]

The process of reasoning can draw on a variety of devices to bring out our reflected moral judgments. A crucially important device Adam Smith used in this context was that of the "impartial spectator." We are asked to imagine how a spectator who is not directly involved in the competing claims, and who is impartial, may view a situation of conflict, or more generally a situation in which there are both some congruence and some conflict of interest. The demand now is to work out how they would look to an outsider who disinterestedly seeks a just solution. It should be obvious that this too—like the contractarian model (such as that of the Rawlsian original position)—involves impersonality and decisions based on suppressing the diverting influence of vested interests. But in contrast with the contractarian approach, the impartial spectator is not himself or herself a party to the contract. Smith's model of the impartial spectator relates to that of the Kantian-Rawlsian contractarian model in much the same way a model of *arbitration* relates to that of *negotiation*.

Limitations of the Contractarian Approach: An Illustration

It is interesting that the fair-arbitration model of the impartial spectator has a reach that the fair-negotiation oriented model of the original position lacks. Consider, for example, the ethics of population policy. The basic problem for the mode of reasoning involving the original position arises from the incoherence of trying to include in the original position all the affected parties where some people would be present in one society if one decision were taken about population, who would never exist if a different decision were to be taken. People who would not be born under some social arrangement cannot be seen to be evaluating that arrangement—a "non-being" cannot assess a society from the position of never having existed (even though there would have been such a person had history been different).

For example, consider a case in which there would be a million people if one decision were taken and a million and a half people if another population policy were to be pursued. Do the extra half a million people participate in the original position in deciding on which society to choose, including which population decision to take? Suppose we presume that they should be involved. If that is the case and if, it so happens, that the decision that emerges is to have the restrictive population policy, then these people would simply not be brought into existence, and it would then not be obvious what status to accord these people who allegedly participated in the original position without actually existing. On the other hand, if they are not to be included in the original position and the decision to emerge is that the more expansive population policy is to be followed, then this additional half a million people would actually exist, but would not have participated in the deliberations in the original position. Indeed, since the deliberations are held together as an integral whole, their fate and their future would be decided without their participation. In either formulation, therefore, the original position is quite incapable of dealing with such issues as the population problem, and an as-if contract between the affected parties is, thus, not possible.

The same difficulty applies to other uses of the contractarian approach. Consider, for example, the powerful approach that Thomas Scanlon has explored as a discipline of moral reasoning. He sees the contractarian requirement as a matter of selecting general rules "which no one can reasonably reject as a basis for informed, unforced general agreement."[10] The problem, in this case, lies in identifying the potential "rejecters" (*who* are to be accorded the standing of being able to "reasonably reject"?). People who would never exist if a particular substantive arrangement were selected cannot be invoked as rejecting (or refusing to reject) rules that yield that arrangement. Indeed, the difficulty is endemic in the contractarian approach that is now so dominant in contemporary moral philosophy. Since the contractarian method requires the congruence of the set of judges and the set of lives that are being judged, it is fundamentally ill-suited for helping us resolve any problem that deals with a varying of participants. But it is hard to think of any substantial economic or social decision that will not have an influence—direct or indirect—on the size or composition of the population.

Can Adam Smith's model of the impartial spectator deal with the population problem? Would it not be subject to the same difficulty as the contractarian reasoning? The answer is no. The impartial spectator is impartial between the parties (or would-be parties), but is not required to do her observing—not to mention negotiation—in the form of *being* each of the parties, as in the contractarian method. There is, therefore, no similar problem in this mode of reasoning as it would apply in the contractarian approach. The impartial spectator can place herself in different situations (without having to be present in any of them), and thus the problem of varying participants does not cripple the Smithian approach.

There are, thus, real advantages in taking a leaf from Adam Smith's book, rather than Immanuel Kant's, and I hope I am not being influenced by the fact that I am primarily an economist and only secondarily a philosopher. The reach of the impartial spectator model is larger, at least in this respect. This is an issue that is quite important in dealing with plural affiliations, since there too the groups would be to some extent ambiguously defined. Also the same person can easily belong to different groups, for example as a citizen of a nation, on the one hand, and as a feminist activist, on the other. Both roles may be important in different contexts, and the person involved can invoke the more permissive model of impersonality both to help in the analysis of justice within each group and also to assess possibly competing loyalties to which individuals are subject as members of two different groups.

Institutions and Multiplicity of Agencies

Leaving aside these issues of philosophical formulations, the important question that needs major emphasis in understanding global justice is the presence of different groups and different associations, with their respective delineations of "borders." Many of the associations are informal, and include loyalties related to one's identity, say, as a worker, or as a peasant, or as a person with liberal convictions (or conservative ones), or as a woman (or as a feminist), and so on. These associations have significance in the understanding of justice across borders that must not be submerged in the allegedly canonical grouping of individuals as members of particular nations and citizenry.

There are also many associations that are formal and organizationally structured. A great many agencies can influence global arrangements and consequences. Some of them are clearly "national" in form, including domestic policies of particular states, and also international relations (contracts, agreements, exchanges, etc.) between states, operating *through* the national governments. Other cross-border relations and actions, however, often involve units of economic operation quite different from national states, such as firms and businesses, social groups and political organizations, nongovernmental organizations (NGOs), and so on, which may operate locally as well as beyond national frontiers. Transnational firms constitute a special case of this. There are also international organizations, which may have been set up directly by the individual states acting together (such as the League of Nations or the United Nations), or indirectly by an already constituted international organization (such as the ILO, UNICEF, or UNDP). Once formed, these institutions acquire a certain measure of independence from the day-to-day control of the individual national governments.

Still other institutions involve the working of nongovernmental, nonprofit entities that operate across borders—organizing relief, providing immunization, arranging education and training, supporting local associations, fostering public discussion, and a whole host of other activities. Actions can also come from individuals in direct relation to each other in the form of communication, argumentation, and advocacy that can influence social, political, and economic actions (even when the contacts are not as high profile as, say, Bertrand Russell's writing to John Kennedy and Nikita Kruschev on the nuclear confrontations of the cold war).

The demands of justice—and that of fairness—can be investigated in several distinct though interrelated ways, invoking various groups that cut across national boundaries. These groups need not be as universally grand as the collectivity of "all" the people in the world nor as specific and constrained as national states. Many policy issues cannot be reasonably addressed in either of these two extremist formats. Individuals live and operate in a world of institutions, many of which operate across borders.[11]

Concluding Remarks

Let me end with some general remarks. First, I have argued that justice across borders must not be seen merely as "international justice"—as the issue is often formulated. Even though that is the way mainstream ethical thinking (led by Kantian-Rawlsian contractarian analysis) has gone, that line of reasoning is fundamentally defective. It is normatively unsatisfactory, since not all of our ethical commitments and obligations are mediated through relations between nations. A feminist activist in America who wants to help, say, to remedy some features of female disadvantage in Africa or Asia, draws on a sense of identity that goes well beyond the sympathies of one nation for the predicament of another. A person can see herself as an Italian, as a woman, as an agnostic, as a doctor, and so on; there is no contradiction in this richer understanding of a person's identity.

Second, the international contractarian line of reasoning is also institutionally obtuse in taking little note of the variety of institutions (such as markets, religious groupings, political organizations, etc.). These institutions operate through affiliations that may be quite different from national groupings, and they certainly can influence relations between people across borders. Indeed, many NGOs— Médecins sans Frontières, OXFAM, Amnesty International, Human Rights Watch, and others—explicitly focus on affiliations and associations that cut across national boundaries.

Third, turning to somewhat more general theory, the contractarian line of reasoning is inherently defective in dealing with variable groups and cannot deal at all adequately with some standard problems of ethical and political decision *even* for a given society. The difficulty it has in dealing with population policy—or any decision that influences the size or the composition of the population—illustrates its limited reach.

Fourth, if we shift our philosophical focus from Immanuel Kant's influential line of thinking to that of the more neglected theories of his contemporary, Adam Smith, we get a model of reasoning that is better able to cope with these problems of variable and varying groups. The discipline of the "impartial spectator" has much to offer to this range of ethical issues, and this applies also to justice across borders.

Finally, it is very important to note that "grand universalism" is not the only alternative to "national particularism." The noninstitutional and utopian nature of grand universalism is sometimes invoked to provide an alleged justification of the nationally particularist line of thinking, based on the false presumption that national particularism would be the only alternative left if grand universalism were taken to be unduly demanding. This is not the case.

I have argued in favor of a line of reasoning that is geared to the existence of multiple institutions and the presence of plural identities in the way we see ourselves. This makes it impossible to resolve all problems of justice by one all-encompassing original position (as under grand universalism), or even by two sets of overarching original positions—one within each nation and another among the representatives of all nations (as in the combination of national particularism and the "law of peoples"). The coexistence of many affiliations and diverse identities is a central feature of the world in which we live and cannot be ignored in exploring the demands of global justice. Each of our plural associations entails some general concerns about justice across borders as well as within those respective borders. The borders are defined differently for different groups, and our reasoning about justice has to reflect that reality.

Requirements of global justice offer guidance in diverse voices and sometimes in conflicting directions. Although we cannot escape the need for critical scrutiny of the respective demands, this is not a reason for expecting to find one canonical superdevice that will readily resolve all the diversities of obligations that relate to our various affiliations, identities, and priorities. The oversimplification that must be particularly avoided is to identify global justice with international justice. The reach and relevance of the former can far exceed those of the latter.

Acknowledgments

This essay draws on my lecture for the Centennial Year Celebrations of the De Paul University in Chicago in September 1998 and also on an earlier presentation at a conference of the United Nations Development Programme in New York in 1997.

Notes

1. John Rawls, *A Theory of Justice* (Cambridge. MA: Harvard University Press, 1971); *Political Liberalism* (New York: Columbia University Press, 1993); *The Law of Peoples* (Cambridge, MA: Harvard University Press, 1999).

2. My own combination of admiration and scepticism of the particular Rawlsian formula can be found in my book, *Collective Choice and Social Welfare* (San Francisco: Holden-Day, 1970; republished, Amsterdam: North-Holland, 1997). I was in fact responding to Rawls's papers that preceded his book, which explains how my response could have been published before Rawls's own book.

3.   I have discussed this issue in my "Equality of What?" in S. McMurrin, ed., *Tanner Lectures on Human Values*, vol. I (Cambridge: Cambridge University Press, and Salt Lake City: University of Utah Press, 1980); "Justice: Means versus Freedoms," *Philosophy and Public Affairs* 19 (1990), and *Inequality Reexamined* (Oxford: Clarendon Press, and Cambridge, MA: Harvard University Press, 1992).

4.   I have discussed some of these issues also in "Global Justice: Beyond International Equity," in Inga Kaul, I. Grunberg and M. A. Stern, eds., *Global Public Goods: International Cooperation in the 21st Century* (Oxford: Oxford University Press, 1999).

5.   See Rawls, *The Law of Peoples*.

6.   See Rawls, *The Law of Peoples*. Rawls's strategy and conclusions have been further explored by Alyssa R. Bernstein, "Human Rights Reconceived: A Defence of Rawls's Law of Peoples." Ph.D. dissertation, Philosophy Department, Harvard University, May 2000.

7.   On this see Rabindranath Tagore, *Nationalism* (London: Macmillan, 1917; new edition with an introduction by E. P. Thompson, 1991).

8.   Indeed, as a matter of historical interest, I should also mention that Smith had outlined his ideas on impersonality earlier than Kant's own formulations, and there is even some evidence that Kant was actually influenced by Smith's mode of reasoning. Kant discusses Smith's model of the impartial spectator in his book on anthropology which had preceded Kant's definitive writings on ethics and practical reason.

9.   Adam Smith, *An Inquiry Into the Nature and Causes of the Wealth of Nations* (1790; republished, London: Home University, 1910), 159, 319.

10.   See also Thomas Scanlon, *What We Owe to Each Other* (Cambridge, MA: Harvard University Press, 1998).

11.   On this see my *Development as Freedom* (New York: Knopf, and Oxford and Delhi: Oxford University Press, 1999).

2

The Legitimacy of Peoples

Leif Wenar

In John Rawls's *Law of Peoples* we find unfamiliar concepts, surprising pronouncements, and what appear from a familiar Rawlsian perspective to be elementary errors in reasoning.[1] Even Rawls's most sensitive and sympathetic interpreters have registered unusually deep misgivings about the book.[2] Most perplexing of all is simply the character of the view that Rawls sets out to justify. For in this book Rawls—perhaps America's leading egalitarian liberal—advances a theory that shows no direct concern for individuals and requires no narrowing of global material inequality.

I believe that *Law of Peoples* does present a coherent and powerful argument, if neither a perfect nor a complete one. There are two points crucial to understanding its strengths and weaknesses. The first is that Rawls in this work is concerned more with the legitimacy of global coercion than he is with the arbitrariness of the fates of citizens of different countries. This connects *The Law of Peoples* much more closely to *Political Liberalism* than to *A Theory of Justice*. The second point relates to Rawls's unusual conception of the nature and interests of peoples. A people in Rawls's view is startlingly indifferent to its own material prosperity, and this fact gives Rawls's "law of peoples" much of its distinctive cast.

This essay will develop these two points by contrasting Rawls's "law of peoples" with the Rawlsian cosmopolitan theories of Charles Beitz and Thomas Pogge. I begin with a brief review of Rawls's theory of justice for a single country (justice as fairness) and the cosmopolitan theories that developed out of it. I then summarize Rawls's law of peoples and some of his puzzling statements about its justification. The bulk of the essay explains how Rawls's fundamental norm of legitimacy forced him away from the cosmopolitan alternative, and how Rawls's conception of a people led him to reject international egalitarianism. Toward the end I will suggest that Rawls's theory of global institutions is, although consistent and forceful, incomplete. To make up for Rawls's lack of attention to individuals, I propose a supplemental original position argument that grounds principles of global economic justice and human rights.

Justice as Fairness

The subject of justice as fairness is the basic structure of a modern democratic nation.[3] Rawls focuses on the basic structure because its institutions have such pervasive and unchosen effects on the life chances of the people who live within them. The problem of the justice of the basic structure arises because while citizens realize that social cooperation within its institutions produces great advantages, they are not indifferent to how the benefits and burdens of this cooperation (rights, opportunities, recognition, income, and wealth) will be divided up.

Rawls's solution to the problem of the justice of the domestic basic structure can be stated in one sentence: a just society will be a fair scheme of cooperation among citizens regarded as free and equal. Social cooperation is to be fair in that all who do their part are to benefit according to public and agreed standards. Citizens are free and equal in that each is an equally valid source of claims on social institutions regardless of religious affiliation, philosophical commitments, and personal preferences. To these characterizations of society and citizens, Rawls also adds what could be called the "strong egalitarian proviso": the distribution of benefits and burdens (rights, income, and other goods) should not be based at the deepest level on citizens' race, gender, class of origin, or endowment of natural talents. As Rawls famously put it, in justice as fairness the distribution of social goods will not be grounded in factors "arbitrary from a moral point of view."[4]

In Rawls's original position thought-experiment, representatives of free and equal citizens are placed in fair conditions for choosing the basic terms of social cooperation. Rawls holds that two principles of justice would be selected in this original position. The first principle guarantees citizens equal basic rights and liberties. The second principle requires equal opportunities for obtaining positions of power, and requires that any inequalities of income and wealth work to the greatest benefit of the worst-off members of society. The second part of the second principle is known as the difference principle.

Rawls and the Cosmopolitan Egalitarians

Justice as fairness is a theory for the institutions of one self-contained national society. In *Theory of Justice* Rawls discussed only briefly how this theory might be extended to the global order.[5] For a number of Rawlsian theorists, however, the proper method of extension was clear. Global justice should be just as liberal, and just as egalitarian, as justice as fairness says domestic justice should be.

Two of the most astute Rawlsian theorists, Charles Beitz and Thomas Pogge, argued as follows.[6] There is an international basic structure just as there is a domestic basic structure, with political, economic, military, and cultural institutions linking citizens of different countries together in a worldwide system of social cooperation. Moreover this global basic structure has deep and unchosen effects on the life chances of the people within it.[7] The problem of global justice is thus the same, *mutatis mutandis*, as the problem of domestic justice. What is therefore needed is a theory to specify what counts as a fair distribution of the benefits and burdens of global cooperation.

Fortunately, Beitz and Pogge claimed, Rawls's justice as fairness can be transformed directly into a theory of international justice. Beitz and Pogge proposed a *cosmopolitan* reformulation of domestic justice as fairness, which takes as its protagonists not citizens of a liberal society but instead all human beings regarded as "citizens of the world." In the cosmopolitan view a just global society will be a fair system of cooperation among global citizens, all of whom are regarded as free and equal. Indeed global citizens are to be considered "strongly" equal to each other. The fact that one citizen is born in an affluent and abundant country while another is born in an impoverished and barren land is just as arbitrary from a moral point of view as are the facts that fellow countrymen are born to different genders, races, and classes. A cosmopolitan theory of justice aims to justify a distributive principle that will overcome this arbitrariness.

The cosmopolitans thus proposed a global original position in which each "world citizen" has a representative, just as in the domestic original position every "domestic citizen" has a representative. Such a global original position will endorse, they claimed, a globalized difference principle: inequalities of income and wealth should be allowed only if these inequalities work to the greatest benefit of the world's worst-off individuals. Beitz in particular championed such an international difference principle, which would—given the vast inequalities in global income and wealth—require drastic restructuring of the world's economic institutions.[8]

When Rawls finally published his own theory of global institutions, the shape and the conclusions of the theory greatly disappointed the cosmopolitans. Contrary to the cosmopolitan interpretation, Rawls stipulated that the parties in the global original position should *not* be thought to represent individual human beings. Rather, each party in the global original position should represent an entire domestic society—or a "people" as Rawls prefers to say.[9] Worse still, the principles that Rawls claimed would be agreed upon in such a global original position bore little resemblance to the principles of justice as fairness. They instead looked very much like "familiar and largely traditional principles . . . from the history and usages of international law and practice."[10] Given Rawls's radical egalitarianism for liberal democracies, his conservatism in the international realm was most unwelcome to those who had tried to develop justice as fairness into an international egalitarian theory. As Pogge remarked in discouragement on an early version of Rawls's theory of global relations, "I am at a loss to explain Rawls's quick endorsement of a bygone status quo."[11]

The Puzzle of Rawls's Rejection of Global Egalitarianism

Rawls's vision of a well-ordered society of peoples is, in essence, that each people should be just by its own lights within the bare constraints of political legitimacy, and that peoples should be good neighbors to each other.

Domestically, this means that each government must respect basic human rights, apply its own laws impartially, and be responsive to the grievances of its citizens. Beyond these minimal constraints, each national society is left to work out the justice of its domestic institutions as it sees fit. Internationally, Rawls's principles state that peoples have a right to self-defense and to the proper conduct of war; that peoples should keep their treaties and fund a world bank; and that peoples should ensure that trade among them is fair (a provision we will examine more closely later). Rawls does add to these international principles a moderate "principle of assistance." According to this principle, wealthier peoples have a duty to assist those "burdened" societies which, because of natural disaster or an impoverished political culture, are not able to sustain minimal conditions of legitimate government. But Rawls includes no principles whatsoever that are intended to narrow the economic gap between richer and poorer countries.[12] Once a society has become self-sustaining and self-guiding, any duty to transfer resources to it ceases. There is no requirement for permanently redistributive, much less egalitarian, international institutions.

Rawls's reasons for resisting more egalitarian proposals initially sound very odd indeed. Rawls first criticizes Beitz's global difference principle for not having a "target" state after which its demands cut off—as Rawls says, Beitz's global difference principle is meant to apply "continuously and without end."[13] Yet this seems a peculiar objection for Rawls to make to a principle of distributive justice. If Beitz's globalized difference principle is flawed because it lacks a target and a cutoff point, then one would think that Rawls's own domestic difference principle would be flawed for the same reason, whatever that reason turns out to be.

Rawls also ventures that redistribution among peoples would be unacceptable because it would not respect peoples' political autonomy.[14] He asks us to imagine two societies, initially equally well-off. The first society decides to industrialize and increase its real rate of savings; the second society prefers a more pastoral and leisurely existence. After a few decades, the first society is twice as well-off as the second. It would be inappropriate, Rawls says, to tax the first society and redistribute the proceeds to the second—for this would not respect each society's right to self-determination.

The strangeness of Rawls making this reply can be shown by conjuring up an old debate in which Nozick attempts to use an analogous example against the principles of justice as fairness. Imagine two citizens of the same society, Nozick might say, initially equally well-off. The first citizen works hard at the factory and saves, the second has a leisurely life as a shepherd. After a few years, the first citizen is twice as well-off as the second. Would it not impinge on the industrious citizen's "self-determination" to tax his earnings to give to the shepherd?

What Rawls should say in response to this sort of example is by now familiar. He should say that it is acceptable for differential effort and savings to bring differential rewards, but only when background institutions like taxes keep the overall distribution from reflecting factors arbitrary from a moral point of view. Since this would obviously be Rawls's response in the domestic case, it is hard to see how he could have a different view internationally. Yes an industrializing and abstemious society may be allowed to become better off, but only if background institutions assure that any inequalities work to the advantage of all.

In opposing the cosmopolitan egalitarian interpretation, Rawls faces the general problem of identifying the asymmetry between the international order where he rejects egalitarian redistribution and the domestic order where he requires it. Until he identifies such an asymmetry, any objection he makes to international egalitarianism will simply boomerang as an objection to justice as fairness. So how can Rawls resist the demand for international egalitarian redistribution?

One thought is that Rawls might point to the decent but deeply inegalitarian cultures of the world, with worries about foisting alien

Western ideas of equality on unwilling foreigners, but he does not in fact pursue this strategy. Indeed Rawls says he would reject international egalitarian redistribution *even for a world populated only by liberal peoples all of whom accepted justice as fairness.*[15] So the existence of illiberal peoples is not relevant to our puzzle, and we can simply ignore the existence of illiberal peoples from now on.

Alternatively, Rawls might have resisted international egalitarianism by claiming that—in contrast to the domestic case—the affinity among citizens of different countries could never grow to be strong enough for citizens of wealthier countries to support continuous redistribution to the poor of the world. Although he gestures toward this sort of skepticism in a footnote, Rawls appears to think that he cannot rest too much weight on it.[16] To make plausible his own duty of assistance he must maintain that "The relatively narrow circle of mutually caring peoples in the world today may expand over time and must never be viewed as fixed."[17] This leaves him in a weak position to assert the impossibility of an extension of fellow feeling sufficient for a globalized difference principle.

Finally, Rawls might have voiced misgivings that global institutions could be constructed capable of administering any egalitarian principle. And he does endorse Kant's thesis that a centralized global government with legal powers like those of domestic governments would be either despotic or riven by unmanageable civil strife.[18] Yet Rawls does not cite the impossibility of stable global government as a reason to resist global egalitarianism. Nor do the egalitarian proposals of Beitz and Pogge call for a centralized world government, but rather for dispersed and overlapping agencies that together realize the egalitarian ideal.

So far we have made little progress in clarifying Rawls's motives. Yet Rawls's final remark on the differences between his own and the cosmopolitan approach to global justice provides us with a clue. The cosmopolitan egalitarian views are concerned with *the well-being of individuals,* Rawls says, while his own law of peoples is concerned with *the justice of societies.*[19] To understand this enigmatic comment, we must look more closely at why Rawls populates his global original position with representatives of peoples rather than representatives of individual human beings. And to see this clearly, one must explore other parts of the Rawlsian architectonic, leaving justice behind and turning to the idea of legitimacy.

Rawls's Fundamental Norm of Legitimacy

Let us put to one side for the moment justice as fairness, which was Rawls's project in the 1970s and early 1980s. In the late 1980s and 1990s, Rawls worked out a very different kind of theory: a theory of political legitimacy.[20] Legitimacy is a much weaker standard than justice: institutions may be legitimate without being just, and no doubt many nations' institutions are exactly this way. Legitimacy sets a ground-level criterion for basic structures, whose institutions are always backed by coercive powers of enforcement. The coercion employed within a legitimate basic structure may not be wholly justifiable—as just mentioned, a basic structure may be legitimate without being just. But the coercion of a legitimate basic structure is justifiable enough that outsiders ought not themselves use coercive force to try to change the institutions that employ it. Legitimacy is a primitive concept of normative recognition: a legitimate regime imposes duties on its citizens instead of merely issuing commands to them. When we recognize a government, we recognize it as a government instead of as merely a powerful gang.

Rawls's fundamental norm of legitimacy for the institutions of a basic structure states that the coercive force that these institutions employ is legitimate only insofar as it is exercised on grounds that are reasonably or responsibly acceptable to those who are coerced.[21] I believe this norm is the source from which all of Rawls's later theorizing flows. It underlies his criteria for the legitimacy of both national and international institutions. In this section, I describe how Rawls's fundamental norm bears on national institutions.

In *The Law of Peoples* Rawls says that legitimate national institutions must recognize core human rights, enforce the rule of law, and be genuinely responsive to citizen dissent. These are the minimal requirements for any national basic structure to be reasonably or responsibly acceptable to all citizens.[22] Beyond this minimum—and every society will include coercive institutions that go beyond this minimum—coercion can only be based on ideas that are acceptable to the citizens of that particular society. In a traditional or hierar-chical society the problem of finding generally acceptable ideas may be less acute, since citizens may, for example, adhere to the same religion. But the problem of acceptability is more severe for modern liberal societies, in which citizens hold a wide variety of views and allegiances.

This is the problem of *Political Liberalism*.[23] In any pluralistic society, Rawls explains, it would be unreasonable to expect all citizens to accept coercive institutions based on any subgroup's particular views. This is clearest in the religious case: Unitarians can reasonably reject the basic structure of their society being based on the Catholic tenets of their neighbors, and vice-versa. Indeed no citizen's comprehen-sive view of the good will be reasonably acceptable to all citizens, and so no citizen's comprehensive view may be used as the basis for legitimate coercion.[24]

Given that no comprehensive doctrine can provide the content of a liberal society's basic structure, Rawls believes that there remains only one other source of ideas for ordering its institutions. This is what he calls the society's *public political culture*. The public political culture is made up of the political institutions of the regime and the public traditions of their interpretation as well as historic texts and documents that have become part of common knowledge and common knowledge itself.[25] All citizens can reasonably accept coer-cion based on ideas in the society's public political culture, Rawls writes, because the public culture is "a shared fund of implicitly rec-ognized basic ideas" that are likely to be "congenial to [citizens'] most firmly held convictions."[26] In other words, all citizens can accept ideas drawn from the public political culture as a reasonable basis for their common institutions because—in view of the pluralism of liberal societies—the public culture is the only available focal point of doctrine.

In a liberal democracy, the public political culture will contain at the deepest level the abstract ideas that citizens ought to be treated fairly as free and equal. From this fact Rawls infers that any legiti-mate liberal regime must protect familiar civil and political rights and ensure all citizens sufficient means to take advantage of these rights.[27] Beyond this minimum of liberal legitimacy, each society will choose a particular scheme of justice built from the materials in its political culture that are acceptable to its particular citizenry. Rawls's own justice as fairness is then one proposal for how to order a liberal society's institutions justly—a proposal based on a specific understanding of "fair, free, and equal" and the strong egalitarian proviso.

Why Rawls Is Not a Cosmopolitan

Returning to the global arena, we can now see how Rawls's fundamental norm of legitimacy explains his populating his global original position with peoples instead of individuals. A global original position will select principles for institutions of the global basic structure. Since these institutions are coercive, they will have to meet the fundamental standard of legitimacy. Which means that these global institutions will have to be acceptable to all those individuals who will be coerced by them. But the plurality of comprehensive doctrines is even greater globally than it is within any liberal society.[28] So, analogously to the liberal domestic case, Rawls must draw on the *global* public political culture for ideas that can be reasonably or responsibly acceptable to all.

But this, I believe, is where Rawls turns away from a cosmopolitan original position, constructed from ideas concerning the nature and relations of "world citizens." For while documents in the global public political culture such as the *Universal Declaration of Human Rights* proclaim the freedom and equality of all, these ideas are deployed almost exclusively to establish how citizens should be treated by their own national governments. They are not as a rule used to explain how citizens of different countries should regard and relate to one another. In the main the political institutions of international society are framed in terms not of individual citizens but of states—or (as Rawls prefers) "peoples." The public political culture of global organizations, conventions, and treaties is primarily *international*, not interpersonal.

There simply is no robust global public political culture emphasizing that citizens of different countries ought to relate fairly to one another as free and equal in a single scheme of social cooperation— much less that the distribution of global resources and wealth should not be based on factors "arbitrary from a moral point of view." There is no conceptual focal point comparable, that is, to the central idea in the public political culture of a liberal democracy that citizens ought to relate fairly to one another as free and equal, regardless of their more particular characteristics. It is peoples, not individuals, whom international political institutions regard as free and equal, and this is why Rawls makes peoples the subject of his global political theory.

Rawls doubtless believes as much as anyone that all humans should be regarded as free and equal. But he believes more deeply that humans should be coerced only according to a self-image reasonably acceptable to them. This far, Rawlsian politics is identity politics. Since "global citizens" cannot be presumed to view themselves as free and equal individuals who should relate fairly to each other across the board, we cannot build coercive social institutions that assume they do.[29] Using the ideas from the global political culture about how free and equal *peoples* should relate fairly to each other, Rawls is able to construct what he believes to be a more legitimate original position argument.

Moreover, theorizing in terms of peoples has further and related benefits. For theorizing in terms of peoples also allows Rawls to construct a global original position argument with the same justificatory advantages as his domestic original position. Rawls's international original position first affirms principles of international relations that we already believe are extremely important: that aggressive wars of aggrandizement are wrong, that treaties should be kept, and that trade should be fair. This is like his domestic original position, which first affirms a principle—which we already believe is extremely important—securing all citizens' basic rights and liberties. Rawls's international original position then aims to extend our less confident intuitions on the issue of global economic distribution by favoring a limited duty of assistance. This is much as the domestic original position aimed to extend our less confident intuitions about domestic economic redistribution by favoring the domestic difference principle. Both original position arguments are meant to gain their justificatory power from first reinforcing and then expanding our reflective equilibria. Working in terms of peoples instead of individuals thus enables Rawls's global original position, like his domestic original position, to "accommodate our firmest convictions and . . . provide guidance where guidance is needed."[30]

By contrast, the cosmopolitans' original position endorses a highly progressive economic principle (the globalized difference principle) without first showing that it can confirm the basic rules of international relations that keep our global order even minimally stable and tolerable. The cosmopolitans, that is, use their original position to derive a radical distributive result without a prior demonstration that this original position can validate the most fundamental norms of global justice and peace. Nor will it be easy for cosmopolitans to overcome this deficiency, for they cannot simply staple the basic norms of international relations into their individualistic theories. To redeem principles like "nations should keep their treaties," cosmopolitans would have to explain why and in what circumstances the principles of their theories should be framed in terms of nations instead of persons. And this would require a general account of the ideal role of the nation-state in a world that is just to individuals regardless of their nationality—a formidable challenge indeed. Yet until they meet this challenge, cosmopolitans will appear to be advancing a theory that tries to leap before it can stand.

In searching for legitimacy, Rawls hit on an original position with greater immediate plausibility, yet this plausibility comes at some price. Because Rawls's global theory works exclusively in terms of peoples, it cannot show any direct concern for individuals. This is clear in Rawls's account of human rights and humanitarian intervention. When a Rawlsian people intervenes in another people's affairs, to stop human rights abuses or to provide food aid, the intervention is *not* for the sake of the well-being of the oppressed or the starving individuals in the other country.[31] Rather, the intervenor aims at bringing the "outlaw" or "burdened" people up to the level of legitimacy, so that it can play its role in the society of peoples. It is as if societies were individuals, with their members being merely the cells of their bodies, and one society intervened to give medical treatment to another to enable it to rejoin the scheme of social cooperation.[32] The fact that the concerns of peoples cannot "trickle down" to become concern for individuals gives Rawls's accounts of human rights and humanitarian intervention a bloodless, institutional character. And it limits the range of his theories of human rights and humanitarian intervention to those rights and occasions where national legitimacy is at stake.

How much of a price this is I leave for the reader to judge. But we can now understand much better Rawls's enigmatic comment that, while the cosmopolitan views are concerned with the well-being of individuals, his own law of peoples is concerned with the justice (or, better, the legitimacy) of societies. The law of peoples orders the relations between peoples, and therefore leaves the interests of individuals as an indirect and rather minimal concern.

Why Rawls Is Not a Global Egalitarian

Understanding Rawls's views on legitimacy makes sense of his focus on peoples instead of individuals. Yet it may now appear even more puzzling why Rawls is not a global egalitarian.

After all, Rawls implies that the international public political culture already contains the fundamental ideas that *peoples* should be regarded as free and equal, and that the society of *peoples* should be fairly regulated.[33] And these are just the ideas of freedom, equality, and fairness that in justice as fairness led to the domestic difference principle. It may or may not be true that the global political culture contains the analogue of what I have called the strong egalitarian proviso: the distribution of benefits and burdens should not depend on arbitrary features of peoples like their place in the distribution of natural resources. But if this idea is not yet in the global political culture, then it might well develop. Since Rawls's fundamental ideas of the global society of peoples so closely resemble those of the liberal society of citizens, should not Rawls be advocating that economic inequalities between peoples are only permissible if they work to the advantage of the least advantaged peoples? While we have seen why Rawls is not a cosmopolitan, we still have not found the asymmetry between the global and domestic spheres that produces egalitarian principles in one but not the other.[34]

The asymmetry emerges when we realize how Rawls understands the interests of peoples. As Rawls defines them or discovers them in the relevant public political cultures, peoples and domestic citizens simply have different fundamental interests. Domestic citizens as such want more income and wealth, while peoples as such do not. This is why the distribution of income and wealth is a central problem for citizens, but not for peoples.

Citizens within justice as fairness are assumed to want more income and wealth, not as positional goods but simply as resources with which to pursue their visions of the good life. Peoples within the law of peoples, on the other hand, are not assumed to want more wealth, because peoples have no vision of the good life. Rawls says that peoples have interests only in maintaining their territorial integrity, securing the safety of their citizens, maintaining their free and just social institutions, and securing their self-respect as peoples.[35] He suggests that the idea that peoples must hunger for more territory is left over from the disastrous days of imperial Europe, and the idea that peoples must perpetually pursue wealth is merely the ideology of capitalist businessmen.[36] The right conception of a people is as satisfied within itself, having no projects to further beyond its own material and moral maintenance. Once internal justice is achieved, Rawls says, it is perfectly possible and perhaps even preferable for a people's real rate of economic growth to stop.[37]

A people must be concerned with its level of wealth if this is insufficient to support a free and just political order. A people must also be concerned if economic inequality threatens its political status—if it is being menaced by an aggressive neighbor, for instance. But above the goal of internal justice and given no political knock-on effects, a people as such is totally uninterested in its economic status both absolutely and relative to other peoples.

We can now make more sense of Rawls's earlier example of the initially equal societies, one of which decides to industrialize and the other of which remains pastoral. Rawls said of this example that it would be unjust to tax the first to give to the second, and this appeared odd given his repeated emphasis in the domestic realm on the importance of maintaining background justice. But Rawls's reasoning is now clearer. Above the level of political self-sufficiency, there is no need to redistribute to maintain background justice because peoples are indifferent to that which would be redistributed.

Should a people decide to make itself wealthier through greater savings, then this should be of no official concern whatsoever to other peoples. We can now also understand why Rawls complained that Beitz's globalized difference principle lacks a "target" and a "cut-off point." In Rawls's view a global distributive principle for wealth must have a cut-off, because beyond some minimal level peoples' concern for wealth simply cuts off.

So the members of wealthier peoples, wanting to justify themselves to the members of poorer peoples, could in a Rawlsian world say: "Your society meets the minimal standards of legitimacy and stability. It is just by your own lights, or if it is not it is your task to make it so. We have more wealth than you do, it is true. But this is an indifferent matter from the standpoint of international justice or legitimacy. If you want more wealth, it is up to you and your compatriots to decide to save more, or borrow more, or change your population policy, or whatever. We will guarantee your decency and stability but we need take no notice of your prosperity. That is not what global justice demands."

Rawls's Blind Spot: Individuals in the Global Economy

It is not my aim here to undermine Rawls's assumption that peoples as such are indifferent to greater wealth, or the implications of this assumption for his account of international duties of redistribution. However, this assumption brings us to a fundamental problem with Rawls's anticosmopolitanism. This is that a law of peoples cannot be sensitive to certain crucial individual interests.

We can get a sense of the problem by noticing a disconnect between the motivations of the main players in Rawls's domestic and global theories. Recall that in justice as fairness, citizens are assumed to want more wealth and income. Yet in the law of peoples, peoples as such have no motivation to increase their wealth. This is the disconnect: peoples are not assumed to be motivated to get more of what their citizens want. This implies that peoples as such have no motivation to attend to at least some of the interests of their members. Rawls might try to explain this away by saying that each citizen merely wants more *of the national product that there is* and has no interest in the national product being larger. But this chafes against the rationale he gave for citizens wanting income and wealth in the first place: citizens want wealth and income to be able to pursue their visions of the good life. Citizens as Rawls defines them should rationally desire that the national product become bigger, as this would mean that more could be distributed among them. Yet these are rational desires of which their peoples need take no notice.

In Rawls's account of human rights we found that the concerns of peoples do not "trickle down" to become direct concern for the interests of individuals. Here we are finding that certain interests of individuals do not "trickle up" to become the concerns of peoples, which are the only concerns represented in Rawls's global theory.

This problem goes deeper than merely a theoretical disjunction between Rawls's domestic and global theories. We can see this particularly in Rawls's account of global fair trade. Here Rawls lays out his principles for global economic activity. The principles say essentially that nations should keep their economic treaties, that there should be a world bank, and that obvious market imperfections like monopolies and oligopolies should be discouraged.[38] What is notable is that these are all provisions that allow *peoples* to relate fairly to each other. Indeed, Rawls could have added all of the main World Trade Organization rules to his list, such as the rules that nations should not distinguish among trading partners, the rules that national laws should give equal treatment to foreign and domestic products, and the rules against national subsidies and commodity dumping. These provisions all seem sensible as far as they go. But what they lack is any concern for individuals' economic interests as such.

Because of its exclusive focus on peoples, Rawls's global framework for fair trade cannot recognize individual economic interests as independent interests that give rise to distinctive problems of international justice. None of Rawls's rules could recognize, for instance, an Indian citizen's demand to be compensated for the industrial negligence of an American company; nor could they recognize an Indonesian worker's demand to be paid by her multinational employer for working forced overtime.

And of course individuals do have their own independent interests in gaining the goods and avoiding the bads generated by the international economic basic structure. Individuals have interests not only in increased income and wealth but in employment, employment opportunities, good working conditions, price stability, clean air, and more. Equally obviously, the structure of the coercive institutions that regulate international economic activity can affect these interests significantly. Yet within a law of peoples these interests cannot percolate up to become peoples' concerns, nor are these interests addressed in justice as fairness, which is framed for a self-contained domestic society. This means that the important interests that individuals have in how they are affected by global economic activity have no place anywhere in Rawls's theorizing.

This is why Rawls's theorizing needs supplementation. In the next section I sketch an original position argument to complement Rawls's arguments in justice as fairness and the law of peoples, which addresses the interests of individuals in the global economy.

A Corporatist Global Original Position

Original position arguments are simply devices to move from a conception of agents and their proper moral relations to principles for regulating the basic structure that distributes the benefits and burdens of their interactions. So far we have seen three such arguments: Rawls's domestic original position, which moves from domestic citizens as free and equal relating fairly to the two principles of justice as fairness; Rawls's global original position, which moves from peoples as free and equal relating fairly to the principles of the law of peoples; and the cosmopolitan original position of Beitz and Pogge, which moves from world citizens as free and equal relating fairly to a globalized difference principle.

Above I claimed that Beitz's and Pogge's conception of persons and their proper moral relations went beyond what is contained in the global public political culture (global political institutions and the public traditions of their interpretation as well as historic texts and documents that have become part of common knowledge and common knowledge itself). This means that coercive enforcement of their globalized difference principle would be illegitimate, being in violation of Rawls's fundamental norm that coercive force is legitimate only when it is exercised on grounds that are reasonably or responsibly acceptable to those who are coerced. Our current task is to construct an original position pertaining to individual economic interests, using conceptions of agents and of their proper relations that do not go beyond what is contained in the global public political culture.

The basic structure to be regulated by this new original position is made up of the institutions—beyond those regulated by Rawls's law of peoples—that distribute internationally generated economic goods and bads. These institutions include national and international laws and bodies that define property and contracts, that make policy regarding employment and liability standards for multinational corporations, that establish levels of global carbon emissions, that set targets for currency exchange rates, and so on. Analogously to justice as fairness, the problem of the justice of this basic structure arises because economic activity within these institutions produces advantages, but individuals are not indifferent to how the benefits and burdens generated by the institutions will be divided. These benefits and burdens include not only products and services but employment, income, profit, pollution, and much besides.

The conceptions of the person that we will use for this original position are persons as producers, consumers, and owners of internationally generated economic goods and bads (hence this original position is "corporatist"). These economic roles are defined by their interests. Producers have interests in income, employment opportunity and stability, decent working conditions, and control over hours of labor. Consumers have interests in the variety, availability, and affordability of goods and services but also in avoiding dangerous products and pollution. Owners have interests in maximizing profit or shareholder value. The individuals inhabiting each of these three roles also have generic interests simply as human beings: interests in their continued health, and in developing and maintaining basic abilities rationally to direct their own activities. I will further assume that there is a limited partial ranking among these interests: for example, physical health is more important than the consumption of luxuries.

These specifications of the interests of consumers, producers, and owners appear innocuous enough. And although any list and ranking of human interests can be challenged as outstripping common-sense acceptability, I don't believe that the account just given faces serious objections. The most difficult challenge for constructing the new original position is to identify the moral relations in which our role bearers are said to be situated. Here the global political culture provides very limited content, and we must be careful not to stray beyond it. I will assume two relations—equality and fairness—which I believe stay within the limits. Our persons are equal, in the restricted sense that each person's interests are assumed to be of equal intrinsic worth regardless of their economic role or at what point in the career of humanity their life is lived. And our persons are to relate fairly, in the following minimal sense: we assume that the mere fact that one person has the power to shape the common rules in his favor (e.g., because he owns capital) is not in itself a good reason for the rules to be so shaped.

These two relations of equality and fairness produce a thin veil of ignorance. The representatives of our economic agents have veiled from them the economic roles of the individuals they represent. That is, they do not know whether those they represent are producers, consumers, owners, or some combination of the three. They also do not know when in time those they represent live (this screens out intergenerational discrimination). But that is all. We cannot knit a thicker veil by assuming that individuals are robustly "free and equal," or that their class positions or access to natural resources are arbitrary from a moral point of view. These ideas are not a deep part of the international political culture, so it would not be legitimate by Rawls's standard to coerce people in terms of them.

The parties so veiled will try to come to an agreement on principles, based on what each sees as the rational advantage of the individual she represents. Since the interests of producers, consumers, and owners conflict in obvious ways, the parties will face familiar questions about what economic principles to choose.[39] In many areas they will not be able to answer these questions. But there are two types of cases in which agreement should be possible: cases in which there is a convergence of interests, and cases where there is a clear hierarchy of interests. It is the parties' attention to convergent and hierarchical interests, along with their rational concern for the worst possible outcomes, that makes this original position an effective moral heuristic.

The interests of producers, consumers, and owners do sometimes converge: for instance, they converge on the importance of maintaining a predictable and stable economic environment. Because of this convergence the parties will favor principles aimed at securing property rights, making contracts enforceable, punishing fraud, and promoting price stability. To take price stability as a particular example,[40] the parties might further specify principles that require greater transparency in international markets, encourage central banks to counteract inflationary and deflationary pressures, promote diversification in countries heavily dependent on single-commodity exports, and discourage financial instruments which increase exchange-rate volatility.

Now it might be denied that there is complete convergence of interests on all of these more practical suggestions: perhaps some individuals will lose out if certain of these policies are implemented. Yet here we can also appeal to the other source of agreement in this original position: a hierarchy of interests. Price stability is a strong general interests of producers, consumers, and owners—especially of the economically worst-off in these categories. By comparison, increasing profit from factors that tend to make prices unstable is a less urgent interest. This ranking is what makes it rational for the parties to choose principles securing price stability even foreseeing the possibility that its implementation might reduce the potential profits of those they represent.

Hierarchies of interests will also generate some of this original position's more progressive principles. From the basic and profound human interests in health and rational self-direction we should expect at least the following: prohibitions on slavery and child prostitution; penalties for industrial negligence; requirements for minimally decent working conditions and hours; and employment (if not necessarily job) security. The interests here are so strong that the parties would wish to secure them at the cost of almost any other interest. Here we find a much more robust foundation than in Rawls's law of peoples for economic human rights.[41]

There are also familiar trade-offs within this class of urgent interests. The parties would not want to burden industry with so much liability insurance and safety regulation, for example, that employers could not afford to offer any jobs at all. Yet it seems to me that this original position is a useful tool for considering how these trade-offs should rightly be made. For the parties in this original position will have their attention focused on the worst that could happen to those they represent; and this will require that trade-offs, when they must be made, will be made among the interests that are genuinely the most urgent (e.g., employment versus safety). This kind of moral reasoning stands in contrast to the real world "race to the bottom" where poor countries compete to cheapen their labor costs to attract international capital. In this real world process urgent interests are traded off against those less urgent, such as increased profitability of first-world corporations. And this trade-off is made because these corporations and their supporters have the power to shape the rules in their favor. This is just the sort of power-based reason that the corporatist veil of ignorance filters out, leaving individual interests to be balanced by their true human importance.[42]

Whether the addition of the corporatist original position completes the Rawlsian global theory, or whether further supplementation is still required, are questions for further research. Yet we might be encouraged that the corporatist original position can produce results that we are confident are correct (protections against slavery, theft, and fraud) while plausibly extending our intuitions where they may have been less certain (on, for example, the importance of price stability). This original position thus appears able—as Rawls's own two original positions are able—to "accommodate our firmest convictions and . . . provide guidance where guidance is needed." This suggests that the corporatist original position may be a constructive extension of Rawls's law of peoples and may help us to order our thoughts about global economic justice for individuals.

Notes

1. John Rawls, *The Law of Peoples* (Cambridge: Harvard University Press, 1999). The current essay is an expanded version of the discussion of *Law of Peoples* in my "Contractualism and Global Economic Justice" (*Metaphilosophy* 32.1 [2001]; and in *Global Justice* ed. T. Pogge [Oxford: Blackwell, 2001]), which also discusses T. M. Scanlon's contractualism.

2. See for example the papers by Charles Beitz and Allen Buchanan in the "Symposium on John Rawls's *Law of Peoples*," *Ethics* 110.4 (2000); Thomas Pogge, "John Rawls: The Law of Peoples," forthcoming in *Philosophical Quarterly*.

3. John Rawls, *A Theory of Justice* rev. ed. (Cambridge: Harvard University Press, 1999); John Rawls, *Justice as Fairness: A Briefer Restatement* [manuscript, 1994]; see also *Law of Peoples*, 30–32.

4. *Theory of Justice*, 63.

5. *Theory of Justice*, 331–333.

6. Charles Beitz, *Political Theory and International Relations* with a new afterword (Princeton: Princeton University Press, 1999); "Cosmopolitan Ideas and National Sentiment," *Journal of Philosophy* 80.10 (1983). Thomas Pogge, *Realizing Rawls* (Ithaca, N.Y.: Cornell University Press, 1989); "An Egalitarian Law of Peoples," *Philosophy and Public Affairs* 23.3 (1994). I am here ignoring some significant differences between Beitz's and Pogge's approaches.

7. To take an example of Pogge's, "The current distribution in national rates of infant mortality, life expectancy and disease . . . [can] be accounted for, in large part, by reference to the existing world market system" (*Realizing Rawls*, 237).

8. Pogge also supported a globalized difference principle, but he suggested that a Rawlsian should favor a more modest "global resource tax" as a step toward an egalitarian world order. Pogge is no longer engaged in the Rawlsian project, although he would welcome support from Rawlsians for his current proposal, a "global resource dividend." See Pogge, "A Global Resource Dividend," in *Ethics of Consumption*, eds. D. A. Crocker and T. Linden (Lanham, MD: Rowman & Littlefield, 1998).

9. *Law of Peoples*, 23–30. Many have objected that Rawls's category of "peoples" is not apt for a global normative theory because its use ignores the arbitrariness of international boundaries and the existence of subnational groups. Although I share some of these misgivings, I will not discuss the difficulties here.

10. *Law of Peoples*, 57.

11. *Realizing Rawls*, 246.

12. *Law of Peoples*, 35–43.

13. *Law of Peoples*, 117.

14. *Law of Peoples*, 117–118.

15. *Law of Peoples*, 119–120.

16. *Law of Peoples*, 112, footnote 44.

17. *Law of Peoples*, 113.

18. *Law of Peoples*, 36.

19. *Law of Peoples*, 119–120.

20. The turning point in the subject matter of Rawls's theorizing occurs with "Justice as Fairness: Political not Metaphysical," *Philosophy & Public Affairs* 14.3 (1985). Rawls's attention to legitimacy deepened in the essays over the next four years: "The Idea of an Overlapping Consensus" (1987), "The Priority of Right and Ideas of the Good" (1988), and "The Domain of the Political and Overlapping Consensus" (1989) [now all in Rawls, *Collected Papers* (Cambridge: Harvard University Press, 1999)], and finally found its full expression in *Political Liberalism* (New York: Columbia University Press, 1993). On the centrality of legitimacy in Rawls's later theorizing, see David Estlund, "The Survival of Egalitarian Justice in John Rawls' *Political Liberalism*," *Journal of Political Philosophy* 4.1 (1996).

21. I infer this generalized principle of legitimacy, which applies to both liberal and nonliberal societies, from Rawls's liberal principle of legitimacy (*Political Liberalism*, 137). The phrase "reasonably or responsibly" reflects Rawls's usage in *Law of Peoples* that ties "reasonable" to liberal societies and "responsible" to decent (i.e., non-liberal) societies. Coercive force must be "reasonably or responsibly" acceptable to those who are coerced because it must be acceptable to the citizens of both liberal and decent societies. I explore the role of this general principle of legitimacy more thoroughly in "The Unity of Rawls's Work" (forthcoming).

22. *Law of Peoples*, 65–67.

23. *Political Liberalism*, xvi–xviii.

24. *Political Liberalism*, 36–38. For more thorough treatments of Rawls's idea of the "reasonable," see Wenar, "*Political Liberalism*: An Internal Critique," *Ethics* 106.1 (1995); David Estlund, "The Insularity of the Reasonable: Why Political Liberalism Must Admit the Truth," *Ethics* 108.2 (1998); Larry Krasnoff, "Consensus, Stability, and Normativity in Rawls's *Political Liberalism*," *Journal of Philosophy* 115.6 (1998).

25. *Political Liberalism*, 8–15. I have added the phrase "common knowledge itself" to accommodate the recurring theme in Rawls's work that in working up the content of a political conception we may use premises that are widely accepted and uncontroversial. Common knowledge fits comfortably within Rawls's norm of legitimacy, since the use of common knowledge (so long as it genuinely is so) should be acceptable in political argument by all reasonable and responsible agents. See, e.g., *Political Liberalism*, 224.

26. *Political Liberalism*, 8.

27. *Political Liberalism*, 156–157; *Law of Peoples*, 141.

28. *Law of Peoples*, 18.

29. For the view that peoples should be treated as free and equal, regardless of how they view themselves as represented in the "public political culture," see Beitz, "Cosmopolitan Ideas and National Sentiment," 596; Pogge, *Realizing Rawls*, 270; and Andreas Follesdal, "The Standing of Illiberal States, Stability and Toleration in John Rawls' 'Law of Peoples,' " *Acta Analytica*, 18 (1997), 152–153.

30. *Theory of Justice*, 18.

31. Pogge, "An Egalitarian Law of Peoples," 209–210.

32. As Beitz puts it, "Respect for human rights is, so to speak, part of the price of admission to international society." Beitz, "Rawls's Law of Peoples," *Ethics* 110.4 (2000), 684.

33. *Law of Peoples*, 33–34.

34. See Buchanan, "Rawls's Law of Peoples: Rules for a Vanished Westphalian World," *Ethics* 110.4 (2000), 708.

35. *Law of Peoples*, 29, 34.

36. *Law of Peoples*, 25–28, 107.

37. *Law of Peoples*, 106–107.

38. *Law of Peoples*, 37, 42–43.

39. Analogously to justice as fairness, where the parties have no knowledge of the likelihood of persons they represent being in any particular economic class, the parties here have no idea how likely it is that those they represent will be consumers, producers, owners, or some combination of the three. They cannot therefore gamble based on the probabilities that the persons they represent are in one group or another.

40. I am here imagining that the parties engage in a process similar to Rawls's "four-stage sequence" in justice as fairness, in which they specify general principles more exactly as appropriate to the circumstances of a particular time and place. See *Theory of Justice*, 171–176.

41. Since this corporatist original position is supplemental to the one set out in *Law of Peoples*, it assumes that Rawls's global principle of assistance is already in effect—and therefore that individuals' most basic needs (decent food, clothing, shelter) are already met either locally or through international aid.

42. Not everyone will be satisfied with the way this original position is set out. In particular, some may suspect that this original position is biased in favor of labor over capital. But capital is represented through its owners, and also, importantly, through the interests of future producers and consumers. We should therefore expect restrictions on international entrepreneurship, but not blindness to the interests of its current or future beneficiaries.

II

Strong Universalism and Transnational Commitments

3

Intervention and Civilization: Some Unhappy Lessons of the Kosovo War

David Luban

Twenty years ago I published a paper on just-war theory, arguing that military intervention in foreign countries to defend basic human rights is just, even if it violates national sovereignty and therefore amounts in legal terms to aggression. I was, as I recall, rather proud of the paper.[1]

As the Kosovo War unfolded in 1999, I was more than once haunted by the ironic slogan, "Be careful what you wish for." The Kosovo War was a military intervention to defend basic human rights. The Kosovo War was also a near disaster, for reasons that go to the heart of its moral justification: legitimate political concerns led the NATO allies to wage war in a way that endangered the very people the war was supposed to defend. Understanding that these political concerns were legitimate is one unhappy lesson of the Kosovo War. The lesson, more generally, is that practical and political limitations on effective warfare can amount to moral limitations as well—and limitations on effective warfare can, in turn, weaken the humanitarian rationale for intervening in the first place.

I have nevertheless come to believe that the Kosovo intervention was, in the end, morally justified. It would have been shameful not to intervene, because the Kosovar Albanians were being treated in a way that is not civilized. As we shall see, this turns out to be an uncomfortably fragile basis for humanitarian intervention, because the distinction between civilized and barbaric behavior, drawn by all peoples at all times, nevertheless varies greatly among societies and epochs. It is a distinction based in social sentiment rather than universal reason. Even the judgment that mass expulsion and ethnic cleansing are uncivilized is fundamentally sentimental. Yet, sentimental or not, the conclusion that gross human rights violations are an affront to civilized standards may well be the *only* basis for humanitarian intervention. Fighting for human rights proves to be far more precarious, both practically and philosophically, than friends of humanitarian intervention would like to believe. This is the second unhappy lesson of the Kosovo War.

1 Introduction: Circumspect Humanitarianism in Kosovo

The American-led NATO attack on Kosovo began on March 24, 1999. Within two days, it appeared that the immediate result was a humanitarian catastrophe of incredible proportions. As if the air attack was their cue, Serbian police and military units joined with Serb Kosovar militias and opportunistic thugs to drive Kosovar Albanians from their homes (a process that had been happening before, although on a much smaller scale). Tales of horror followed the hundreds of thousands of miserable refugees streaming to the borders. Their homes had been looted or burned, men were separated from women, and an unknown number of men (several thousand, it now appears) were murdered. Young women were gang-raped. The Serbian forces moved quickly but systematically to eradicate the Albanian presence from Kosovo. Hedging against the day the Albanians might return, the Serbs methodically destroyed birth records, deeds, auto registrations, and other documents that Albanians might use to prove that they had once existed in Kosovo and owned property there.

The NATO forces appeared helpless to stop the disaster. NATO had not prepared an expeditionary force of ground troops, having apparently concluded that bombings alone would cause Serbian President Milosevic to fold quickly. Indeed, President Bill Clinton had incautiously announced that America would never send ground troops. That left air power, but bad weather too often prevented NATO aircraft from bombing Serbian troops and armor without flying so low that they would be vulnerable to surface-to-air missiles.

NATO leaders proved unwilling to take the risk, and the astounding fact is that no NATO aircraft were shot down. Weeks later, when American Apache helicopters were brought in, they sat unused on the ground for similar reasons.

To those of us following the news from Kosovo aghast, it seemed that the NATO incursion had turned into an unmitigated disaster, ruining the very people it was supposed to help. It was hard not to share the sentiment of Noam Chomsky, who circulated a lengthy e-mail message during the first week of the bombing in which he assailed NATO for violating the fundamental Hippocratic principle that should govern all humanitarians: "First do no harm!"[2] Even though President Clinton and Secretary of State Madeline Albright assured us that the Serb campaign of ethnic cleansing would have unfolded in much the same way without the NATO attack, it appeared likely that it would not have happened so soon or so quickly—which means that it might have been blunted or even prevented.[3]

Soon NATO began to bomb Serbia proper in order to raise the stakes and bring the war home. Even so, American spokespersons declared that Milosevic's presidential palace was off limits because of its historical and cultural significance, including the Rembrandt on its first floor.[4] Like the refusal to take any military risks, this announcement appeared to signal a lack of seriousness on the part of NATO's political leaders—a determination to fight a war that in some sense was not a war, a politically correct war that would raise no objections on the home front.[5]

The Serbian surrender on June 3, 1999, was as unexpected as the ferocious Serb attack on the Albanians. It appeared to give bragging rights to President Clinton and the NATO leadership; the political commentator Hendrik Hertzberg, writing in *The New Yorker*, argued soon after that it proved the wisdom of Clinton's entire approach to the Kosovo crisis.[6]

Of course, it proved no such thing. NATO's cautious, low-risk-of-casualties, air-power-only approach may well have prolonged the war, inflicted needless suffering on the civilian population of Serbia, permitted additional atrocities to be visited on the Albanian Kosovars, and thereby provoked them to revenge-atrocities and reverse ethnic cleansing when they returned, thereby prolonging the task of NATO peacekeepers and perhaps making it an impossible one. It also sent a message that could hardly be lost on the world: that Americans considered one American life to be worth thousands of Yugoslav lives—hardly a resounding endorsement of the doctrine of universal human rights.[7]

2 The Abiding Tension between Statism and Human Rights

The reply is that a more aggressive warfare strategy was politically impossible, both because America's NATO allies were unwilling to go along with it and—more importantly—because the American public (and, presumably, the publics in the other NATO nations) would be unwilling to accept very many casualties in a war justified in purely humanitarian terms.

This last point seems to me a philosophically important one. Throughout human history, wars have been fought mostly, perhaps exclusively, to advance the perceived interests of the states or rulers whose soldiers fought them. This is no less true in the United Nations era, even though the U.N. Charter prohibits wars motivated by the age-old quests for plunder, tribute, empire, colonies, and slaves, the traditional national interests advanced by war. The Charter reduces the permissible interests to self-defense and collective self-defense, but these remain national interests nonetheless. Significantly, President Clinton occasionally found it necessary to justify the intervention in explicitly antialtruistic terms of American commercial interests in European stability. Ironically, perhaps, it seemed necessary for the president to position himself on the moral *low* ground to set minds at ease.[8]

The fact is that a war fought to protect human rights is deeply subversive as a matter of theory. International law and the international order are founded on the ultimacy of sovereign states. It is states that public international law regulates, states whose consent via treaties and customs creates the stuff of international norms, states whose interactions are the subject matter of diplomacy. International law also recognizes substate national groups, and the principle of national—that is, ethnic—self-determination is in notable tension with the principle of state sovereignty. But even national self-determination is fundamentally state-centered: it is the claim that national minorities deserve states of their own. Within this state-centered order, individual human beings amount to little more than an ontological curiosity.

I do not mean that human rights are unimportant in public international law. That is plainly untrue. I mean instead to highlight the embarrassing fact that the coercive protection of human rights is profoundly subversive of the ultimate ground of the international order, state sovereignty.[9]

Nowhere is this more apparent than in the Nuremberg Charter, in some sense the foundational document of contemporary human rights law. In addition to traditional war crimes, Article 6 of the Charter introduced two novel crimes, crimes against peace (Article 6(a)) and crimes against humanity (Article 6(c)). The Charter also abolished the act of state defense (Article 7) and the defense of superior orders (Article 8). Abolishing these defenses displaces the sovereign as the sole lawgiver and denies that sovereign acts are above the law, so the Charter plainly seems like an anti-sovereignty, pro-human-rights document. Furthermore, crimes against humanity can be committed by a sovereign against his own subjects, so that Article 6(c) is likewise an encroachment on sovereignty. Finally, Nuremberg instituted a system of individual, not just state, responsibility for violations of international law—another innovation that undercuts the view that only states matter.

Yet all these achievements are nullified, at least in part, by Article 6(a), which the framers of the Nuremberg Charter regarded as their greatest accomplishment, because they imagined that it would bring war to an end. Crimes against peace are crimes that plan or execute an aggressive war. The Nuremberg Charter gave this clause of Article 6 priority over Article 6(c), by restricting crimes against humanity to persecutions committed in execution of crimes against peace and war crimes. In effect, the tribunal subordinated its cosmopolitan demands to the statist demand of Article 6(a), that all states must respect the sovereignty of other states.[10]

I am not implying that the Kosovo intervention violated international law. Lawyers will argue about this, but the question is not really so important, because the actions of great powers are as much sources as subjects of international law.[11] The Kosovo intervention certainly violated whatever law the authors of the Nuremberg Charter thought they were framing; but the fact that heirs of the Nuremberg powers conducted the intervention may show that Nuremberg law has been superseded by something else. The important point is not that humanitarian intervention violates Nuremberg law, but that it violates the statist order that the Nuremberg Charter aimed to protect. Indeed, United Nations Secretary-General Kofi Annan, in a widely heralded address to the General Assembly, claims that "[s]tate sovereignty, in its most basic sense, is being redefined by the forces of globalization and international cooperation."[12] Now, he believes, the aim of sovereignty is to protect human rights as well as the rights of states. It follows that a state that fails to protect human rights forfeits at least part of its sovereignty. On that basis, Annan defends humanitarian interventions, but he recognizes that doing so requires fundamentally recasting the basic terms of international law.

3   Unromantic Statism and the Requirement of Domestic Legitimacy

Some years ago, I argued that there is nothing regrettable about violating the statist order to protect human rights; the justice and injustice of war should be assessed along the dimension of human rights protection, not state sovereignty protection. The rights of government derive from the rights of the governed through the process of consent; because people do not consent to their own repression, human rights violation undercuts the very basis of sovereignty.[13]

This argument, which harmonizes with Annan's address, subordinates states to individuals as a matter of what might rather grandly called social ontology. However, while I continue to accept the argument, I now believe that it is incomplete and one-sided. The supremacy of states cannot be wished out of just-war theory. It takes an army to fight an army, and it will be states, not heroic little bands like the Abraham Lincoln Brigade, that carry out whatever humanitarian interventions ought to be carried out.[14] This is as it should be, not only because heroic little bands do not win wars but also because no reasonable law of peoples can tolerate vigilante interventions. To say this is not to say that vigilantes act wrongly when they place their lives on the line in a foreign land to defend the basic rights of people dwelling there. It is that they are the wrong actors. When self-appointed saviors use force to pursue their own political aims, it gets hard in principle to distinguish Abraham Lincoln Brigades from Symbionese Liberation Armies, or, for that matter, from mafias.[15]

For anyone other than anarchists (who believe that states are themselves mafias), states or multilateral organizations of states must be the normal military actors. The focus remains on states rather than multilateral organizations, because, for the foreseeable future, multilateral organizations must rely on states to provide their military forces voluntarily, so that the individual state remains the gatekeeper of intervention. Equipping multilateral organizations like the U.N. with standing armies might alleviate this difficulty, but for just that reason the idea is unlikely to be adopted without states retaining the power to veto the use of their own troops in any given conflict. No state will tolerate the prospect of its own troops being ordered into combat against the wishes of its people or leadership, nor is it obvious that states should tolerate this prospect. Like it or not, the state remains the center of gravity for legitimate warfare abroad.

This, let me underline, is not the romantic defense of statism, which argues that the state simply is the nation or people in its political form. The qualified defense of statism I offer here is little more than a recognition that the anarchist "romance of the people militant" is just as dangerous as the "romance of the nation-state," while the "romance of world government" (dangerous in its own way) is too utopian for the world we live in.

Once we acknowledge that it will be states that intervene, however, we must acknowledge as well that the domestic political process by which a state decides whether or not to commit its children and its fisc to war is relevant to just-war theory. The decision to intervene must be politically legitimate back home as well as morally legitimate abroad.[16] In a democracy, the political support of citizens is a morally necessary condition for humanitarian intervention, not just a regrettable fact of life.[17] If the folks back home reject the idea of altruistic wars, and think that wars should be fought only to promote a nation's own self-interest, rather narrowly conceived, then an otherwise-moral intervention may be politically illegitimate. If the folks back home will not tolerate even a single casualty in an altruistic war, then avoiding all casualties becomes a moral necessity. That is why President Clinton's low-casualty tactics and his arguments that flip-flopped between morality and national self-interest were more than a concession of morality to politics. They represented the twin demands for international and domestic legitimacy.

4 Altruism and National Interest: A False Dichotomy

What just-war theory must offer, then, is an argument within deliberative democracy—an argument addressed to citizens, not just governments, explaining why they should support an altruistic foreign intervention. To whet our intuitions, we may pose the question in melodramatic terms: what explanation can be offered to American soldiers and their parents about why the soldiers should stand ready to die (not to mention to kill) in defense of the rights of Kosovar Albanians? After all, the same liberal regard for the value of individual human lives that commends humanitarian intervention should make us justifiably reluctant to send young men and women into combat.

In one way, of course, the question is misleading. Nothing will ever justify a child's death to a parent. So the question is rather whether there is some explanation that can be offered that is as strong as the time-honored justifications based on national self-interest. Self-defense against foreign conquest offers the best example of a satisfactory explanation, one that only strict pacifists would reject.

However, most Americans probably accept a broader justification of military force than mere defense against foreign conquest, which indeed has never been a genuine risk in twentieth-century wars, including the world wars. The broader justification is that military force can be used in defense of America's vital strategic interests.[18]

Should an American soldier or his parents accept this as a justification for risking death in a far-off land? What is meant by "vital interests" for a country whose physical and political existence is not in any realistic sense imperiled? What were America's vital interests in

Grenada, Panama, Haiti, and Kuwait? In fact, the geopolitical interests of a superpower have changed little since the days of the Roman or Han empires. They are economic interests in securing trade routes, access to raw materials and markets, investment opportunities, and commercial advantages; buttressing allies; and discouraging challenges from potential economic rivals. These interests are not vital to national existence as such; they are vital only to the rather elevated standard of living that superpowers enjoy.

Now, it seems to me odd to tell someone that her son or daughter should risk death so that their neighbors should continue to be able to gas up their sport utility vehicles at a comfortable price. The idea is particularly jarring in a country like the United States, which exhibits a relatively weak commitment to institutions of social welfare. Why should people who resent having their taxes raised to support social welfare policies be expected to go into combat on behalf of their countrymen's luxuries?

I raise this question for two reasons. First, it suggests that there is nothing intuitive or straightforward about justifying wars fought in defense of national strategic interests—nothing, that is, to make the justification more plausible than altruistic reasons. Second, it calls into question the assumption that fighting on behalf of vital economic interests really *is* in the interest of the soldier, even in the extended sense in which defending his country's liberty against foreign invaders is in his moral if not material interest. Both points, I think, weaken the intuitive case for thinking that wars of national interest stand on a firmer and more common-sense ground than wars of altruism. They stand on the same plane, and if arguments of vital national interest are acceptable, there is no reason why arguments of humanitarian interest should not be.

5 American Hegemony and Limiting Principles

The question then becomes what kind of altruistic reasons should properly move American citizens to support humanitarian intervention. To put it another way, which human rights violations rise to a level that demands a military response? If war in defense of basic rights is permissible, which permissible wars should be fought?

Before turning to this question, however, it will be useful to address some preliminary issues.

First, one might wonder why I am focusing exclusively on Americans. One answer is that these thoughts apply to citizens of other democracies as well, and I think this is true. But there is an important reason for focusing on America, a reason given in the title of Lea Brilmayer's book *American Hegemony*.[19] For the time being, at least, America is the world's reigning hegemon (or, since the word is awkward, let me say "superpower").

From the point of view of humanitarian intervention, American hegemony has profound consequences. First, it means that other potential interveners—I am thinking of the Europeans—are unlikely to move without America taking the lead, even when they are better situated to intervene and have more of a stake in doing so, as in the Balkan wars. Second, other potential interveners are likely to believe that America is economically, militarily, and diplomatically in the better position to intervene. Why should they absorb the costs when America can do it with less pain? For better or for worse—mostly for worse, I expect—humanitarian intervention will chiefly be American-led intervention.[20] This is good reason for focusing on the moral justifications for American citizens in particular to commit themselves to humanitarian intervention.

A third consequence of hegemony, however, is a problem of overcommitment. America simply cannot intervene everywhere that humanitarian debacles might warrant it, because humanitarian debacles are everywhere. During the 1990s, one could readily justify humanitarian interventions in Bosnia, Kosovo, Somalia, Rwanda, Burundi, Sierra Leone, Congo, Sudan—and these are only the headline catastrophes. Since the end of the Cold War, American military planning calls for the capacity to fight two regional campaigns simultaneously. That appears to be a lot, but it obviously does not begin to come near the need.

Even a superpower needs limiting principles, by which I mean principles for selecting among all the morally permissible humanitarian interventions those that are truly imperative. The issue here concerns which human rights violations demand a military response and which do not; but this is not the only issue, and before turning to it I wish to say at least a few words about other principles that should guide decisions about where to intervene. Each of them represents a moral constraint on otherwise-permissible humanitarian intervention.

There is, first, Chomsky's Hippocratic principle: the intervention should not make matters worse for those it aims to help (of course, it will make matters worse for those it aims to hinder). This implies that the war should be winnable—winnable, moreover, without undue damage to its intended beneficiaries, and winnable without escalating into a regional or global conflict.[21]

Second, the intervention must be winnable without violating the just-war principle of proportionality: the enemy's interests count as well. One consequence of this condition is that only large-scale human rights violations are likely to call for intervention; otherwise, the intervention will probably be disproportionate to its aim. (Obviously, there can be exceptions to this rule of thumb: intervening against a small and weak human rights violator like Haiti might succeed with very few if any enemy casualties.)

Third, if the aftermath of intervention is anarchy or an unstable truce, the war should be waged only if the interveners are prepared for a lengthy occupation or an exercise in state building. This is a crucial point: no follow-through, no intervention. Otherwise, intervention is like tossing a life jacket to a shipwreck victim but then leaving the victim adrift in the middle of the ocean. One might respond that it is always acceptable to stop a murder in progress even if you do not know what your next move will be. But if the only way to stop the murder is by waging war, the burden of justification surely demands more than "we'll cross that bridge when we come to it."

Fourth, American hegemony notwithstanding, the United States should not intervene when another nation, or a multinational organization, is better situated or morally obligated to lead the intervention. The principle is analogous to the idea in tort theory that liability should lie with the party that can guard against accidents at lowest cost to itself: interventions, too, should be undertaken by the least-cost avoider. Of course, this will create a wrenching dilemma if the least-cost avoider refuses to intervene, for then following the limiting principle will mean that the victims of catastrophe are left to their fates. Unfortunately, the alternative is always picking up the ball when someone else drops it, which heightens the problem of overcommitment, and creates a perverse incentive for nations to engage in a game of humanitarian chicken where each waits for another to take up the burden of intervention.

Even if all these principles are honored, it may well turn out that too many morally legitimate humanitarian interventions remain, so that triage is required. If so, then it appears permissible for an intervener to use its own national interests as a tiebreaker. Suppose that humanitarian intervention would be appropriate in two different countries, but that the intervener can commit the resources to at most one of the two. In that situation, it would be entirely reasonable to choose the country in which the intervener has interests of its own at stake—and using self-interest as a tiebreaker does not make the intervention any less humanitarian.

Recognizing these principles can help address a difficult issue that triage inevitably raises, namely the charge that the intervener picks and chooses among equally compelling cases for unprincipled and unworthy motives. Yes to intervention in Kosovo and Somalia; no to intervention in Bosnia and Rwanda. The Rwanda case is instructive because the American role in Rwanda was shameful—not merely failing to intervene, but frantically maneuvering to stop others from intervening as well.[22] As is now well understood, the Clinton administration was afraid of acknowledging the Rwanda genocide, which would have triggered the 1948 Genocide Convention's requirement to take action. Humiliated by failure in Somalia, the administration was willing to play the scoundrel's part to avoid humanitarian overcommitment. On the one hand, this repulsive episode underlines the problem of overcommitment; but it also confirms suspicions about selective intervention and hypocrisy. Limiting principles, publicly acknowledged, seem far superior.[23] In Rwanda, the moral burden of intervention arguably rested on France and Belgium, whose foreign and colonial policies were in large part responsible for Hutu-Tutsi hatreds.[24] (Instead, France engaged in what one observer calls "blatant complicity in the preparation and implementation of the butchery,"[25] and France's ultimate intervention helped the *géno-cidaires* as much as their Tutsi victims.[26])

Some readers may object that I have been implicitly writing as though the United States always aims to do the right thing. The history of American military intervention hardly inspires confidence in American altruism and humanitarianism, and critics might argue that a blanket rule against intervention would do far more good than a rule riddled with controversial and easy-to-manipulate humanitarian exceptions, which might do little more than provide a fig leaf for superpower realpolitik.[27] Yet even if American interventions have often been purely self-interested, there is no reason to doubt that the Kosovo intervention (like the intervention in Somalia) was fundamentally a humanitarian effort. It is not a given that American intervention is self-interested, and exploring the rationale and limits of good-faith humanitarian intervention makes no assumption one way or the other about which interventions are humanitarian.

The limiting principles I have mentioned are all based in common sense and require no elaborate philosophical argument. According to these limiting principles, what should we think of the Kosovo War? I regard it as a very close call. The interveners were the "right" countries—only Russia was a lesser cost-avoider than NATO, but Russia was backing Milosevic. Furthermore, the war was winnable with little risk of escalation. But, as I have suggested, it is far from obvious that it satisfied Chomsky's Hippocratic principle *given the tactics that the NATO publics were willing to back.* Moreover, it is too soon to tell whether the victorious countries are prepared for the potentially long-term occupation and protection mission that the international security force in Kossovo (KFOR) and the United Nations have assumed. A year after the war, it appears that they are not—the head of the U.N. civil administration has had to beg the reluctant NATO countries to pay their shares; American policymakers complain that policing Kosovo is "mission creep," even though custodial governance *is* the mission. These were all foreseeable problems, and if in hindsight the postwar reconstruction turns out well, that will be largely a matter of moral luck. If it does not, the failure may retroactively rob the war of whatever moral legitimacy it had.

6   Legitimacy or Morality?

One possible limiting principle that I have deliberately omitted from this untidy catalogue is one that would restrict interventions to cases in which the target is a regime lacking domestic legitimacy. In my own earlier work, I argued that regimes lacking the consent of the governed have no moral claim to military immunity, because a state maintained only by force cannot claim to represent the nation, that is, its people. The argument proceeds in three simple steps: no consent, no legitimacy; no legitimacy, no sovereignty; no sovereignty, no immunity to intervention. The converse of this argument might be used to defend a limiting principle based on state legitimacy: with consent comes legitimacy, with legitimacy comes sovereignty, and with sovereignty comes immunity.

I have now come to doubt this argument in both directions. The purpose of intervention is supposed to be protecting human rights; but the legitimacy argument makes no mention of human rights. Even a legitimate regime can engage in repulsive human rights violations, and the legitimacy argument would immunize it against humanitarian intervention.

One might object that a truly consent-based state will not engage in human rights violations. Regimes engage in repression as a substitute for consent, and so we can infer illegitimacy from brutality. This is an error, however. Even if consent is the ultimate basis of legitimacy, the fact remains that people can consent to hierarchical legitimation principles that authorize nonconsensual or even anticonsensual governments, including repressive ones. I do not mean that even the dissenters who are being repressed "really" consent to the government that represses them. The point is rather that in politics consent is never unanimous, and widespread support, which even repressive governments can enjoy, is all that can reasonably be required for consent-based legitimacy.[28] The post-1979 Iranian theocracy met the consent requirement, and even a regime as horrible as the Argentinian junta of the Dirty War enjoyed widespread support until the Falklands defeat.

This last example exposes the problem, for the Argentinian junta was one of the most atrocious and murderous regimes in the world.

It seems to me that the junta should have enjoyed no moral immunity from intervention: even if a murderous regime like the Argentinian junta was legitimate, that does not make it wrong for outsiders to halt its atrocities if they can. The point of limiting principles is to limit overcommitment to morally worthwhile causes. The point is emphatically *not* to replace moral concerns, grounded in human rights, with political concerns, grounded in the consensual basis of the state that is violating human rights. For that reason, I am now inclined to reject the focus on legitimacy. Legitimacy is no substitute for morality.

7 Why Universal Obligation Does Not Follow from the Concept of a Human Right

That leaves the democratic citizen with a question: Given that any war on behalf of basic human rights that satisfies the other limiting principles is morally permissible, which is morally compelling?

The worry is that human rights are so important that all wars on their behalf are morally required. In an earlier paper I wrote that a human right is "a right whose beneficiaries are all humans and whose obligors are all humans in a position to effect the right. . . . Human rights are the demands of all of humanity on all of humanity."[29] As a conceptual matter, rights correlate with obligations on others—obligations to respect the rights. Supposing this to be correct, it appears to follow that if a government is violating the human rights of its people, everyone else is duty bound to bring the violations to a halt.

But that conclusion is too quick. The right not to be tortured imposes a demand on all of humanity, and that conclusion follows from the bare acknowledgment that we have a *right* not to be tortured. But from the conceptual point alone all that follows is the negative demand that everyone must refrain from torture, not the positive requirement that anyone must intervene to stop others from torturing. To argue for humanitarian intervention, one needs a substantive moral argument to the citizens of the intervening powers about why they must guarantee the right against torture of people in other countries, perhaps at the cost of their own or their children's lives.[30]

This last point is important. Many philosophers argue for global economic obligations, that is, obligations to aid people in other countries based on global principles of distributive justice. Other theorists disagree. But even those of us who defend global obligations involving economic self-sacrifice will be hard-pressed to defend a strict, justice-based moral obligation to fight for the human rights of strangers, that is, to put one's life on the line for them. Distributive justice may require your money, but it cannot require your life.

Apart from distributive justice, the natural analogy to a duty to intervene is the "duty to rescue" embodied in so-called good Samaritan laws. Good Samaritan laws make it a punishable offense to stand idly by while another person perishes if the bystander could rescue the victim at no peril to himself. Such laws are controversial, and they have attracted a large philosophical and legal literature. But even proponents agree that "at no peril to himself" is a crucial condition for a valid good Samaritan law. Requiring one person to sacrifice his life for another's, or even to run substantial risk to life or limb for the sake of a stranger, would undermine the very physical security such laws aim to secure.

Put it more simply: If there was a genuine obligation to intervene militarily on behalf of the basic rights of foreigners, a people would have no right *not* to go to war when the basic rights of foreigners are imperiled. But a people always has the right not to go to war.

8 Why Human Rights Nevertheless Provide Reasons for Intervening

For those who favor humanitarian intervention, the challenge must be explaining why, even in the absence of a justice-based obligation to intervene, intervention may be morally vital.

The reason emerges when we ask why rights correlate with duties.[31] On one view, this correlation is a formal matter: To speak of a right *just is* to speak of a set of obligations on the part of others. This makes a certain amount of sense when one considers legal rights, because legal rights often take the form of obligations on others to do or refrain from doing something. (The right to free speech in the American constitution reads "Congress shall make no law . . . abridging the freedom of speech.") The legal realists, who analyzed formal notions such as rights in everyday terms of who gets to do what to whom, encouraged this way of thinking.

But human rights are more than abbreviations for a set of obligations. Commonly, a commitment to human rights reflects a commitment to the substantive belief that every human being has a certain intrinsic worth (that all human beings are, in Kant's words, ends in themselves).[32] Without some such belief, it is hard to see why anyone would think that people have distinctively human rights, that is, rights possessed solely by virtue of being human.

To translate a human right into an equivalent set of obligations on others threatens to obscure this basic point by deflecting attention from the rights-bearer to the obligation-bearers. Translating human rights into correlative obligations replaces the claim that human beings are valuable with a supposedly equivalent set of claims—that *you* are obligated not to inflict certain harms on another human being, and *I* am similarly obligated, and so is everyone else. But something vital gets lost in the translation, namely that others are obligated not to violate us because of something about *us*—because we are valuable, and that value demands respect.

Once we grasp this simple point, we see that although the obligation to refrain from violating a right is one aspect of the fact that people are valuable, it is not the only aspect. The obligation does not capture the entire meaning of the right, because it does not exhaust all the reasons for action that respecting the value of other people generates. In addition to the obligation not to violate rights, we have (for example) a moral reason for helping other people in hard times; and a moral reason for trying to impede those who are violating human rights; and a moral reason for taking steps to forestall rights violations in advance; and a moral reason to support institutions that promote human rights; and so on.[33] These reasons need not rise to the level of obligations—after all, not every reason for doing something is an obligation to do it. But if I am right, to recognize the rights of others is necessarily to recognize a reason for acting when those rights are threatened.

9 Metaphysical Guilt and Bystander Shame

In the moral imaginations of most, I expect, the Holocaust looms large when we think of such matters. In Washington's Holocaust Museum, buttons are sold reading "Remember" and "Never Again," and America's turning its back on the Holocaust is now a familiar and bitter part of the story.[34] The impetus for intervening, many would say, is the guilt that accrues from standing idly by in the face of barbarism. Karl Jaspers, in his post–World War II masterpiece *The Question of German Guilt*, called this "metaphysical guilt," and described it in the following way:

There exists a solidarity among men as human beings that makes each co-responsible for every wrong and every injustice in the world, especially for crimes committed in his presence or with his knowledge. If I fail to do whatever I can to prevent them, I too am guilty. If I was present at the murder of others without risking my life to prevent it, I feel guilty in a way not adequately conceivable either legally, politically or morally. That I live after such a thing has happened weighs upon me as indelible guilt.[35]

To be sure, Jaspers's idea is hardly a model of analytic rigor, but that is not the problem. His lectures on German guilt were the first straight talk that had been heard in a German university in years; and their fearless, unaffected honesty would by itself require us to consider his idea seriously. The problem lies in understanding why Jaspers thinks there is such a thing as metaphysical guilt. In the discussion that follows, I will suggest some corrections to Jaspers's idea, but I have become convinced that it contains an important insight at its core.

Jaspers distinguishes between metaphysical and moral guilt, and he is careful to insist that people can be metaphysically guilty even if they have done nothing morally wrong. He clearly had in mind the guilt of Germans who had done nothing worse than passively acquiesce, perhaps out of terror, to the Nazi crimes being committed around them. It seems excessively moralistic to insist on an obligation to resist; but it seems inadequate to regard the passive Germans as merely blameless. That is the dilemma that leads Jaspers to introduce the notion of metaphysical guilt.[36]

Jaspers insists that theirs is metaphysical rather than moral guilt because no-one is morally required to throw his or her life away "without chance of success and therefore to no purpose," which he believes would have been the outcome of resistance under the conditions of totalitarian terror.[37] Repeatedly, he tells us that the only way a German could have escaped metaphysical guilt was by resisting the Nazis at the cost of his own life. This, he says, is "an indelible claim beyond morally meaningful duty."[38] At one point Jaspers speaks of "the capacity to live only together or not at all."[39]

Here, however, his focus on the situation of Germans under totalitarianism makes Jaspers run off the rails. All he sees is people who must choose between metaphysical guilt and heroic suicide, and that leads him to conclude that metaphysical guilt is guilt at the bare fact of remaining alive.[40] That, presumably, is what makes it metaphysical—too metaphysical, in my view. When Jaspers says "We are guilty of being alive," when he calls metaphysical guilt "something that is always present," and when he adds that without it we would be angels, he confirms the suspicion that by metaphysical guilt he means nothing less than original sin.[41]

The problem with this is not that it is an essentially theological concept. It is that there is something deeply wrong with the idea that the mere desire to live exhibits inadequate solidarity with the dead, and thus is sin. While I think I understand what Jaspers means, thoughts like this should be resisted. Perhaps with the murder of a human being something of incalculable value has been erased from the world; and perhaps the very idea of human rights requires us to regard the murder as, literally, intolerable, so that one feels ashamed to go on, as if going on is a falsehood, a denial of the fact of murder, a final betrayal of the victim.[42]

But isn't it also a splendid thing that the living bury the dead and then go on living? That the widow remarries? That at the same moment the hero breathes his last, teenagers are making out in a park nearby? George Steiner once praised Verdi and Shakespeare for writing dramas in which even in the midst of tragedy someone somewhere is throwing a party or seducing the maid. He contrasted Verdi's sensibility favorably with Wagner's, whose hero takes the whole world with him when he goes. Jaspers is, in Steiner's terms, too Wagnerian.

Suppose, then, that we scrap the intimations of original sin. It still seems to me that Jaspers has identified an authentic moral phenomenon. It is the sense that I am besmirched by failing to take a stand against evil. If it is not metaphysical guilt, then call it bystander guilt or, more accurately, bystander shame. As Adam Roberts comments about the Kosovo War, "The main underlying explanation for the willingness of NATO's 19 members states to take action over Kosovo is not their interpretation of particular events. . . . Nor was it a shared vision as to what the future of the province should be. Rather, the NATO states were united by a sense of shame. . . ."[43]

According to Jaspers, the basis of bystander shame is that we have an ideal of unconditional human solidarity that our passivity betrays. This diagnosis is controversial; but I think there is something to it. It traces our passivity in the face of evil to the separateness of persons: the fact that I will not imperil *me* to prevent *you* from being murdered arises simply because you are not me. The separateness of persons is a deep fact about us, one that perhaps even deserves to be called "metaphysical". Liberals such as John Rawls and Robert Nozick celebrate the separateness of persons and invoke it to explain the limits of moral obligation. In this sense, Jaspers is also a liberal, because he too insists that no-one has a moral obligation to throw his or her life away because others are dying. But, unlike Rawls and Nozick, Jaspers recognizes that people find something curiously shameful about limiting our obligations through separateness.[44] When we fail to stand up against evil, we find ourselves saying "it wouldn't have done any good" or "it's too much to ask" or "what could I have done?" or even "it's none of my business"—and we recognize the defensiveness in all these responses, the telltale sign that we are ashamed.

The reason, I think, is this. Whether or not we have an ideal of unconditional human solidarity, the question of whether we should act in the face of evil assumes that we have *some* moral ideals and principles by which we recognize and condemn evil. If we do not, the question simply does not arise. Bystander shame is the sense that permitting horrors to be perpetrated without doing anything about it reveals an overly weak commitment to these ideals and gives the lie to our claim that they matter very much to us. Oliver Wendell Holmes called ideals "fighting faiths," and, although Holmes was notoriously and excessively fond of military metaphors, in this case his label appears apt. We do distinguish between walking the walk and talking the talk; and bystander shame is our recognition that when we are not willing to back talk with action, the talk itself becomes cheap and in a way false. Even we ourselves can no longer be confident that evil bothers us sufficiently. Perhaps it does not— so long as it is happening to someone else.

Now we can see more clearly why bystander shame is not metaphysical guilt. Guilt is a response of self-accusation at wrongdoing; and metaphysical guilt at the separateness of persons identifies existing separately from others as a kind of wrongdoing: human plurality becomes original sin. This is the part of Jaspers's idea that we should reject.

But shame is different from guilt. Shame betokens inadequacy, not wrongdoing. We experience shame when we fail (and especially when we are seen by others to fail), and by failing reveal that we are less than we set ourselves up to be. We shame ourselves by not living up to important standards that we have advertised to others; even if failure is not culpable, it diminishes us. Professing to believe in the value of human beings, then refusing to protect them as they are murdered or driven from their homes, is paradigmatically shameful. Likewise, professing moral standards, then proving ourselves unwilling to react when others spit on them, is paradigmatically shameful.

These two shameful failures—failure to protect victims, and failure to react to perpetrators—correspond to two distinct but interlocking aspects of human rights: that human beings are valuable, and that violating human beings is evil. Focusing on the first directs our attention to the victims; focusing on the second, to the perpetrators. Jaspers focuses exclusively on solidarity with the victims of evil. In this sense, our shame at inaction is no different than the bystander shame we would experience if we failed to assist the victims of a hurricane. But Jaspers's account is incomplete, because human rights principles also take into account the conduct of the perpetrator. We should (and do) feel bystander shame at allowing the perpetrator to work his will unhindered, because inactivity appears to condone the crime. In this sense, the purpose of intervention is not just saving the victims but frustrating the perpetrators and declaring their conduct off limits. If we do not do that, we should be ashamed of ourselves.[45]

To forestall misunderstanding: I am not suggesting that one's reason for intervening is shame avoidance, as though the point of acting well is merely being thought by others to act well, or thinking well of ourselves. That would be narcissism, not morality. Shame avoidance provides a political and psychological *motivation* for intervening, but the moral *reasons* for intervening are the two I have just set out: protecting the victims and frustrating the perpetrators. The experience of bystander shame should tip us off when the reasons are strong; but it is the reasons, not the shame, that matter.

Couching the issue of intervention as a matter of honoring our own principles perhaps sounds too insufferably high-minded for foreign policy. There is, however, a political dimension to bystander shame. Unlike guilt, shame is essentially a public rather than an inner or private phenomenon: to be shamed is to stand revealed as subpar along some dimension that matters. For that reason, shame undermines other people's confidence in the person or group that is shamed. I have argued that to stand idly by in the face of evil is a kind of performative contradiction of our claim that human rights matter a great deal to us—a contradiction that makes us uncertain how much human rights do matter to us. How, then, can a nation that throws up its hands in the face of massive human rights violations maintain a credible pro-human-rights foreign policy (let alone a leadership role in world affairs)? Indifference to human rights catastrophes abroad may even weaken a nation's domestic culture of human rights. After all, maintaining any legal culture requires citizens' mutual trust and mutual reassurance that others honor the fundamental values of the legal culture. When citizens show themselves unwilling to sacrifice for those values, their own neighbors are entitled to doubt whether the values matter to them.

Not every failure to intervene against human rights violations shames us. Human rights violations go on everywhere all the time, and no nation need be ashamed merely because its armies are not like Batman and Superman, eternally on call to fight malefactors whenever they threaten the innocent. The question of intervention turns on the degree of evil we face, on what the human rights violations are that we confront. Let us turn to that question.

10   Conduct Unbecoming of Civilized People

Over the decades, the United Nations and other authoritative bodies have promulgated many lists of human rights, beginning with the 1948 United Nations Universal Declaration of Human Rights. To read them is to discover a compendium of liberal and democratic political ideals, rule-of-law principles, and the economic and cultural components of a decent human life. The lists are aspirational in a strong sense: much of the world comes nowhere near satisfying any of these rights, and few if any countries satisfy them all. The Universal Declaration includes the right to participate in the arts and sciences (Article 27), the right to universal suffrage with secret ballots (Article 21), and the right to comprehensive social security in the event of disability (Article 25). As a distillation of nearly four centuries of political thought and experience, these ideas deserve the utmost respect. Historically, they have all been fighting faiths, and for good reason. Yet long lists are wish lists, and it appears farfetched that any deviation from them requires a military response from outsiders.

Instead, I want to suggest a very old-fashioned answer to the question: "which human rights are worth going to war over?" The answer is: those human rights the violation of which is uncivilized, so that standing idly by while they are violated calls into question our very commitment to civilization over barbarism.

The distinction between civilized and barbaric behavior is not the same as the distinction between right and wrong. Eating stew with your hands is uncivilized but not wrong; tax fraud is wrong but not uncivilized. I am suggesting that the acts calling for military intervention are those that are not merely wrong but wrong to the point of being barbaric. Before considering in greater detail which rights those might be, it is important to understand what this suggestion means as a matter of theory.

I regard the distinction between civilized and uncivilized behavior as a kind of anthropological primitive, like the distinction between food that is fit and unfit for human consumption, or between the clean and the dirty, the wholesome and the disgusting, the pure and the impure. Every human culture draws lines like these, making them in that sense universal; and the various distinctions often have some nonconventional basis—for example, you can not simply declare poisons to be edible or excrement to be clean. But various cultures draw the lines in different places, so that the distinction between civilized and uncivilized is culturally relative and in that respect insusceptible to rational or philosophical argument.

Let me illustrate with a familiar human-rights example. All the Western European nations have for practical purposes abolished the death penalty; the United States has not. My impression is that contemporary European revulsion to America's death penalty rest very little on philosophical argument; instead, Europeans tend to regard the death penalty as uncivilized. Americans obviously do not.

The American philosopher Jeffrey Reiman has argued, convincingly to my mind, that there is no stronger argument against a fairly administered death penalty than the insistence that it is uncivilized.[46] Arguments about mistaken executions, tainted trials, and racial bias implicitly concede that if these problems could be remedied the death penalty would be acceptable; and philosophical arguments against the death penalty are inconclusive at best. The institution of criminal punishment, I am assuming, can be justified; it can best be justified on retributive grounds; and the permissible upper limit of retribution is the *lex talionis*, which would sanction executing murderers. That, in brief, is the case Reiman makes that the death penalty is just punishment for murder.

But there is another side to the story. Nothing requires administering the maximum justified punishment; and we have typically understood the move toward greater civilization as a move toward greater moderation in punishment. In Reiman's words, *"though the death penalty is a just punishment for murder,* abolishing the death penalty is part of the civilizing mission of modern states."[47]

This is a historicist argument, not a philosophical one. After all, it is only a few decades since Europeans too saw nothing uncivilized about capital punishment. Americans have likewise become noticeably more restrained in their outlook. Today, capital punishment for property offenses would horrify us; a hundred years ago we hung horse thieves. Today, we would be outraged at the spectacle of executions staged as public entertainments—but what Nietzsche rightly called "festivals of cruelty" were standard fare everywhere for most of human history. Dramatists in Shakespeare's time complained because executions emptied the theaters; as recently as the 1920s, American lynch mobs were proud to be photographed in action, and their members mailed picture postcards to their friends. The line between civilization and barbarism is a shifting divide, not a philosophical fixed point.

11   Universal Rights and Relative Civilization

To say this is not to endorse moral relativism which, as Stuart Hampshire notes, "has always rested on an under-estimate of universal human needs."[48] As Hampshire elaborates, "There is nothing ... culture-bound in the great evils of human experience, reaffirmed in every age and in every written history and in every tragedy and fiction: murder and the destruction of life, imprisonment, enslavement, starvation, poverty, physical pain and torture, homelessness, friendlessness."[49] These great evils, universally recognized, form the basis of moral argument in every culture and every epoch, regardless of how much the cultures' positive ideals and conceptions of the good vary. There is no society, and I will venture to assert that there could be no society, in which gratuitous infliction of the great evils is tolerable.

The entry point for relativism lies instead in the fact that in all societies it is thought permissible under some circumstances to inflict great evils on people. At the very least, hard-core violent criminals must be isolated from society, even though imprisonment is one of the great evils. Once this is admitted, then the question of which evils may be inflicted under which justifications arises, and disagreements among societies blossom. In Singapore, unlike the United States, flogging is permissible to punish crimes; in Saudi Arabia, shari'a-based law permits punishment by amputation. Punishments like these are thought barbaric in the United States, but apparently the death penalty is fine. So are savagely long prison sentences: the U.S. Supreme Court has upheld a life sentence for repeated petty frauds, and life without parole for a first-offense drug possession.[50] In the United States, favoring life without parole for murderers makes you a humanitarian. Elsewhere, people shake their heads at American practices of punishment.

It is hard to find a principled rationale for such distinctions. I am suggesting that there is none. Torture and mutilation are per se barbaric, uncivilized; imprisonment is not—and that's the end of the story. To repeat the basic point: there is nothing culturally relative about recognizing the great evils, which are the same everywhere and at all times. What is culturally relative is the recognition of which great evils are off limits for civilized people. Controversial practices such as capital punishment and female genital mutilation, which some cultures find morally revolting and others applaud, make visible the bedrock arbitrariness of the nevertheless necessary distinction between civilization and barbarism.

What about the commonplace idea that what makes practices uncivilized is that they violate human dignity? Isn't that a principled rationale for the distinction? Torture, mutilation, and similar atrocious acts involve an assault on the human body. Confinement at least leaves the inmate in possession of an undisturbed body and a free mind—for the Stoics, all that is necessary for a decent human life. Mutilation dishonors the body; torture overwhelms the mind with distraction. Both, like rape, coercive medical experiments, and other crimes against humanity (the legal term for uncivilized acts) humiliate and mock. These are all crimes against humanity because they are assaults on human dignity.

In the same way, one might argue that the notion of human dignity underlies the other principal category of crimes against humanity (the first category being acts like torture and mutilation that are per se atrocious[51]). These are persecutions on ethnic, racial, or religious grounds, including genocide.[52] Group persecutions visit evils on people regardless of anything they may have done. In this respect, group persecutions are very different from political repression and persecution which, abhorrent though it is, attacks people for choices they have made or actions they have performed. Human dignity, which demands that people be treated as individuals, requires no less.

So, of the three major categories of serious human rights violations—atrocious acts, group persecutions, and political repressions—only the first two represent basic assaults on human dignity. Only they are uncivilized. Although no record remains of how the term "crimes against humanity" was chosen by the framers of the Nuremberg Charter, it seems clear that the term was intended to register the judgment that these crimes represent a basic boundary-crossing from civilization to barbarism.[53]

Now, I do not disagree that the special barbarism of crimes against humanity is their affront to human dignity, over and above the tangible evils they inflict. But the concept of human dignity is too abstract to provide a principled basis for distinguishing civilized from uncivilized behavior. Human dignity is not a self-explanatory and self-executing notion; neither is the famous Kantian formula of treating people as ends in themselves rather than means. Social meaning matters immensely in giving content to ideas like these; we will never be able to deduce from the Kantian formula alone that flogging violates human dignity while confinement does not. It is more plausible that our catalogue of crimes against humanity defines what we mean by violations of human dignity. In effect, then, we recognize offenses against human dignity because they are uncivilized, rather than the other way around.

12 Intervention and Civilization: Is the Argument Neocolonialist?

It is time to make explicit the connection between civilization and bystander shame. The hypothesis is that we should be ashamed to remain bystanders in the face of evil when evil rises to the level of barbarism. As democratic citizens, we should support intervention to stop human rights violations when they seem not just wrong but barbaric to us, because it is shameful to remain uninvolved.

This is a disquieting conclusion, because we also recognize that our distinction between the civilized and the barbaric is fluctuating and fraught with relativism. In other words, one of the gravest steps we can take—going to war—rests on a judgment that has no philosophical foundation and that others may reasonably disagree with. It is a judgment, one might say, based largely on sentiment.[54] To some observers, it was simply soft-headed emotionalism to support the Kosovo intervention because the ethnic cleansing looked sufficiently Holocaust-like, with boxcars of refugees and tragic columns of displaced Albanians walking their trail of tears to the border. But on the view defended here, sentimental criteria like these are signs that civilization is under attack, and acting on them is not soft-headed at all. It is, I fear, the best reason NATO had for going into Kosovo.

I find these conclusions troubling for reasons that are obvious, including the ease with which sentiments can be manipulated; but I want to address explicitly one important objection that does not worry me.

The objection is that the proposal smacks of neocolonialism. America and countries that share its conception of human rights are supposed to invade Kosovo or Rwanda to plant the flag of civilization. Is this not just a newfangled version of taking up the white man's burden?

I believe that it is not, for two reasons. First, and most important, humanitarian intervention does not have as its aim the conquest of colonies, the installation of an exploitative foreign elite, or the exaction of tribute and plunder. Colonialists hope to stay in the driver's seat as long as possible, but contemporary interveners wish desperately to get out fast. Intervention simply is not colonialism. Second, the aim is not to force an alien vision of the good on reluctant people. Recall Hampshire's crucial distinction between pluralism of visions of the good—which is indisputable—and monism when it comes to recognizing the great evils—which is also indisputable. It is crucial that the aim of intervention is to stop the infliction of evils, not to convert the heathen to an alternative conception of the good. There is no reason to believe that Rwandans think murder is a central practice of their civilization, or that the Somalis think deliberate starvation is, or the Serbs think that mass expulsion is. To suppose otherwise is to suppose something truly grotesque about Orthodox or Islamic or sub-Saharan civilizations.

In addition, the protection of human rights has been agreed to, at least at the level of international agreements and political lip service, throughout the world. That fact by itself pulls much of the sting of the cultural imperialism argument.

13 Conclusion

The stance toward civilization I have been describing here resembles what Richard Rorty has called "liberal irony"—liberal, because it attaches primary importance to human rights and human dignity; irony, because coupled with liberalism is an ironic awareness that alternative stances are equally possible and, in an analytical sense, equally defensible. Civilization is worth fighting for; civilization is also culturally relative: Rorty's liberal ironist embraces both propositions.

But Rorty also understands that as a stance for democratic citizens deliberating about war, or for makers of military policy, irony is a little too precious and a little too anemic.[55] Ironists, according to Rorty, are "never quite able to take themselves seriously because [they are] always aware . . . of the contingency and fragility of their final vocabularies. . . ."[56] The ironist's stance nests withdrawal within commitment within withdrawal in an endless series of Chinese boxes. This is not true to our experience.

For, in an important sense, relativist hesitations make life more complicated than it actually is. As an intellectual matter, one can recognize that standards of civilized behavior vary greatly among times and places, and that no a priori argument is going to settle the question. When we witness barbaric evil in action, matters assume a different aspect. The perpetrators become incomprehensible to us; the victims' sufferings overwhelm our imaginations. At that point, the distinction between the civilized and the barbaric appears like a bright line inscribed in the world; relativistic doubts evaporate.

But of course the perpetrators of barbaric evil are no more incomprehensible than any of us. One unhappy lesson of Kosovo, Bosnia, and Rwanda is that getting people to murder and torment their neighbors is not hard; in some ways, it turns out to be ridiculously easy. Our neighbors could do it; so could we. Civilization, we realize, is a perilously thin membrane between us and the lord of the flies.[57] All the more reason to be ashamed if we are not willing to defend it.

Acknowledgments

I have had the benefit of comments on an earlier draft of this essay by many friends more knowledgeable than me. Although to varying extent they all disagree with my conclusions, their patience and generosity has made the essay better than it started out. Thanks go to Alex Aleinikoff, David Crocker, Heidi Feldman, Pablo De Greiff, Paul Kahn, Neil Katyal, David Koplow, Jane Stromseth, Dan Tarullo, and Robin West. I presented this essay at Harvard's Seminar on Ethics and International Affairs and Stanford's Program on Ethics in Society, and I wish to thank the participants for their many helpful questions and suggestions.

Notes

1. "Just War and Human Rights," *Philosophy & Public Affairs* 9 (1980): 160–181; revised version in Charles Beitz, Marshall Cohen, Thomas Scanlon, and A. John Simmons, eds., *International Ethics: A Philosophy & Public Affairs Reader* (Princeton: Princeton University Press, 1985). When I cite to "Just War and Human Rights," I use the later version, which corrects errors in the first. The paper also appears in Thomas Morawetz, ed., *Justice* (Aldershot, UK: Dartmouth Publishing, 1992), 329–350, and Micheline R. Ishay, ed., *The Human Rights Reader: Major Political Essays, Speeches, and Documents from the Bible to the Present* (London: Routledge, 1997), 368–377.

2. "A standard argument is that we had to do something: we could not simply stand by as atrocities continue. That is never true. One choice, always, is to follow the Hippocratic principle: 'First, do no harm.' If you can think of no way to adhere to that elementary principle, then do nothing. There are always ways that can be considered. Diplomacy and negotiations are never at an end." Noam Chomsky, "The Current Bombings: Behind the Rhetoric," e-mail, March 29, 1999. Subsequently, Chomsky expanded on his views in *The New Military Humanism: Lessons from Kosovo* (Monroe, ME: Common Courage Press, 1999).

3. See Adam Roberts, "NATO's 'Humanitarian War' over Kosovo," *Survival* 41 (1999), 113–114 (arguing that atrocities and expulsions have always been worse under cover of warfare).

4. Michael R. Gordon, "Crisis in the Balkans: The Overview; NATO Plans Weeks of Bombing to Break Grip of Serb Leader," *New York Times*, April 1, 1999, A1 (reporting on NATO guidelines on choice of bombing targets).

5. Although I seldom find myself agreeing with columnist Charles Krauthammer, he seemed to me largely correct when, in a series of angry articles during the war, he

excoriated the Clinton administration for the drastic disconnect between its chosen means and humanitarian ends in Kosovo. On the present point: "In and of themselves, pacifism, humanitarianism, even sentimentalism are not to be denigrated. People who hate war . . . deserve the highest respect. But they shouldn't be running wars. . . . When will we know our leaders have become serious? When they are prepared to hit a Rembrandt." Charles Krauthammer, "Bombing Empty Buildings," *Washington Post*, April 8, 1999, A31. See also Krauthammer, "The Road To Hell: Clinton, Kosovo and Good Intentions," *Washington Post*, April 2, 1999, A29 ("Has there ever been a clearer case of foreign policy means and ends so mismatched . . . ?"); Krauthammer, "Fighting to Feel Righteous," *Washington Post*, April 23, 1999, A37 ("This disconnection between means and ends is more than simply a military failure. It constitutes a colossal moral failure. . . . [I]f your ends are humanitarian, you are obliged to supply the means you propose to save.") Krauthammer's well-taken admonitions were not entirely fair criticisms of the Clinton administration, however, because—as was widely reported at the time and subsequently confirmed—many of the restrictions on NATO tactics were at the insistence of other NATO members; France in particular exercised a veto power over targets. Dana Priest, "Bombing by Committee; France Balked at NATO Targets," *Washington Post*, September 20, 1999, A1.

6. Hendrik Hertzberg, "On Patrol in the Kosovo Precinct," *The New Yorker* 75, July 12, 1999: 21, 24.

7. "What kind of humanitarianism is it that makes its highest objective ensuring that not one of our soldiers is harmed while the very people we were supposed to be saving are suffering thousands of dead and perhaps a million homeless?" Charles Krauthammer, "Fighting to Feel Righteous," *Washington Post*, April 23, 1999, A37. On the same point, see Paul Kahn, "War and Sacrifice in Kosovo," *Report from the Institute for Philosophy and Public Policy* 19, nos. 2–3 (Spring/Summer 1999): 1–6. Michael Ignatieff has elaborated this argument in *Virtual War: Kosovo and Beyond* (New York: Henry Holt, 2000): 62, 161–215.

8. In a speech on Kosovo given just hours before the war began, Clinton referred to a "Europe that is safe, secure, free, united, a good partner with us for trading"; he also stated that "If we're going to have a strong economic relationship that includes our ability to sell around the world, Europe has got to be a key." Remarks at the Legislative Convention of the American Federation of State, County, and Municipal Employees, March 23, 1999, 35 Comp. Pres. Doc. 491. A week later, however, Clinton defended his policy on explicitly moral grounds: "If there's one pledge that binds the past and future generations, it is that we cannot allow people to be destroyed because of their ethnic or racial or religious groups when we have the power to do something about it." Radio address, April 3, 1999, 35 Weekly Comp. Pres. Doc. 579. Most commonly, Clinton combined humanitarian arguments with nonaltruistic arguments based on the possibility of the Balkan wars escalating and igniting a tinderbox. See, e.g., the Letter from the President to the Speaker of the House and the President Pro Tempore of the Senate, March 26, 1999, 35 Weekly Comp. Doc. 527; Radio address, March 27, 1999, 35 Weekly Comp. Pres. Doc. 531.

One frequently offered justification of the Kosovo campaign was that NATO's credibility was on the line. This sounds like an argument of interest rather than morality, but it is not: if NATO had not undertaken pro-human-rights policy commitments in the Balkans, the alliance's credibility would never have been on the line. Thus, I regard the appeal to NATO credibility as a worthwhile moral argument masquerading as an argument of self-interest—a perfect illustration of setting minds at ease by positioning oneself on the moral low ground.

9. Each of the three fundamental values of public international law—state sovereignty, national self-determination, and human rights—can be allied or opposed to the other two, both in theory and in practice. State sovereignty and national self-determination are alike in that both are antiindividualistic, and they subordinate the interest in human rights to national or political communities that they take to be ontologically prior to individual humans. Conversely, when an existing state engages in violent repression of ethnic separatist movements, human rights advocates will join with nationalists to condemn the state; implicitly, their condemnation places the state on a lower plane than either individual human beings or national groups. Finally, political liberals sometimes insist that political significance is to be found only in the interests of human individuals and the states they choose to govern them; nationalists who insist that ethnic identity is thicker than liberal political bonds will be regarded as tribalist fanatics. It is hardly surprising that the protection of human rights appears to garner the least political support of the three. States have the guns, and ethnicities have the numbers.

10. I have argued this interpretation at greater length in my essay, "The Legacies of Nuremberg," in David Luban, *Legal Modernism* (Ann Arbor: University of Michigan Press, 1994), 335–378.

11. For discussions of the legality of the intervention see, e.g., Roberts, "NATO's 'Humanitarian War' Over Kosovo," 103–108; Catherine Guicherd, "International Law and the War in Kosovo," *Survival* 41 (1999): 19–34.

12. "Secretary-General Presents His Annual Report to General Assembly," U.N. Press Release SG/SM7136, GA/9596, September 20, 1999.

13. "The Romance of the Nation-State," *Philosophy & Public Affairs* 9 (1980): 392–397; reprinted in *International Ethics: A Philosophy & Public Affairs Reader.*

14. As Stanley Hoffman objected to Charles Beitz's antistatist view, "it is blissfully unpolitical, since he keeps forgetting that it is the very states he distrusts that will have to carry out the principles of justice." Stanley Hoffman, *Duties Beyond Borders: On the Limits and Possibilities of Ethical International Politics* (Syracuse: Syracuse University Press, 1980), 57.

15. The Kosovo Liberation Army (KLA) offers a case in point: the KLA was simultaneously a defender of human rights, a rebel force with political ambitions of its own, and (as Milosevic charged) a criminal enterprise engaged in smuggling, terrorism, and drug trafficking.

16. On this point, see Allen Buchanan, "The Internal Legitimacy of Humanitarian Intervention," *Journal of Political Philosophy* 7 (1999), 71–87.

17. One reason Kant favored a republican constitution was that it would remove the decision to go to war from bellicose princes to the ordinary citizens who actually bear the burdens of war and would therefore not consent. Kant, "Perpetual Peace," in Hans Reiss, ed., *Kant's Political Writings*, 2nd ed. (Cambridge: Cambridge University Press, 1991), 100.

18. For a strong defense of this view in the context of Kosovo, see David Fromkin, *Kosovo Crossing: American Ideals Meet Reality on the Balkan Battlefields* (New York: Free

Intervention and Civilization

Press, 1999), 168. Fromkin believes that interventions should be limited to regions where the United States has vital strategic interests at stake.

19. Lea Brilmayer, *American Hegemony: Political Morality in a One-Superpower World* (New Haven: Yale University Press, 1994).

20. Obviously there are exceptions, most recently the Australian intervention in East Timor.

21. In practice, it may often turn out that Fromkin's "vital interests" test provides a useful rough-and-ready proxy for winnability: regions where a nation has no vital interests are very likely regions that are logistically remote and hard to campaign in. But this was not the case in Kosovo.

22. Philip Gourevitch, *We Wish to Inform You That Tomorrow We Will Be Killed With Our Families: Stories From Rwanda* (New York: Picador, 1998), 149–154; Gérard Prunier, *The Rwanda Crisis: History of a Genocide* (New York: Columbia University Press, 1997), 274–275.

23. British Prime Minister Tony Blair has offered a slightly different list of five necessary conditions for humanitarian intervention: that the intervener is sure of the facts; that diplomacy has been exhausted; that the intervention is militarily feasible; that the intervener is ready for the long term and not simply seeking an exit strategy; and that national interests are involved. Speech, April 22, 1999, quoted in Roberts, 119. The Clinton administration's criteria for participating in United Nations peace-keeping operations is set out in Presidential Decision Directive 25 (May 1994).

24. Prunier, 1–41, 89n, 102–107.

25. Gourevich, 155.

26. Ibid., 154–161. For a slightly less hostile account by a participant in the French intervention, see Prunier, 277–311.

27. I examine this argument in David Luban, "Action and Reaction in International Law," *Proceedings of the American Society of International Law, 1987* (1987): 420–426.

28. David Hume incisively objects to social contract theory that neither tacit nor explicit consent is ever tendered to governments, and that far from consent being the source of loyalty, consent possesses no more moral force than loyalty. Hume, "Of the Original Contract," in *Essays: Moral, Political, and Literary*, ed. Eugene F. Miller (Indianapolis: Liberty Classics, 1985), 465–487. The view I present here acknowledges Hume's point; but unlike Hume, I regard loyalty and support for a government as the form consent assumes in politics.

29. "Just War and Human Rights," 209.

30. I was thus wrong when I wrote, "Such rights are worth fighting for . . . not only by those to whom they are denied but, if we take seriously the obligation which is indicated when we speak of human rights, by the rest of us as well (although how strictly this obligation is binding on 'neutrals' is open to dispute)." "Just War and

Human Rights," 210. The final parenthetical comment shows some awareness that the argument is not as simple as I was making it out to be.

31. The argument that follows closely follows the reasoning of Buchanan, "The Internal Legitimacy of Humanitarian Intervention," 84–85.

32. Most people who believe in human rights also believe that human beings are of *equal* intrinsic worth, but this is not essential. A caste-ridden or patriarchal society can still be committed to the idea that even unequal people are entitled to a certain basic level of decent treatment. Believing that human beings are ends in themselves does not by itself guarantee believing in human equality: some ends in themselves may be more valuable than others.

33. In his recent book *What We Owe to Each Other* (Harvard University Press, 1999, ch. 2), T. M. Scanlon argues that there is no way to read off from the bare claim that something is valuable the particular reasons for action that it generates. Artworks are valuable in a different way from friendship, and we honor the value of artworks differently than we honor the value of friendship; the value of art and friendship provide different reasons for action. For that reason, the proposition that something is valuable functions as something like a placeholder for a more specific set of reasons for action, and when we inquire what we should do to honor the value of something, the claim of value "passes the buck" to the reasons that it summarizes. If Scanlon is right, then my claim that the value of humans provides a reason for intervening against rights-violations begs the question by passing the buck back to the value of humans. Not every kind of value is honored by being actively promoted, so we cannot assume that human value provides reasons for promoting the rights of other people. However, it seems to me uncontroversial that the value of humans *is* honored by being actively promoted; and, even on Scanlon's view, once we recognize that some action is an appropriate way to respect a value, the value can still rightly be deemed the source of the reasons.

34. The standard source is David S. Wyman, *The Abandonment of the Jews: America and the Holocaust, 1941–1945* (New York: Pantheon, 1984).

35. Karl Jaspers, *The Question of German Guilt*, trans. E. B. Ashton (New York: Dial Press, 1947), 32.

36. One important interpretive question is whether Jaspers is talking about humanity-wide guilt or community-wide guilt. In his sense, are we coresponsible (as he says) for "every wrong and every injustice in the world," or only (as he also says) for crimes committed in our presence—by extension, crimes committed within our own community? One of Jaspers's most distinguished present-day exponents interprets metaphysical guilt along communitarian lines, as a kind of guilt for what others in my group have done—it is a guilt based on recognizing that group identity is founded on shared group attitudes, including attitudes like racism that led to the crimes. Larry May, *Sharing Responsibility* (Chicago: University of Chicago Press, 1992), 152–155. If that is what Jaspers meant, his idea will not be of use in explaining the response of many people to the events in Bosnia, Rwanda, and Kosovo—that we are sullied if we stand by and allow atrocities to happen, even when the perpetrators and victims are all strangers in a strange land with whom we share very little.

But I don't think this gets at the core of Jaspers's idea. Remember that Jaspers was addressing fellow-Germans about their own guilt, and his theme naturally leads him to emphasize guilt within the community. Elsewhere in his book, however, Jaspers expands his discussion to "the responsibility of the inactive bystander" outside of Germany, and speaks about "solidarity not only among fellow-citizens but also among Europeans and among mankind." Jaspers, 92. He adds: "We have the right to recall that the others, not under terrorism, also remained inactive—that they let pass . . . events which, as occurring in another country, they did not regard as their concern." Ibid., 95; see also 96. When Jaspers writes that "[m]etaphysical guilt is the lack of absolute solidarity with the human being as such" (ibid., 71), he plainly has humanity-wide guilt in mind. Moreover, even when he is speaking only of German metaphysical guilt, Jaspers is not referring to attitudes that ordinary Germans shared with the Nazis. He is referring to their failure to "go into the streets when our Jewish friends were led away; [to] scream until we too were destroyed." Ibid., 72. He is talking about the guilt of cautious anti-Nazis, not unconscious Nazis.

37. Jaspers, 32, 71–73. It is important, however, that Jaspers *did* think that there was a moral obligation to take risks. "I may be morally bound to risk my life . . . but there is no moral obligation to sacrifice one's life in the sure knowledge that nothing will have been gained. Morally we have a duty to dare, not a duty to choose certain doom." Ibid., 71.

38. Ibid., 71.

39. Ibid., 32.

40. "That I live after such a thing has happened weighs on me as indelible guilt." Ibid., 32. Again: "I know from a voice within myself: I am guilty of being still alive." Ibid., 71. Again: "We are guilty of being alive." Ibid., 72.

41. Ibid., 33.

42. Robert Nozick goes so far as to say that because of the Holocaust, "Humanity has lost its claim to continue." Robert Nozick, *The Examined Life: Philosophical Meditations* (New York: Simon and Shuster, 1989), 238. Setting to one side the bathos in Nozick's reflection, it appears to me that Nozick is framing the same intuition as Jaspers, that the Holocaust is a kind of stain on those who were not murdered. There is no bathos in Jaspers.

43. Roberts, 104. For a similar thought, see Ignatieff, *Virtual War*, 178.

44. There is an important difference between Jaspers's ideal of unconditional solidarity and the more individualist Kantian ideal of respect for human beings as ends in themselves. The Kantian ideal regards human beings as possessors and sources of value, whereas Jaspers's ideal of unconditional solidarity needs to assume nothing about the value of human beings. Even on the nihilistic assumption that human beings are without any value at all, we may nevertheless prize the ideal of solidarity: there can be solidarity among the damned (a theme touchingly explored in literature from Dante's *Inferno* to *Waiting for Godot*). Conversely, respect for individual human beings as ends in themselves need not—and, in many versions of liberalism, does not—require stronger forms of solidarity than mutual respect and tolerance. This difference may account in part for the difference between Jaspers and Kantian liberals such as Rawls and Nozick.

45. The importance of frustrating perpetrators over and above helping victims has overtones of general deterrence, that is, responding punitively to wrongdoing to

deter future wrongdoing by others. This raises delicate issues, however: if general deterrence were the main point of the Kosovo intervention, then it might be justified even if intervening made matters worse for both the Kosovar Serbs and Albanians. Thus, general deterrence cannot be the *only* point. Thanks to Neal Katyal for raising this issue.

46. Jeffrey Reiman, "Justice, Civilization, and the Death Penalty: Answering van den Haag," *Philosophy and Public Affairs* 14 (1985): 115–148.

47. Ibid., 115.

48. Stuart Hampshire, *Innocence and Experience* (Cambridge: Harvard University Press, 1989), 90.

49. Ibid.

50. Rummel v. Estelle, 445 U.S. 263 (1980) (sustaining life sentence for repeated petty frauds totaling $228); Hutto v. Davis, 454 U.S. 370 (1981) (sustaining 40-year sentence for possession of less than nine ounces of marijuana); Harmelin v. Michigan, 501 U.S. 957 (1991) (sustaining life without parole for first-offense cocaine possession, and holding that although cruel, the sentence is not cruel and unusual).

51. Article 6(c) of the Nuremberg Charter includes as crimes against humanity "murder, extermination, enslavement, deportation and other inhumane acts," among which we might include deliberate starvation (such as the Somali warlords practice), enforced disappearance, the theft of children, and coercive medical experimentation. My list does not correspond exactly with the extension given by law to the concept "other inhumane acts." For details, see M. Cherif Bassiouni, *Crimes against Humanity in International Criminal Law*, 2nd ed. (The Hague: Kluwer, 1999), 330–368.

52. I take this language from Article 18 of the International Law Commission's 1996 Draft Code of Crimes against the Peace and Security of Mankind, quoted in Bassiouni, 192. In international law, genocide and crimes against humanity are distinct offenses, but it makes conceptual sense to classify genocide together with lesser forms of group persecution as one distinct kind of crimes against humanity. By contrast, I deliberately treat the category of political persecution separately, even though it is lumped together with racial and religious persecution in all the legal definitions of crimes against humanity, because political persecutions seem different in kind from persecutions on the basis of membership in an ascriptive group.
    Roughly speaking, my distinction between atrocious acts and group persecutions corresponds with the two conceptually distinct but overlapping types of crimes against humanity: treating people in atrocious ways, regardless of their group membership, and persecuting people because of their group membership, regardless of whether the persecution consists of atrocious acts.

53. According to Bassiouni, the term was chosen by Robert Jackson in consultation with Hersch Lauterpacht, and the choice to say virtually nothing about its origin grew at least in part out of something akin to bystander shame on the part of the Allies for having ignored the crimes against humanity during most of the war. Bassiouni, 17–18.

54. Richard Rorty has argued that the human rights culture is entirely the product of sentimental education. Richard Rorty, "Human Rights, Rationality, and Senti-

mentality," in Stephen Shute and Susan Hurley, eds., *On Human Rights: The Oxford Amnesty Lectures 1993* (New York: Basic Books, 1993). I would add: education backed by the possibility of force.

55. Richard Rorty, "Private Irony and Liberal Hope," in *Contingency, Irony, and Solidarity* (Cambridge: Cambridge University Press, 1989), 85–88.

56. Rorty, *Contingency, Irony, and Solidarity*, 73–74.

57. Whether this turns out to be for reasons grounded in rational behavior, in social psychopathology, or in collective myths is an all-important question. For sophisticated examples of these three explanatory strategies see Russell Hardin, *One for All: The Logic of Group Conflict* (Princeton: Princeton University Press, 1995), 142–182 (rational choice explanation); Ervin Staub, *The Roots of Evil: The Origins of Genocide and Other Group Violence* (Cambridge: Cambridge University Press, 1989) (social psychology); Julie A. Mertus, *Kosovo: How Myths and Truths Started a War* (Berkeley: University of California Press, 1999) (collective mythology).

4

Capabilities and Human Rights

Martha Nussbaum

Introduction

When governments and international agencies talk about people's basic political and economic entitlements, they standardly use the language of rights. When constitutions are written in the modern era, and the framers wish to identify a group of particularly urgent interests that deserve special protection, once again it is the language of rights that is standardly preferred.

The language of rights has a moral resonance that makes it hard to avoid in contemporary political discourse. But it is certainly not on account of its theoretical and conceptual clarity that it has been preferred. There are many different ways of thinking about what a right is, and many different definitions of "human rights."[1] For example, rights are often spoken of as entitlements that belong to all human beings simply because they are human, or as especially urgent interests of human beings as such that deserve protection regardless of where people are situated.[2] Within this tradition there are differences. The dominant tradition has typically grounded rights in the possession of rationality and language, thus implying that nonhuman animals do not have them, and that mentally impaired humans may not have them. Some philosophers have maintained that sentience, instead, should be the basis of rights; thus all animals would be rights bearers.[3] In contrast to this entire group of natural-rights theorists, there are also thinkers who treat all rights as artifacts of state action.[4] The latter position would seem to entail that there are no human rights where there is no state to recognize them. Such an approach appears to the holders of the former view to do away with the very point of rights language, which is to point to the fact that human beings are entitled to certain types of treatment *whether or not* the state in which they happen to live recognizes this fact.

There are many other complex unresolved theoretical questions about rights. One of them is the question whether the individual is the only bearer of rights, or whether rights belong as well to other entities, such as families, ethnic, religious, and linguistic groups, and nations. Another is whether rights are to be regarded as side-constraints on goal-seeking action, or as parts of a goal that is to be promoted.[5] Still another unresolved question is whether rights (thought of as justified entitlements) are correlated with duties. If A has a right to S, then it would appear there must be someone who has a duty to provide S to A. But it is not always clear who has these duties—especially when we think of rights in the international context. Again, it is also unclear whether all duties are correlated with rights. One might hold, for example, that we have a duty not to cause pain to animals without holding that animals have rights—if, for example, one accepted one of the classic accounts of the basis of rights that makes reference to the abilities of speech and reason as the basis, and yet still believed that we have other strong reasons not to cause animals pain.

Finally, there are difficult theoretical questions about what rights are to be understood as rights *to*. When we speak of human rights, do we mean, primarily, a right to be treated in certain ways? A right to a certain level of achieved well-being? A right to certain resources with which one may pursue one's life plan? A right to certain opportunities and capacities with which one may, in turn, make choices regarding one's life plan? Political philosophers who debate about the nature of equality standardly tackle a related question head on, asking whether the equality most relevant to political distribution should be understood, primarily, as equality of well-being, or equality of resources, or equality of opportunity, or equality of capabilities.[6] The language of rights to some extent cuts across this debate and obscures the issues that have been articulated in it.

Thus one might conclude that the language of rights is not especially informative, despite its uplifting character, unless its users link their references to rights to a theory that answers at least some of these questions.[7] It is for this reason, among others, that a different language has begun to take hold in talk about people's basic entitlements. This is the language of capabilities and human functioning. Since 1993 the *Human Development Reports* of the United Nations Development Programme (UNDP)[8] have assessed the quality of life in the nations of the world using the concept of people's capabilities, by which is meant their abilities to do and to be certain things deemed valuable. Under the influence of economist and philosopher Amartya Sen, they have chosen that conceptual framework as basic to intercountry comparisons and to the articulation of goals for public policy.

Along with Sen, I have been one of the people who has pioneered what is now called the "capabilities approach," defending its importance in international debates about welfare and quality of life. My own use of this language was originally independent and reflected the fact that Aristotle used a notion of human capability (Greek *dunamis*) and functioning (Greek *energeia*) to articulate some of the goals of good political organization.[9] But the projects soon became fused: I increasingly articulated the Aristotelian idea of capability in terms pertinent to the contemporary debate,[10] while Sen increasingly emphasized the ancient roots of his idea.[11] In a variety of contexts, we argued that the capabilities approach was a valuable theoretical framework for public policy, especially in the international development context. We commended it to both theoreticians and practitioners as offering certain advantages over approaches that focus on opulence (GNP per capita), or welfare (construed in terms of utility or desire satisfaction), or even the distribution of basic resources.[12]

Both Sen and I stated from the start that the capabilities approach needs to be combined with a focus on rights. Sen wrote about rights as central goals of public policy throughout the period during which he developed the approach.[13] I stressed from the start that Aristotle's theory was grossly defective because it lacked a theory of basic human rights, especially rights to be free from government interference in certain areas of choice.[14] More recently, responding to communitarian critics of rights-based reasoning and to international discussions that denigrate rights in favor of material well-being, both Sen and I have even more strongly emphasized the importance of rights to our own capabilities approach, stressing the various roles liberty plays within our respective theories and emphasizing the closeness of our approach to liberal theories such as that of John Rawls.[15]

Moreover, rights play an increasingly large role inside the account of what the most important capabilities are. Unlike Sen, who prefers to allow the account of the basic capabilities to remain largely implicit in his statements, I have produced an explicit account of the most central capabilities that should be the goal of public policy. The list is continually being revised and adjusted in accordance with my methodological commitment to cross-cultural deliberation and criticism. But another source of change has been an increasing determination to bring the list down to earth, so to speak, making the "thick vague conception of the good"[16] a little less vague, so that it can do real work guiding public policy. At this point, the aim is to come up with the type of specification of a basic capability that could figure in a constitution,[17] or perform apart from that the role of a constitutional guarantee. In the process, I have increasingly used the language of rights, or the related language of liberty and freedom, in fleshing out the account of the basic capabilities.

Thus, in HC I speak of "legal guarantees of freedom of expression . . . and freedom of religious exercise" as aspects of the general capability to use one's mind and one's senses in a way directed by one's own practical reason. I also speak of "guarantees of noninterference with certain choices that are especially personal and definitive of selfhood," and of "the freedoms of assembly and political speech."[18] In a forthcoming paper, I use the language of rights itself in articulating the capability to seek employment outside the home, and several of the other important capabilities.[19] In part, this is a rhetorical choice, bringing the list of capabilities into relation with international human rights instruments that have a related content. But in part it also reflects a theoretical decision to emphasize the affiliations of the approach with liberal rights-based theories in an era of widespread reaction against the Enlightenment and its heritage.

But there are still some large questions to be answered. The relationship between the two concepts remains as yet underexplored. Does the capabilities view supplement a theory of rights, or is it intended to be a particular way of capturing what a theory of rights captures? Is there any tension between a focus on capabilities and a focus on rights? (Are the two approaches competitors?) On the other hand, is there any reason why a capabilities theorist should welcome the language of rights—that is, is there anything in the view itself that leads naturally in the direction of recognizing rights? (Would a natural-law Catholic theorist who used an Aristotelian language of capability and functioning but rejected liberal rights-based language be making a conceptual error?)[20] Does the capabilities view help us to answer any of the difficult questions that I sketched above, which have preoccupied theorists of rights? Does the capabilities view incline us to opt for any particular set of answers to the various questions about rights or any particular conception of rights? (For example, is Sen right to think that the capabilities view supports a conception of rights as goals, rather than as side constraints?[21]) Finally, is there any reason, other than a merely rhetorical one, why we should continue to use the language of rights in addition to the language of capabilities?

In short, this conceptual relationship needs further scrutiny.[22] Commenting on Sen's Tanner Lectures in 1987, Bernard Williams expressed sympathy with the capabilities approach, but called for a conceptual investigation:

I am not very happy myself with taking rights as the starting point. The notion of a basic human right seems to me obscure enough, and I would rather come at it from the perspective of basic human capabilities. I would prefer capabilities to do the work, and if we are going to have a language or rhetoric of rights, to have it delivered from them, rather than the other way around. But I think that there remains an unsolved problem: how we should see the relations between these concepts.[23]

This essay is a contribution to that project. I shall not be able to answer all the outstanding questions, and I shall certainly not be able to offer a theory of rights that solves all the problems I outlined. But I hope to illuminate some of the issues that must be faced when one attempts to connect the two ideas, some of the options one has, some of the problems that arise, and some of the positive dividends one may reap.

I shall begin by describing the capabilities approach and the motivations for its introduction: what it was trying to do in political philosophy, how it commended itself by contrast to other standard ways of thinking about entitlements. Then I shall briefly clarify the connection between the capabilities approach and liberal theories of justice. Finally I shall turn to my central topic.

1 The Capabilities Approach: Motivation and Argument

Why, then, should there be a theory of human capabilities? What questions does it answer, and what is its practical point? Why should an international agency such as the UNDP use a measure of quality of life based on human capability and functioning, rather than other more traditional measures: those based, for example, on opulence (GNP per capita), on utility (construed as the satisfaction of preference and desire), or on a distribution of resources that satisfies some constraint, whether it be a social minimum, or the Rawlsian "difference principle," or some more exacting egalitarian condition?

The account of human capabilities has been used as an answer to a number of distinct questions, such as: What is the living standard?[24] What is the quality of life?[25] And, What is the relevant type of equality that we should consider in political planning?[26] It has also been closely linked to discussion of a theory of justice: in particular, with the need such a theory has for an account of what it is trying to achieve for people. I believe that the most illuminating way of thinking about the capabilities approach is that it is an account of the space within which we make comparisons between individuals and across nations as to how well they are doing. This idea is closely linked with the idea of a theory of justice, since one crucial aim of a theory of justice typically is to promote some desired state of people; and in "Aristotelian Social Democracy" I linked it closely to an account of the proper goal of government, to bring all citizens up to a certain basic minimum level of capability. But up to a point the approach is logically independent of a theory of justice, since a theory of justice may acknowledge many constraints with regard to how far it is entitled to promote people's well-being. (For example, Robert Nozick could grant that capabilities are the relevant space within which to make comparisons of well-being, while denying that this has anything at all to do with a theory of justice, since he rejects theories of justice based on a "patterned end-state" conception, preferring to define justice solely in terms of procedures and entitlements.[27]

The capabilities idea is also closely linked to a concern with equality in that Sen has always used it to argue that people are entitled to a certain level of rough material and social equality. But, strictly speaking, these two concerns of Sen's are logically independent. One might agree that capabilities are the relevant space within which to compare lives, and nations, and yet hold that equality of capability is not the appropriate goal. Capabilities inform us as to what type of equality might be thought pertinent; they do not by themselves tell us whether we should value an equal distribution or some other distribution.

As a theory of the relevant space within which to make comparisons, the capabilities approach is best understood by contrasting it with its rivals in the international development arena. The most common method of measuring the quality of life in a nation, and making cross-national comparisons, used to be simply to enumerate GNP per capita. This crude method is reminiscent of the economics lesson imagined by Charles Dickens in *Hard Times* (and used by Sen and me to introduce our volume on *The Quality of Life*):

> "And he said, Now, this schoolroom is a Nation. And in this nation, there are fifty millions of money. Isn't this a prosperous nation? Girl number twenty, isn't this a prosperous nation, and a'n't you in a thriving state?"
> "What did you say?" asked Louisa.
> "Miss Louisa, I said I didn't know. I thought I couldn't know whether it was a prosperous nation or not, and whether I was in a thriving state or not, unless I knew who had got the money, and whether any of it was mine. But that had nothing to do with it. It was not in the figures at all," said Sissy, wiping her eyes.
> "That was a great mistake of yours," observed Louisa.[28]

In short, the crude approach does not even tell us who has the money, and thus typically gave high marks to nations such as South

Africa, which contained enormous inequalities. Still less did it provide any information at all about elements of human life that might be thought very important in defining its quality but that are not always well correlated with GNP per capita: eduational opportunities, health care, life expectancy, infant mortality, the presence or absence of political liberties, the extent of racial or gender inequality.

Somewhat less crude is an economic approach that measures quality of life in terms of utility, understood as the satisfaction of preference or desire. This approach at least has the advantage of concerning itself to some degree with distribution in the sense that it looks at how resources are or are not going to work to make people's lives better. But it has severe shortcomings. First, there is the familiar problem that utilitarianism tends to think of the social total (or average) as an aggregate, neglecting the salience of the boundaries between individual lives.[29] As Rawls pointed out, this means that it can tolerate a result in which the total (or average) is good enough, but where some individuals suffer extremely acute levels of deprivation, whether of resources or of liberty. In that sense, it doesn't tell Sissy "who has got the money and whether any of it is mine," any more than does the GNP-based approach. (Indeed, Sissy's teacher was clearly a Benthamite Utilitarian.) Rawls was convinced that the failure of utilitarianism to justify adequately strong protections for the basic political liberties, given this propensity to aggregate, was by itself sufficient reason to reject it. Bernard Williams, similarly, has considered utilitarianism's neglect of the "separateness of persons" to be a cardinal failure and a reason why the theory cannot give an adequate account of social well-being.[30]

A second problem with utilitarianism is its commitment to the commensurability of value, the concern to measure the good in terms of a single metric and thus to deny that there are irreducibly plural goods that figure in a human life. Both Sen and I have pursued this question extensively apart from our work on capabilities.[31] But it has also had importance in justifying the capabilities approach, since the quality of life seems to consist of a plurality of distinct features, features that cannot be simply reduced to quantities of one another. This limits the nature of the trade-offs it will be feasible to make.[32]

But a third feature of utilitarianism has been even more central to the capability critique. As Sen has repeatedly pointed out, people's satisfactions are not very reliable indicators of their quality of life. Wealthy and privileged people get used to a high level of luxury and feel pain when they do not have delicacies that one may think they do not really need. On the other hand, deprived people frequently adjust their sights to the low level they know they can aspire to, and thus actually experience satisfaction in connection with a very reduced living standard. Sen gave a graphic example: In 1944, the year after the Great Bengal Famine, the All-India Institute of Hygiene and Public Health did a survey. Included in this survey were a large number of widows and widowers. The position of widows in India is extremely bad in all kinds of ways but notoriously in terms of health status. But on the survey only 2.5 percent of widows, as against 48.5 percent of widowers, reported that they were either ill or in indifferent health. And when the question was just about "indifferent health," as opposed to illness (for which we might suppose there are more public and objective criteria), 45.6 percent of widowers said their health was "indifferent," as opposed to zero percent of the widows. The likely explanation for this is that people who have standardly been malnourished, who have in addition been told that they are weak and made for suffering, and who, as widows, are told that they are virtually dead and have no rights, will be unlikely to recognize their fatigue and low energy as a sign of bodily disease; not so males, who are brought up to have high expectations for their own physical functioning. Sen concludes: "Quiet acceptance of deprivation and bad fate affects the scale of dissatisfaction generated, and the utilitarian calculus gives sanctity to that distortion."[33]

This phenomenon of "adaptive preferences" has by now been much studied in the economic literature,[34] and it is now generally recognized as a central problem, if one wants to use the utilitarian calculus for any kind of normative purpose in guiding public policy.[35] This is especially likely to be true when we are studying groups that have been persistent victims of discrimination, who may as a result have internalized a conception of their own unequal worth. It is certain to be true when we are concerned with groups who have inadequate information about their situation, their options, and the surrounding society—as is frequently the case, for example, with women in developing countries. For these reasons, then, the utility-based approach seems inadequate as a basis for offering comparisons of quality of life.

More promising by far is an approach that looks at a group of basic resources and then asks about their distribution, asking, in particular, how well even the worst-off citizens are doing with respect to the items on the list. Such is the approach of John Rawls, who, in *A Theory of Justice* and subsequent works, advanced a list of the "primary goods," intended to be items that all rational individuals, regardless of their more comprehensive plans of life, would desire as pre-requities for carrying out their plans of life.[36] These items include liberties, opportunities, and powers; wealth and income; and the social basis of self-respect. (More recently, Rawls has added freedom of movement and the free choice of occupation.[37]) The idea is that we measure who is better off and less well off by using such a list of primary resources; that information is used, in turn, by the parties who are choosing principles of justice. Notice that this list is heterogeneous. Some of its items are capacities of persons: liberties, opportunities, powers; the social basis of self-respect is a complex property of society's relation to persons; but income and wealth are pure resources. And income and wealth frequently play a central role in the measurement of who is better and worse off.[38] Rawls was at pains, moreover, to state that this list of "primary goods" is not a comprehensive theory of what is good or valuable in life.[39] The attraction of operating with a list of resources, for Rawls, is that it enables the approach to steer clear of prescribing the basic values of human life, which individuals must be able to select for themselves, in accordance with their own more comprehensive religious or ethical conceptions.

Sen's basic argument against Rawls, for the past twenty years, has been that the space of resources is inadequate as a space within which to answer questions about who is better and who worse off. This is so because individuals vary greatly in their need for resources and in their ability to convert resources into valuable functionings. Some of these differences are physical. Nutritional needs vary with age, occupation, and sex. A pregnant or lactating woman needs more nutrients than a nonpregnant woman. A child needs more protein than an adult. A person whose limbs work well needs few resources to be mobile, whereas a person with paralyzed limbs needs many more resources to achieve the same level of mobility. Many such variations escape our notice if we live in a prosperous nation that can afford to bring all individuals to a high level of physical attainment; in the developing world we must be highly alert to these variations in need. Some of the variations, again, are social, and have to do with traditional social hierarchies. If we wish to bring all citizens of a nation to the same level of educational attainment, we will need to devote more resources to those who encounter obstacles from traditional hierarchy or prejudice: thus women's literacy will prove more expensive than men's literacy in many parts of the world. This means that if we operate only with an index of resources, we will frequently reinforce inequalities that are highly relevant to well-being. An approach focusing on resources does not go deep enough to diagnose obstacles that can be present even when resources appear to be adequately spread around, causing individuals to fail to avail themselves of oportunities that they in some sense have (such as free public education, or the vote, or the right to work).

For this reason, we argue that the most appropriate space for comparisons is the space of capabilities. Instead of asking "How satisfied is person A?" or "How much in the way of resources does A command?" we ask the question, "What is A actually able to do and to be?" In other words, about a variety of functions that would seem to be of central importance to a human life, we ask, is the person capable of this or not? This focus on capabilities, unlike the focus on GNP, or on aggregate utility, looks at people one by one, insisting on locating empowerment in *this* life and in *that* life, rather than in the nation as a whole. Unlike the utilitarian focus on satisfactions, it looks not at what people feel about what they do, but about what they are actually able to do.[40] Nor does it make any assumptions about the commensurability of the different pursuits: indeed, it denies that the most important functions are all commensurable in terms of a single metric, and it treats the diverse functions as all important and all irreducibly plural.[41] Finally, unlike the focus on resources, it is concerned with what is actually going on in the life in question: not how many resources are sitting around, but how they are actually going to work in enabling people to function in a fully human way.[42]

2 The Central Human Capabilities

Sen has focused on the general defense of the capability space, and he has not offered any official account of what the most central human capabilities are, although in practice he has to some extent done so by focusing on some areas of human life and not others in constructing the measures used in the *Human Development Report*. Again, his recent book on India gives many concrete examples of the importance and the interrelationships of various different concrete human capabilities.[43] I, by contrast, have focused on the task of producing such a working list, describing a methodology by which we might both generate and justify such a list[44] and defending the whole project of giving such a list against the objections of relativists and traditionalists.[45] The list is supposed to be a focus for political planning, and it is supposed to select those human capabilities that can be convincingly argued to be of central importance in any human life, whatever else the person pursues or chooses.

The central capabilities are not just instrumental to further pursuits: they are held to have value in themselves, in making a life fully human. But they are held to have a particularly central importance in everything else we plan and choose. In that sense, they play a role similar to that played by primary goods in Rawls's more recent account: they support our powers of practical reason and choice, and they have a special importance in making any choice of a way of life possible. They thus have a special claim to be supported for political purposes in societies that otherwise contain a great diversity of views about the good. I do not think of the political sphere in exactly the way that Rawls conceives it, since I do not make the assumption that the nation-state should be the basic deliberative unit,[46] and the account is meant to have broad applicatibility to cross-cultural deliberations. Nonetheless, the basic point of the account is the same: to put forward something that people from many different traditions, with many different fuller conceptions of the good, can agree on as the necessary basis for pursuing their good life.[47]

The list is an attempt to summarize the empirical findings of a broad and on-going cross-cultural inquiry. As such, it is open-ended and humble; it can always be contested and remade. It does not claim to read facts of "human nature" off of biological observation, although it does of course take account of biology as a relatively constant element in human experience. Nor does it deny that the items on the list are to some extent differently constructed by different societies. Indeed part of the idea of the list is that its members can be more concretely specified in accordance with local beliefs and circumstances. (In that sense, the consensus it hopes to evoke has many of the features of the "overlapping consensus" described by Rawls.[48])

Here is the current version of the list, revised as a result of my recent visits to development projects in India:[49]

1. *Life.* Being able to live to the end of a human life of normal length; not dying prematurely, or before one's life is so reduced as to be not worth living.

2. *Bodily health.* Being able to have good health, including reproductive health; to be adequately nourished; to have adequate shelter.

3. *Bodily integrity.* Being able to move freely from place to place; to be secure against violent assault, including sexual assault and domestic violence; having opportunities for sexual satisfaction and for choice in matters of reproduction.

4. *Senses, imagination, and thought.* Being able to use the senses to imagine, think, and reason—and to do these things in a "truly human" way, a way informed and cultivated by an adequate education, including, but by no means limited to, literacy and basic mathematical and scientific training. Being able to use imagination and thought in connection with experiencing and producing works and events of one's own choice, religious, literary, musical, and so forth.

5. *Emotions.* Being able to have attachments to things and people outside ourselves; to love those who love and care for us, to grieve at their absence; in general, to love, to grieve, to experience longing, gratitude, and justified anger. Not having one's emotional development blighted by fear and anxiety. Supporting this capability means supporting forms of human association that can be shown to be crucial in their development.

6. *Practical reason.* Being able to form a conception of the good and to engage in critical reflection about the planning of one's life. This entails protection for the liberty of conscience and religious observance.

7. *Affiliation.*

A. *Friendship.* Being able to live with others, to recognize and show concern for other human beings, to engage in various forms of social interaction; to be able to imagine the situation of another and to have compassion for that situation; to have the capability for both justice and friendship. Protecting this capability means protecting institutions that constitute and nourish such forms of affiliation, and also protecting the freedom of assembly and political speech.

B. *Respect.* Having the social bases of self-respect and non-humiliation; being able to be treated as a dignified being whose worth is equal to that of others. This entails provision of non-discrimination on the basis of race, sex, ethnicity, caste, religion, and national origin.

8. *Other species.* Being able to live with concern for and in relation to animals, plants, and the world of nature.

9. *Play.* Being able to laugh, to play, to enjoy recreational activities.

10. *Control over one's environment.*

A. *Political.* Being able to participate effectively in political choices that govern one's life; having the right of political participation, protections of free speech and association.

B. *Material.* Being able to hold property (both land and movable goods); having the right to employment; having the freedom from unwarranted search and seizure.

The list is, emphatically, a list of separate components. We cannot satisfy the need for one of them by giving a larger amount of another one. All are of central importance and all are distinct in quality. (Practical reason and affiliation, I argue elsewhere, are of special importance because they both organize and suffuse all the other capabilities, making their pursuit truly human.)[50] This limits the trade-offs that it will be reasonable to make, and thus limits the applicability of quantitative cost-benefit analysis. At the same time, the items on the list are related to one another in many complex ways. One of the most effective ways of promoting women's control over their environment, and their effective right of political participation, is to promote women's literacy. Women who can seek employment outside the home have more resources in protecting their bodily integrity from assaults within it.

3   Capabilities as Goals

I have spoken both of functioning and of capability. How are they related? Getting clear about this is crucial in defining the relation of the "capabilities approach" both to liberalism and to views of human rights. For if we were to take functioning itself as the goal of public policy, the liberal would rightly judge that we were precluding many choices that citizens may make in accordance with their own conceptions of the good and perhaps violating their rights. A deeply religious person may prefer not to be well-nourished but to engage in strenuous fasting. Whether for religious or for other reasons, a person may prefer a celibate life to one containing sexual expression. A person may prefer to work with an intense dedication that precludes recreation and play. Am I declaring, by my very use of the list, that these are not fully human or flourishing lives? And am I instructing government to nudge or push people into functioning of the requisite sort no matter what they prefer?

It is important that the answer to these questions is no. Capability, not functioning, is the political goal. This is so because of the very great importance the approach attaches to practical reason as a good that suffuses all the other functions, making them human rather than animal,[51] and figures, itself, as a central function on the list. It is perfectly true that functionings, not simply capabilities, are what render a life fully human: if there were no functioning of any kind in a life, we could hardly applaud it, no matter what opportunities it contained. Nonetheless, for political purposes it is appropriate for us to aim for capabilities and those alone. Citizens must be left free to determine their course after that. The person with plenty of food may always choose to fast, but there is a great difference between fasting and starving, and it is this difference that we wish to capture. Again, the person who has normal opportunities for sexual satisfaction can always choose a life of celibacy, and we say nothing against this. What we do speak against (for example) is the practice of female genital mutilation, which deprives individuals of the opportunity to choose sexual functioning (and indeed, the opportunity to choose celibacy as well).[52] A person who has opportunities for play can always choose a workaholic life; again, there is a great difference between that chosen life and a life constrained by insufficient maximum-hour protections and/or the "double day" that makes women unable to play in many parts of the world.

I can make the issue clearer, and also prepare for discussion of the relationship between capabilities and rights, by pointing out that there are three different types of capabilities that figure in my analysis.[53] First, there are what I call *basic capabilities*: the innate equipment of individuals that is the necessary basis for developing the more advanced capability. Most infants have from birth the *basic capability* for practical reason and imagination, though they cannot exercise such functions without a lot more development and education. Second, there are *internal capabilities*: that is, states of the person herself that are, so far as the person herself is concerned, sufficient conditions for the exercise of the requisite functions. A woman who has not suffered genital mutilation has the *internal capability* for sexual pleasure; most adult human beings everywhere have the *internal capability* to use speech and thought in accordance with their own conscience. Finally, there are *combined capabilities*,[54] which I define as internal capabilities *combined with* suitable external conditions for the exercise of the function. A woman who is not mutilated but is secluded and forbidden to leave the house has internal but not combined capabilities for sexual expression (and work, and political participation). Citizens of repressive nondemocratic regimes have the internal but not the combined capability to exercise thought and speech in accordance with their conscience. The aim of public policy is the production of *combined capabilities*. This means promoting the states of the person by providing the necessary education and care; and it also means preparing the environment so that it is favorable for the exercise of practical reason and the other major functions.[55]

This explanation of the types of capabilities clarifies my position. I am not saying that public policy should rest content with *internal capabilities*, but remain indifferent to the struggles of individuals who have to try to exercise these in a hostile environment. In that sense, my approach is highly attentive to the goal of functioning and instructs governments to keep it always in view. On the other hand, I am not pushing individuals into the function: once the stage is fully set, the choice is up to them.

The approach is therefore very close to Rawls's approach that uses the notion of primary goods. We can see the list of capabilities as like a long list of opportunities for life-functioning, such that it is always rational to want them whatever else one wants. If one ends up having a plan of life that does not make use of all of them, one has hardly been harmed by having the chance to choose a life that does. (Indeed, in the cases of fasting and celibacy it is the very availability of the alternative course that gives the choice its moral value.) The primary difference between this capabilities list and Rawls's list of primary goods is its length and definiteness, and in particular its determination to place upon the list the social basis of several goods that Rawls has called "natural goods," such as "health and vigor, intelligence and imagination."[56] Since Rawls has been willing to put the social basis of self-respect on his list, it is not at all clear why he has not made the same move with imagination and health.[57]

Rawls's evident concern is that no society can guarantee health to its individuals—in that sense, saying that the goal is full external capability may appear unreasonably idealistic. Some of the capabilities (e.g., some of the political liberties) can be fully guaranteed by society, but many others involve an element of chance and cannot be so guaranteed. My response to this is that the list is a list of political *goals* that should be useful as a benchmark for aspiration and comparison. Even though individuals with adequate health support often fall ill, it still makes sense to compare societies by asking about actual health capabilities, since we assume that the comparison will reflect the different inputs of human planning and can be adjusted to take account of more and less favorable natural situations. (Sometimes it is easier to get information on health achievements than on health capabilities; to some extent we must work with the information we have, while not forgetting the importance of the distinction.)

In saying these things about the political goal, we focus on adults who have full mental and moral powers—what Rawls calls "normally cooperating members of society." Children are different, since we are trying to promote the development of adult capabilities. We may in some cases be justified in requiring functioning of an immature child, as with compulsory primary and secondary education (see below); but we must always justify coercive treatment of children with reference to the adult capability goal.

Earlier versions of the list appeared to diverge from the approach of Rawlsian liberalism by not giving as large a place to the traditional political rights and liberties—although the need to incorporate them was stressed from the start.[58] This version of the list corrects that defect of emphasis. These political liberties have a central importance in making well-being human. A society that aims at well-being while overriding these has delivered to its members a merely animal level of satisfaction.[59] As Amartya Sen has recently written, "Political rights are important not only for the fulfillment of needs, they are crucial also for the formulation of needs. And this idea relates, in the end, to the respect that we owe each other as fellow human beings."[60] This idea of freedoms as need has recently been echoed by Rawls: primary goods specify what citizens' needs are from the point of view of political justice.[61]

The capability view justifies its elaborate list by pointing out that choice is not pure spontaneity, flourishing independently of material and social conditions. If one cares about people's powers to choose a conception of the good, then one must care about the rest of the form of life that supports those powers, including its material conditions. Thus the approach claims that its more comprehensive concern with flourishing is perfectly consistent with the impetus behind the Rawlsian project, which has always insisted that we are not to rest content with merely formal equal liberty and opportunity, but must pursue their fully equal worth by ensuring that unfavorable economic and social circumstances do not prevent people from availing themselves of liberties and opportunities that are formally open to them.

The guiding thought behind this form of Aristotelianism is, at its heart, a profoundly liberal idea,[62] and one that lies at the heart of

Rawls's project as well: the idea of the citizen as a free and dignified human being, a maker of choices. Politics here has an urgent role to play, providing citizens with the tools that they need, both in order to choose at all and in order to have a realistic option of exercising the most valuable functions. The choice of whether and how to use the tools, however, is left up to the citizens in the conviction that this is an essential aspect of respect for their freedom. They are seen not as passive recipients of social patterning but as dignified free beings who shape their own lives.[63]

4 Rights and Capabilities: Two Different Relationships

How, then, are capabilities related to human rights? We can see, by this time, that there are two rather different relations that capabilities have to the human rights traditionally recognized by international human rights instruments. In what follows, I shall understand a human right to involve an especially urgent and morally justified claim that a person has, simply in virtue of being a human adult, and independently of membership in a particular nation, class, sex, or ethnic, religious, or sexual group.

First, there are some areas in which the best way of thinking about what rights are is as what I call *combined capabilities* to function in various different ways. The right to political participation, the right to religious free exercise, the freedom of speech, the freedom to seek employment outside the home, the freedom from unwarranted search and seizure, all of these are best thought of as human capacities to function in ways that we then go on to specify. The further specification will usually involve both an internal component and an external component: a citizen who is systematically deprived of information about religion does not really have religious liberty, even if the state imposes no barrier to religious choice. On the other hand, internal conditions are not enough: women who can think about work outside the home, but who are going to be systematically denied employment on account of sex, or beaten if they try to go outside, do not have the right to seek employment. In short, in these areas to secure a right to a citizen is to put them in a position of capability to go ahead with choosing that function if they should so desire.

Of course, there is another way in which we use the term "right" in which it is could not be identified with a capability. We say, that is, that A has "a right to" seek employment outside the home, even when her circumstances obviously do not secure such a right to her. When we use the term "human right" this way, we are saying that just in virtue of being human, a person has a justified claim to have the capability secured to her: so a right in that sense would be prior to capability and a ground for the securing of a capability. "Human rights" used in this sense lie very close to what I have called "basic capabilities," since typically human rights are thought to derive from some actual feature of human persons, some untrained power in them that demands or calls for support from the world. Different rights theories differ about which basic capabilities of the person are relevant to rights, but the ones most commonly chosen are the power of reasoning and the power of moral choice; and reasoning is generally understood to be moral reasoning.[64]

On the other hand, when we say, as we frequently do, that citizens in country C "have the right of free religious exercise," what we typically mean is that this urgent and justified claim is being answered, that the state responds to the claim that they have just by being human. It is in this sense that capabilities and rights should be seen to be equivalent, for I have said that combined capabilities are the *goals* of public planning.

Why is it a good idea to understand rights, so understood, in terms of capabilities? I think this is a good idea because we then understand that what is involved in securing a right to people is usually a lot more than simply putting it down on paper. We see this very clearly in India, for example, where the Constitution is full of guarantees of Fundamental Rights that are not backed up by effective state action. Thus, since ratification women have had rights of sex equality—but in real life they are unequal not only *de facto*, but also *de jure*, in that most of the religious systems of law that constitute the entirety of the Indian system of civil law have unequal provisions for the sexes, very few of which have been declared unconstitutional.[65] So we should not say that women have equal rights since they do not have the capabilities to function as equals. Again, women in many nations have a nominal right of political participation without having this right in the sense of capability, for they are secluded and threatened with violence should they leave the home. This is not what it is to have a right. In short, thinking in terms of capability gives us a benchmark in thinking about what it is really to secure a right to someone.

There is another set of rights, largely those in the area of property and economic advantage, which appear to be analytically different in their relationship to capabilities. Take, for example, the right to a certain level of income, or the right to shelter and housing. These are rights that can be analyzed in a number of distinct ways, in terms of resources, or utility, or capabilities. We could think of the right to a decent level of living as a right to a certain level of resources; or (less plausibly) as a right to a certain level of satisfaction; or as a right to attain a certain level of capability to function.

Once again, we must distinguish the use of the term "right" in the sentence "A has a right to X" from its use in the sentence "Country C gives citizens the right to X." All human beings may arguably have a right to something in the first sense without being in countries that secure these rights. If a decent living standard is a human right, then American citizens have that right although their state does not give them (or secure to them) such a right. So far, then, we have the same distinctions on our hands that we did in the case of the political liberties. But the point I am making is that at the second level, the analysis of "Country C secures to its citizens the right to a decent living standard" may plausibly take a wider range of different forms than it does for the political and religious liberties, where it appears evident that the best way to think of the secured right is as a capability. The material rights may, by contrast, plausibly be analyzed in terms of resources or possibly of utility.

Here again, however, I think it is valuable to understand these rights, insofar as we decide we want to recognize them, in terms of capabilities. That is, if we think of a right to a decent level of living as a right to a certain quantity of resources, then we get into the very problems I have pointed to: that is, giving the resources to people does not always bring differently situated people up to the same level of functioning. If you have a group of people who are traditionally marginalized, you are probably going to have to expend more resources on them to get them up to the same living standard (in capability terms) than you would for a group of people who are in a favorable social situation.

Analyzing economic and material rights in terms of capabilities would thus enable us to understand, as we might not otherwise, a rationale we might have for spending unequal amounts of money on the disadvantaged or creating special programs to assist their transition to full capability. The Indian government has long done this: indeed, affirmative action in this sense for formerly despised caste and tribal groups was written into the Constitution itself, and it has played a crucial role in creating the situation we have today, in which lower-caste parties form part of the ruling government coalition. (Indeed, one could also argue that even to secure political rights effectively to the lower castes required this type of affirmative action.) If we think of these economic rights while asking the question, "What are people actually able to do and to be?" then I think we have a better way of understanding what it is really to put people securely in possession of those rights, to make them able really to function in those ways, not just to have the right on paper.

If we have the language of capabilities, do we still need in addition the language of rights? The language of rights still plays, I believe, four important roles in public discourse, despite its unsatisfactory features. First, when used in the first way, as in the sentence "A has a right to have the basic political liberties secured to her by her government," this sentence reminds us that people have justified and urgent claims to certain types of urgent treatment no matter what the world around them has done about that. I have suggested that this role of rights language lies close to what I have called "basic capabilities" in the sense that the *justification for* saying that people have such natural rights usually proceeds by pointing to some capability-like feature of persons that they actually have, in at least a rudimentary level, no matter what the world around them has done about that. And I think that without such a justification the appeal to rights is quite mysterious. On the other hand, there is no doubt that one might recognize the basic capabilities of people and yet still deny that this entails that they have rights in the sense of justified claims to certain types of treatment. We know that this inference has not been made through a great deal of the world's history (though it is false to suppose that it only was made in the West, or that it only began in the Enlightenment).[66] So appealing to rights communicates more than appealing to basic capabilities: it says what normative conclusions we draw from the fact of the basic capabilities.

Second, even at the second level, when we are talking about rights guaranteed by the state, the language of rights places great emphasis on the importance and the basic role of these things. To say, "Here is a list of things that people ought to be able to do and to be" has only a vague normative resonance. To say, "Here is a list of fundamental rights," says considerably more. It tells people right away that we are dealing with an especially urgent set of functions, backed up by a sense of the justified claim that all humans have to such things, by virtue of being human.

Third, rights language has value because of the emphasis it places on people's choice and autonomy. The language of capabilities, as I have said, was designed to leave room for choice and to communicate the idea that there is a big difference between pushing people into functioning in ways you consider valuable and leaving the choice up to them. At the same time, if we have the language of rights in play as well, I think it helps us to lay extra emphasis on this important fact: that what one ought to think of as the benchmark are people's autonomous choices to avail themselves of certain opportunities and not simply their actual functionings.

Finally, in the areas where we disagree about the proper analysis of rights talk—where the claims of utility, resources, and capabilities are still being worked out—the language of rights preserves a sense of the terrain of agreement, while we continue to deliberate about the proper type of analysis at the more specific level.

One further point should be made. I have discussed one particular view about human capabilities and functioning, my own; and I have indicated its relationship to Sen's similar view. But of course there are many other ways in which one might construct a view based on the idea of human functioning and capability without bringing capabilities nearly so close to rights. As I have suggested, the view Sen and I share is a liberal view of human capabilities, which gives a strong priority to traditional political and religious liberties, and which focuses on capability as the goal precisely in order to leave room for choice. In addition, as I have more recently stressed, the items on my list of basic capabilities are to be regarded as the objects of a specifically political consensus, rather like a Rawlsian list of primary goods, and not as a comprehensive conception of the good.

A capabilities theorist might construct a view that departed from Sen's and my view in all of these ways. First, the content of the list might be different; it might not give the same importance to the traditional liberal freedoms. Second, government might be given much more latitude to aim directly for functioning as a goal and to penalize people who do not exhibit the desired mode of functioning. Such, indeed, is the strategy of some natural-law thinkers in the Catholic tradition, and in this regard they are closer to Aristotle himself than I am.[67] In that sense, as I have written, they construe the account of the human good as a source of public *discipline* on the choices of citizens, whereas we construe the good as an account of *freedoms* citizens have to pursue a variety of different plans of life. Finally, one might think of the account of human functioning as a comprehensive conception of human flourishing for both public and private purposes rather than as the object of a specifically political consensus. Again, natural law theories sometimes understand the view this way, as does Aristotle himself, although some Catholic thinkers have themselves adopted a political-liberal interpretation of their tradition.[68] Insofar as any of these alternatives is pursued, the relationship between capabilities and rights will shift accordingly.

5 Rights as Goals and Side-Constraints

One final question remains to be discussed. Sen has argued that thinking of rights in terms of capabilities should lead us to opt for a particular way of thinking about rights and to reject another way. Specifically, it should encourage us to think of rights as goals, and thus as part of a more general account of social goals that it is reasonable to promote, rather than to think of them as "side constraints," as justified claims of individuals that should be respected no matter what, and that thus constrain the ways in which we may promote our social goals.[69] Since Sen's target here is the libertarian theory of Robert Nozick, and since I believe his critique has force primarily *ad hominem* against Nozick, not against all versions of a side-constraints view, I must describe Nozick's position.

Nozick's basic argument, in *Anarchy, State, and Utopia*, is that people have rights, in the sense (apparently, since no account of rights is presented) that these rights should not be overridden for the sake of the greater good. The rights people have are a function of their initial *entitlements*, together with a theory of *just transfer*. One of the notoriously frustrating aspects of Nozick's theory is that he refuses to present his own account of initial entitlements, although he alludes to (a controversial interpretation of) Locke to illustrate the type of thing he has in mind. Through this process, he derives the view (which must be advanced tentatively, since the account of initial entitlement has not been given) that people have a right to the property they hold just in case they acquired it by a series of just transfers from the original owners. It is wrong of the state to take any of this property away from them for redistributive purposes. (Nozick focuses on property throughout the book, and says little about political, religious, and artistic liberty.)

Nozick's theory has been criticized in a number of ways. First of all, in the absence of a theory of initial entitlement, it is difficult to see what the upshot will be and thus impossible to know whether a procedural conception of justice like Nozick's will produce results that are acceptable or quite bizarre and unacceptable. And of course one might answer questions about entitlement differently from the way in which Nozick seems inclined to answer them, saying, for example, that individuals are never entitled to any property they do not need for their own use, or that they are never entitled to accumulate a surplus. Such, for example, was Aristotle's view of entitlement, and this meant that for Aristotle the very existence of private ownership of land was a highly dubious business.[70] (In his ideal city, fully half of the land is publicly owned, and the rest is "common in use," meaning its produce can be taken by anyone who is in need.)[71] So Aristotle's view of entitlement, combined with his strong moral distaste for hoarding and accumulation, would certainly not yield the

Nozickian conclusion that "Capitalist acts between consenting adults are no crime."

Second, it has been pointed out that even if individuals do have entitlements to what they have acquired in a just transfer, it does not follow from this that they are entitled to the surplus value of these goods when for contingent reasons they rise in value during the time they hold them. In fact, even the Lockean tradition is much divided on this question.[72]

Third, one might point out that the economic inequalities apparently tolerated in Nozick's minimal state would erode the meaningful possession of other rights that Nozick apparently thinks people have (such as the right to political participation). Nozick nowhere confronted possible tensions between two parts of his libertarian view, so we do not even know whether he would be willing to tax people to get the money to support the institutions that make meaningful political and religious liberties for all a social reality. In these ways, his attitude to rights remained obscure.

Fourth, the view of self-ownership on which much of Nozick's argument rested was rather obscure and somewhat questionable.[73] What does it mean to say of people that they own themselves, and how, precisely, does and should this affect arguments on a variety of topics from the morality of slavery to the legality of prostitution?

These are only some of the ways in which one might criticize Nozick's view. Let me now describe Sen's critique. Sen argues that if we allow rights to function the way Nozick says they should, as "side-constraints" that can almost never be overridden for the sake of the general good, then we will be led to tolerate an unacceptable level of misery.

The question I am asking is this: if results such as starvation and famines were to occur, would the distribution of holdings still be morally acceptable despite their disastrous consequences? There is something deeply implausible in the affirmative answer. Why should it be the case that rules of ownership, etc., should have such an absolute priority over life-and-death questions? . . . But once it is admitted that consequences can be important in judging what rights we do or do not morally have, surely the door is quite open for taking a less narrow view of rights, rejecting assessment by procedures only.[74]

Sen seems to me to be saying two things, not easily made compatible. First, that Nozick has given the wrong account of *what rights people have*: they do not have the right to keep their surplus when others are dying. Second, that the consideration of consequences shows that *the type of view of rights Nozick advances* must be wrong: a side-constraints view is implausible, and we should think of rights as parts of a total system of social goals (as he goes on to argue). But if the first point is correct, as I believe it certainly is, then we have had as yet no reason to accept the second claim. If we question the whole way Nozick thinks about what people's rights and entitlements are, as we most certainly should, then we have no reason to think that a correct list of rights should not be used as side constraints.

This is important, since a list of human rights typically functions as a system of side constraints in international deliberation and in internal policy debates. That is, we typically say to and of governments, let them pursue the social good as they conceive it so long as they do not violate the items on this list. I think this is a very good way of thinking about the way a list of basic human rights should function in a pluralistic society; and I have already said that I regard my list of basic capabilities this way, as a list of urgent items that should be secured to people no matter what else we pursue. In this way, we both conceive of capabilities as a set of goals (a subset of total social goals) and say that they have an urgent claim to be promoted, whatever else we also promote. Indeed, the point made by Sen, in endorsing the Rawlsian notion of the priority of liberty, was precisely this.[75] We are doing wrong to people when we do not secure to them the capabilities on this list. The traditional function of a notion of rights as side constraints is to make this sort of antiutilitarian point, and I see no reason why rights construed as capabilities (or analyzed in terms of capabilities) should not continue to play this role.

Of course there will be circumstances in which we cannot secure to all the citizens the capabilities on my list. Sen and I have argued that the political liberties and liberties of conscience should get a high degree of priority within the general capability set.[76] But we also conceive of the capabilities as a total system of liberty whose parts support one another; thus we also hold that there is something bad about not securing any of the items. The precise threshold level for many of them remains to be hammered out in public debate; but there are surely levels easy to specify beneath which people will have been violated in unacceptable ways if the capabilities are not secured. Viewing capabilities as rather like side constraints also helps here, for it helps us to understand what is tragic and unacceptable in such situations, and why individuals so treated have an urgent claim to be treated better, even when governments are in other ways pursuing the good with great efficiency.

Notes

1. For one excellent recent account, with discussions of other views, see Alan Gewirth, *The Community of Rights* (Chicago: University of Chicago Press, 1995).

2. For just one example, this is the view of Thomas Paine in *The Rights of Man*. Such views ultimately derive from ancient Greek and Roman Stoic views of natural law. The Latin word *ius* can be translated either as "right" or as "law"; Grotius already discussed its manifold applications (in *De Iure Belli Atque Pacis*).

3. See Peter Singer, *Animal Liberation*, new rev. ed. (New York: Avon, 1990).

4. This view is most influentially found in Kant's *Rechtsphilosophie*.

5. An influential example of the first approach is in Robert Nozick, *Anarchy, State, and Utopia* (New York: Basic Books, 1974), ch. 3; see also Samuel Scheffler, *The Rejection of Consequentialism* (New York: Oxford University Press, 1982); for the second approach, see, for example, A. Sen, "Rights as Goals," ref. Below, n. 13.

6. See Amartya Sen, "Equality of What?" in S. McMurrin, ed., *Tanner Lectures on Human Values* 1 (Cambridge: Cambridge University Press, 1980), reprinted in Sen, *Choice, Welfare, and Measurement* (Cambridge, MA: MIT Press, 1982); also Sen, *Inequality Reexamined* (Cambridge, MA: Harvard University Press, 1992), passim; G. A. Cohen, "Equality of Welfare," *Philosophy and Public Affairs*; Ronald Dworkin, "What is Equality? Part 1: Equality of Welfare," *Philosophy and Public Affairs* 10 (1981), 185–246 and 283–345; John Roemer, "Equality of Resources Implies Equality of Welfare," *The Quarterly Journal of Economics* November 1986, 751–783; Richard Arneson, "Equality and Equality of Opportunity for Welfare," *Philosophical Studies* 56 (1989).

7. See for example Bernard Williams, "The Standard of Living: Interests and Capabilities," in Geoffrey Hawthorne, ed., *The Standard of Living* (Cambridge: Cambridge University Press, 1987), 94, 100.

8. *Human Development Reports: 1993, 1994, 1995, 1996*, New York: UNDP.

9. See my "Nature, Function, and Capability: Aristotle on Political Distribution," *Oxford Studies in Ancient Philosophy*, Supplementary Vol. I: 1988, 145–184, hereafter NFC.

10. See "Aristotelian Social Democracy," in *Liberalism and the Good*, ed. R. B. Douglass et al. (New York: Routledge, 1990), 203–252, hereafter ASD; "Non-Relative Virtues: An Aristotelian Approach," in *The Quality of Life*, ed. M. Nussbaum and A. Sen (Oxford: Clarendon Press, 1993), hereafter NRV; "Aristotle on Human Nature and the Foundations of Ethics," in *World, Mind and Ethics: Essays on the Ethical Philosophy of Bernard Williams*, eds. J. E. J. Altham and Ross Harrison (Cambridge: Cambridge University Press, 1995), 86–131, hereafter HN; "Human Functining and Social Justice: In Defense of Aristotelian Essentialism," *Political Theory* 20 (1992), 202–246, hereafter HF; "Human Capabilities, Female Human Beings," in *Women, Culture, and Development*, eds. M. Nussbaum and J. Glover (Oxford: Clarendon Press, 1995), 61–104, hereafter HC; and, most recently, two forthcoming papers: "The Good as Discipline, the Good as Freedom," in *The Ethics of Consumption: The Good Life, Justice, and Global Stewardship*, eds. D. Crocker and T. Linden (Lanham, MD: Rowman & Littlefield, 1998), hereafter GDGF, and "Women and Cultural Universals," chapter 1 in Nussbaum, *Sex and Social Justice* (New York: Oxford University Press, 1999).

11. See, for example, *Inequality Reexamined*, which also contains Sen's most recent formulation of the approach. For other important formulations, see Sen, "Equality of What?" (above); *Commodities and Capabilities* (Amsterdam: North-Holland, 1985); "Well-Being, Agency, and Freedom: The Dewey Lectures 1984," *The Journal of Philosophy* 82 (1985); "Capability and Well-Being," in Nussbaum and Sen, *The Quality of Life* (above), 30–53; "Gender Inequality and Theories of Justice," in *Women, Culture, and Development* (above), 259–273.

12. A good summary of our approaches, and the similarities and differences between Sen's and my views, is in David Crocker, "Functioning and Capability: The Foundations of Sen's and Nussbaum's Development Ethic, Part I," *Political Theory* 20 (1992), 584–612, and "Functioning and Capability: the Foundations of Sen's and Nussbaum's Development Ethic, Part II," in *Women, Culture, and Development*, 153–198.

13. See "Rights and Agency," *Philosophy and Public Affairs* 11 (1982), 3–39 ; "Rights and Capabilities," in T. Honderich, ed., *Morality and Objectivity: a Tribute to J. L. Mackie* (London: Routledge and Kegan Paul, 1985), repr. in Sen, *Resources, Values, and Development* (Cambridge, MA: MIT Press, 1984), 307–324; "Rights as Goals," in S. Guest and A. Milne, eds., *Equality and Discrimination: Essays in Freedom and Justice* (Stuttgart: Franz Steiner, 1985).

14. See ASD, 239.

15. John Rawls, *A Theory of Justice* (Cambridge, MA: Harvard University Press, 1971), and *Political Liberalism* (New York: Columbia University Press, 1993, expanded paperback edition 1996). Sen discusses (and supports) the Rawlsian notion of the priority of liberty in "Freedoms and Needs," *The New Republic*, January 10/17, 1994, 31–38; I discuss the relationship between my own version of the capabilities view and Rawls's theory in ASD and GDGF; in GDGF I emphasize the liberal roots of my own Aristotelianism, contrasting my view with two nonliberal forms of Aristotelianism.

16. My term in ASD, contrasting with Rawls's "thin theory of the good."

17. See HC.

18. HC, 84–85.

19. WC.

20. I put things this way because the most prominent antiliberal natural law theorists do not explicitly reject rights language: see John Finnis, *Natural Law and Natural Rights* (New York: Oxford University Press, 1980), and Robert P. George, *Making Men Moral* (New York: Oxford University Press, 1993); and the most prominent Catholic opponent of rights language, Mary Ann Glendon, does not endorse the capabilities approach (see her *Rights Talk: The Impoverishment of Political Discourse* [New York: Free Press, 1991]). But the combination is easy enough to imagine.

21. See "Rights and Capabilities," 310–312.

22. A valuable beginning, bringing together all that Sen and I have said on the topic, is in Crocker, "Functioning and Capability, Part 2," 186–191.

23. In Hawthorn, ed., *The Standard of Living*, 100.

24. See Sen and others in Hawthorne, eds., *The Standard of Living*.

25. See Nussbaum and Sen, ed., *The Quality of Life*.

26. See Sen, *Inequality Reexamined*.

27. Nozick, *Anarchy, State, and Utopia*, 150–64.

28. Charles Dickens, *Hard Times* (Oxford: Oxford University Press, 1989), 74–75.

29. See Sen and Bernard Williams, eds., *Utilitarianism and Beyond* (Cambridge: Cambridge University Press, 1982), "Introduction," 1, 4–5; John Rawls, *Theory of Justice*, 179–183.

30. Here I am combining arguments from Williams's essay in *Utilitarianism: For and Against* (Cambridge: Cambridge University Press, 1993), with his "Persons, Character, and Morality," in A. Rorty, ed., *The Identities of Persons* (Berkeley: University of California Press, 1976).

31. Nussbaum, "Plato on Commensurability and Desire" and "The Discernment of Perception," in *Love's Knowledge* (New York: Oxford University Press, 1990); chapter 10 in *The Fragility of Goodness* (Cambridge: Cambridge University Press, 1986); Sen, "Plural Utility," in *Choice, Welfare, and Measurement*; *On Ethics and Economics* (Oxford: Blackwell, 1987).

32. See Nussbaum, HC, 85–86; Sen, *On Ethics and Economics*, 63–64.

33. "Rights and Capabilities," 309.

34. See also Sen, "Gender and Cooperative Conflicts," in I. Tinker, eds., *Persistent Inequalities* (New York: Oxford University Press, 1991); J. Elster, *Sour Grapes* (Cambridge: Cambridge University Press, 1983).

35. See Gary Becker, "The Economic Way of Looking at Life," in *The Essence of Becker*, eds. R. Febrero and P. Schwartz (Stanford, CA: Hoover Institution Press, 1995), 633, 636–637, arguing that women and members of racial minorities frequently underin-

vest in their "human capital" because they believe (often wrongly) that they do not have opportunities that would be promoted by education.

36. *Theory of Justice*, 62 ff., 90–95, 396–397. More recently, Rawls has qualified his view by stating that the primary goods are to be seen not as all-purpose means, but as the needs of citizens understood from a political point of view, in connection with the development and expression of their "moral powers"; and he has stressed that the account of the moral powers (of forming and revising a life plan) is itself an important part of the political theory of the good; see *Political Liberalism*, 178–190.

37. *Political Liberalism*, 181.

38. *Theory of Justice*, 97–98.

39. *Political Liberalism*, 188.

40. Sen has insisted, however, that happiness is "a momentous functioning," in "Well-Being, Agency, and Freedom" (sup. n. 11), 200 and I have insisted that emotional functioning is one of the important types of functioning we should consider: see "Emotions and Women's Capabilities," in *Women, Culture, and Development*, 360.

41. See Sen, "Plural Utility," in *Choice, Welfare, and Measurement*; Nussbaum, HC, 85–86.

42. In this sense, the approach takes its inspiration from Marx's discussion of fully human functioning in several early works in which he was in turn much influenced by Aristotle. For discussion of these links, see HN, 119–120.

43. Jean Drèze and Amartya Sen, *India: Economic Development and Social Opportunity* (Oxford: Clarendon Press, 1996), 13–16, 109–139, 155–178. For an enumeration of all the examples Sen has given in a variety of different works, see Crocker, "Functioning and Capability," parts 1 and 2.

44. Especially in HN, 90–95.

45. See HF, 67–72, 93–95, HC, and WC, 12–20.

46. For an excellent discussion of this question and a critique of Rawls with which I largely agree, see Thomas W. Pogge, *Realizing Rawls* (Ithaca: Cornell University Press, 1989), 211–280.

47. See GDGF, 324, where I have stressed this political-liberal role of the capabilities list more than in previous papers.

48. *Political Liberalism*, passim.

49. The primary changes are a greater emphasis on bodily integrity and control over one's environment. Oddly, these features of human "self-sufficiency" are the ones most often critized by Western feminists as "male" and "Western," one reason for their more muted role in earlier versions of the list. See my "The Feminist Critique of Liberalism," the Lindlay Lecture forthcoming in the volume *Women's Voices, Women's Rights: The Oxford Amnesty Lectures 1996*, eds. M. Forey and J. Gardner (Boulder, CO: Westview Press, 1999).

50. See HN, 102–120, ASD, 226–228.

51. See HN, 119–120, with discussion of Marx.

52. See my "Double Moral Standards?" (a reply to Yael Tamir's "Hands Off Clitoridectomy") *The Boston Review* October–November 1996, 28, 30, and "Religion and Women's Human Rights," *Religion and Contemporary Liberalism*, ed. Paul J. Weithman (Notre Dame, IN: Notre Dame University Press, 1997), 93, 107–110.

53. See NFC, 160–164, referring to Aristotle's similar distinctions; and, on the basic capabilities, HC, 88. Sen does not use these three levels explicitly, although many things he says assume some such distinctions.

54. In earlier papers I called these "external capabilities," see, for example NFC, 164; but Crocker has suggested to me that this suggests a misleading contrast with "internal."

55. This distinction is related to Rawls's distinction between social and natural primary goods, see *Theory of Justice*, 62. Whereas he holds that only the social primary goods should be on the list, and not the natural (such as health, imagination), we say that *the social basis of* the natural primary goods should most emphatically be on the list.

56. *Theory of Justice*, 62.

57. Rawls comments that "although their possession is influenced by the basic structure, they are not so directly under its control" (62). This is of course true if we are thinking of health: but if we think of the social basis of health, it is not true. It seems to me that the case for putting these items on the political list is just as strong as the case for the social basis of self-respect. In "The Priority of Right and Ideas of the Good," *Philosophy and Public Affairs* 17 (1988): 251, 257, Rawls suggests putting health on the list.

58. See ASD, 239–240.

59. See HN, 110–120.

60. Sen, "Freedoms and Needs," *The New Republic* January 10/17, 1994, 31–38, at 38.

61. *Political Liberalism*, 187–188.

62. Though in one form Aristotle had it too. See HN, 110–120.

63. Compare Sen, "Freedoms and Needs," 38: "The importance of political rights for the understanding of economic needs turns ultimately on seeing human beings as people with rights to exercise, not as parts of a "stock" or a "population" that passively exists and must be looked after. What matters, finally, is how we see each other."

64. This way of thinking derives from the ancient Stoic tradition, continued through Cicero and on into Grotius and Kant: see my "Kant and Stoic Cosmopolitanism," *Journal of Political Philosophy* 5 (1997) 1–25, and "The Incomplete Feminism of Musonius Rufus," paper presented to the conference on Gender and Sexual Experience in Ancient Greece and Rome, Finnish Academy in Rome, June 22–25, 1997.

65. See my "Religion and Women's Human Rights," 121–126, reviewing this situation. Typically, only small and unpopular religions get their laws thrown out: thus, the Christian inheritance law (or one of them, since Christians in India are governed by a bewildering variety of different systems of Christian law) was declared unconstitutional on grounds of sex equality, but the attempt to set aside a part of the Hindu marriage act on these grounds was reversed at the Supreme Court level.

66. On Indian discussions of religious pluralism and liberty, see Sen, "Human Rights and Asian Values," *New Republic,* July 14 and 21, 1997, 33–40, and "Tagore and His India," *New York Review of Books,* June 26, 1997, 55–56. On the Greek and Roman origins of ideas of human rights, see my NFC, "Kant and Stoic Cosmopolitanism," and also Fred D. Miller, Jr., *Nature and Rights in Aristotle's Politics* (Oxford: Oxford University Press, 1995).

67. See Finnis, *Natural Law and Natural Rights,* and George, *Making Men Moral.* For a detailed discussion of differences between the Sen/Nussbaum view and those views, in a range of areas of public policy, see GDGF.

68. For an eloquent example, see Jacques Maritain, "Truth and Human Fellowship," in *On the Use of Philosophy: Three Essays* (Princeton, NJ: Princeton University Press, 1961).

69. Sen, "Rights and Capabilities," "Rights as Goals," "Rights and Agency."

70. See my discussion in ASD, 203–206, 231–232.

71. See ASD, 205.

72. See Barbara Fried, "Wilt Chamberlain Revisited: Nozick's 'Justice in Transfer' and the Problem of Market-Based Distribution," *Philosophy and Public Affairs* 24 (1995).

73. The best criticism (highly sympathetic to the general idea) is in G. A. Cohen, *Self-Ownership, Freedom, and Equality* (New York: Cambridge University Press, 1995, 1–115).

74. "Rights and Capabilities," 312.

75. "Freedoms and Needs," 32.

76. "Freedoms and Needs," 32–38; GDGF, 314–321.

5

Human Rights and Human Responsibilities

Thomas Pogge

1 The Problem

Various international declarations and treaties offer formulations of human rights that are, for the most part, clear enough to support reasonably precise estimates of the extent to which human rights are unfulfilled worldwide. Piecing together this global human rights record from the available data, one finds that most of the current underfulfillment of human rights is more or less directly connected to poverty. The connection is direct in the case of basic social and economic human rights, such as the right to a standard of living adequate for the health and well-being of oneself and one's family, including food, clothing, housing, and medical care.[1] The connection is more indirect in the case of civil and political human rights associated with democratic government and the rule of law. Desperately poor people, often stunted, illiterate, and heavily preoccupied with the struggle to survive, can do little by way of either resisting or rewarding their rulers, who are therefore likely to rule them oppressively while catering to the interests of other (often foreign) agents more capable of reciprocation.

We have a great wealth of data about how widespread and severe global poverty is today: out of a total of 6 billion human beings, 790 million are malnourished, 880 million lack access to health services, 1 billion are without adequate shelter, 1 billion without access to safe drinking water, 2 billion without electricity, and 2.4 billion without access to basic sanitation; 850 million adults are illiterate.[2] One-quarter of all children between age five and fourteen, 250 million in all, do wage work outside their household, often under harsh or cruel conditions.[3] Some 50,000 human deaths per day, fully one-third of all human deaths, are due to poverty-related causes and therefore avoidable insofar as poverty itself is avoidable.[4]

That a large segment of humankind lives in extreme poverty is nothing new. What is comparatively new, however, is that another large segment is living in considerable affluence. "The income gap between the fifth of the world's people living in the richest countries and the fifth in the poorest was 74 to 1 in 1997, up from 60 to 1 in 1990 and 30 to 1 in 1960." Earlier estimates are 11 to 1 for 1913, 7 to 1 for 1870, and 3 to 1 for 1820.[5] With this tremendous upsurge in global inequality comes a dramatic increase in human capabilities to eliminate severe poverty. It would not cost us much to eradicate the deprivations I have highlighted in the preceding paragraph—perhaps around 1 percent of the disposable incomes of the most affluent tenth of humankind. And this cost would decline over time, as adults who do not have to bear the horrendous mental and physical effects of childhood malnutrition, childhood diseases, child labor, and lack of basic education would be much better able to fend for themselves and to provide for their families. Our opportunity to abolish severe poverty worldwide starkly confronts us then with the question whether we have any responsibilities correlative to the internationally recognized but massively underfulfilled human rights of the global poor.

The world's governments faced up to this question at the World Food Summit in Rome, organized by the U.N. Food and Agriculture Organization (FAO) in November 1996. The principal achievement of this summit was a pledge by the 186 participating governments to reduce the number of undernourished people worldwide by about one-half to 400 million by the year 2015. The opening sentences of this Rome Declaration on World Food Security read as follows:

1. We, the Heads of State and Government, or our representatives, gathered at the World Food Summit at the invitation of the Food and Agriculture Organization of the United Nations, reaffirm the right of everyone to have

access to safe and nutritious food, consistent with the right to adequate food and the fundamental right of everyone to be free from hunger. 2. We pledge our political will and our common and national commitment to achieving food security for all and to an on-going effort to eradicate hunger in all countries, with an immediate view to reducing the number of undernourished people to half their present level no later than 2015. 3. We consider it intolerable that more than 800 million people throughout the world, and particularly in developing countries, do not have enough food to meet their basic nutritional needs. This situation is unacceptable.[6]

The represented governments could not, however, agree on concrete steps toward achieving such progress and did not sign or officially commit to the final document articulating the Summit goals.

Events since 1996 likewise indicate no special eagerness for implementation. The United States has issued an "Interpretive Statement" to clarify its understanding of the Rome pledge: "the attainment of any 'right to adequate food' or 'fundamental right to be free from hunger' is a goal or aspiration to be realized progressively that does not give rise to any international obligations."[7] Challenging the FAO's claim that achieving the Summit goals would require all developed countries combined to increase their official development assistance (ODA) in agriculture by $6 billion annually,[8] the United States has published a competing calculation according to which an annual increase of U.S.$2.6 billion—that is, only $3.30 rather than $7.60 annually for each malnourished person—should be sufficient.[9] The affluent states' foreign aid budgets show an extended down-trend.[10] Workers and imports from the poorest countries continue to be excluded through quotas, tariffs, and regulations.[11] And global poverty has spiked up sharply in the wake of the 1997–98 currency crisis in the emerging markets.[12]

It appears then that the developed countries do not accept any responsibility for severe poverty abroad, either in principle or in practice. Yet, they also seem reluctant to publicize and defend this position, and even suggest the opposite in their rhetorical employment of words such as "intolerable" and "unacceptable." This should heighten interest in the question before us: What are our responsibilities for the massive and avoidable underfulfillment of human rights abroad?

2 A New Universal Declaration?

Great expectations are raised, then, when a prominent group of former heads of state, calling itself the InterAction Council, proposes a *Universal Declaration of Human Responsibilities* for worldwide discussion and for adoption by the General Assembly of the United Nations with the express aim to "complement" the 1948 Universal Declaration of Human Rights on the occasion of its fifth anniversary.[13] In its preamble, the Draft Declaration has the United Nations announce that: "We, the peoples of the world thus renew and reinforce commitments already proclaimed in the Universal Declaration of Human Rights." The new declaration is nevertheless necessary, as the accompanying report points out, for clarifying that human rights correlate with human duties: "Because rights and duties are inextricably linked, the idea of a human right only makes sense if we acknowledge the duty of all people to respect it."

Looking at the Draft Declaration in search for a clarification of the responsibilities for the realization of human rights, one cannot but be severely disappointed. Although one purpose of this declaration is expressed by the compelling idea that rights are meaningless without the specification of corresponding duties, the Draft Declaration is, if anything, less specific about responsibilities than the human-rights documents it seeks to complement. Consider the various articles that spell out our responsibilities about poverty.

Article 7 begins in a promising way: "Every person is infinitely precious and must be protected unconditionally." So who must effect this unconditional protection, how, and against what threats? What are our responsibilities? Article 7 continues: "The animals and the natural environment also demand protection. All people have a responsibility to protect the air, water and soil of the earth for the sake of present inhabitants and future generations." So the only responsibility assigned to us, it appears, is to protect air, water and soil: Animals merely "demand" protection; and humans "must be" protected, though apparently by no one in particular.

Article 9 does somewhat better: "All people, given the necessary tools, have a responsibility to make serious efforts to overcome poverty, malnutrition, ignorance, and inequality." But again, the main issues raised by this statement remain unaddressed: is the directive to *overcome* poverty, malnutrition, and so on, addressed to the poor themselves or to others as well? If the latter, which others: compatriots, all human beings? What counts as making a "serious effort"? And what is the import of the qualification "given the necessary tools"? The other sentence of Article 9 offers little help: "[All people] should promote sustainable development all over the world in order to assure dignity, freedom, security and justice for all people." Nothing is said about what "sustainable development" means or about what counts as promoting it.

Article 10 adds that "Everyone should lend support to the needy, the disadvantaged, the disabled and to the victims of discrimination." Nothing is said about the amount of support, nor about its targeting to ensure that the most urgent needs are actually met.

Article 11, finally, proclaims that "economic and political power must . . . be handled in the service of economic justice and of the social order." The Draft Declaration provides no guidance concerning the highly controversial notion of economic justice. Moreover, since the social order is often itself a major contributor to oppression and economic injustice (however one may wish to understand this notion), the draft assigns potentially counterproductive and conflicting duties to people wielding economic and political power.

While the Draft Declaration expresses awareness of disadvantage and poverty, it fails then to clarify what responsibilities arise therefrom. Perhaps this should not be surprising in a declaration proposed by former heads of state for adoption by present political leaders. For these politicians, any more specific statement of responsibilities might raise awkward questions about how their own decisions have affected global poverty. The former leaders proposing the Draft Declaration can at least adduce the pressures of the Cold War as an excuse. It is unclear what could possibly excuse the increasing tolerance for starvation in the 1990s, when half of the so-called peace dividend would have sufficed to eradicate most of the world hunger problem.[14]

The excessive generality and vagueness of these middle articles is typical of the Draft Declaration as a whole and especially evident also in the opening articles, which have the pomposity and emptiness one might expect in a teenager's first writing attempts. The first four articles are billed as "Fundamental Principles for Humanity." Of these, the third one best exemplifies the problem when it declares that no one stands above good and evil and that every one has a responsibility to promote good and to avoid evil "in all things," but the other principles are not much more meaningful either. The first principle of humanity says that every person has a responsibility to treat all people in a humane way. What does this mean? There are six billion other people out there, and with the vast majority of these I never interact except indirectly. In these cases, am I discharging my responsibility to treat them in a humane way? What if some of them are starving or being tortured for their religious or political views and I do nothing for them—am I treating them humanely? Does it matter here whether they are compatriots or foreigners, or whether I have any general or particular knowledge of their plight? Or consider the people around me: am I discharging my responsibility if I treat them in a humane way at some times and fail to do so at other times? And, most importantly, how is the distinction between humane and inhumane treatment to be drawn?

As if to make up for the vagueness of the prescription, the drafters then add that it applies to every person "regardless of gender, ethnic origin, social status, political opinion, language, age, nationality, or religion." This addition would have a point if it referred to the *objects* of the proclaimed responsibility: to those who are to be treated humanely. It could naturally be taken to mean, then, that one's responsibilities are *equally* strong with regard to all others: the treatment I owe to compatriots, I also owe to foreigners; the treatment I owe to men, I also owe to women; and so forth. The addition is in fact attached, however, to the *subjects* of the proclaimed responsibility: to those who are to accord humane treatment. Here the long verbal addition adds no content at all: The statement that *every person* has a responsibility to treat all people humanely already entails that this responsibility is asserted for male and female persons, rich and poor persons, old and young persons, and so on.

One might think that more clarity can be derived from the draft declaration's endorsement of the Golden Rule in article 4: What you do not wish to be done to yourself, do not do to others. This, of course, is the *negative* version of the Golden Rule. Its *positive* version—

do unto others as you would have them do unto you—is not endorsed, although it is much closer to the "spirit of solidarity" invoked in article 4. Endorsement of the positive version would have made it difficult to deny that persons have a responsibility to help others in distress, even across large distances, when they can do so at comparatively small cost to themselves. Endorsement of the negative version makes this far easier to deny: By *ignoring* the distress of others, I am not *doing* anything to them and hence a fortiori not doing anything I would not wish to be done to myself. What could the point of the selective endorsement of the negative version possibly be, if not to buttress this denial?

To make matters worse, the Golden Rule, in its negative version, often tends to shield and entrench immorality and injustice in situations where exposing them would be painful to their practitioners and beneficiaries. If I had violated some law or some significant ethical rule or principle, or had benefited from another's such violation, I would not wish this fact to become widely known. Does it follow therefrom that I should never expose such violations? Or, to take Kant's related example: should a judge follow the Golden Rule when it enjoins her not to inflict on a defendant any punishment that this judge would not wish inflicted on herself?[15] These problems do not defeat the view that the Golden Rule can be developed into a useful and plausible ethical standard that avoids these and other difficulties; perhaps it can. Without such a development, however, the Golden Rule cannot accomplish any of the purposes appealed to by the drafters. It is far too unclear.[16]

However timely and praiseworthy the project of drafting a universal declaration of human responsibilities may be, this particular draft declaration will not do. It gives no guidance about what our responsibilities are about the massive underfulfillment of human rights today. Let us see, then, whether further reflection on the idea of human rights may lead to a clearer sense of our responsibilities.

3 Understanding Human Rights

It makes sense to begin this inquiry by outlining some plausible competing understandings of human rights, while attending especially to how these differ in their implications about responsibilities for the realization of human rights. This exercise involves distinguishing two different components of any conception of human rights: (1) the *concept* of a human right used by this conception, or what one might also call its *understanding* of human rights, and (2) the *substance* or content of the conception, that is, the goods it selects as objects for a set of human rights.

A conception of human rights addresses then two questions: what are human rights? And what human rights are there? I believe that these two questions are asymmetrically related in this sense: we cannot convincingly justify a particular list of human rights without first making clear what human rights are. Yet we *can* justify a particular understanding of human rights without presupposing more than a rough idea about what goods are widely recognized as worthy of inclusion. This, in any case, is what I will attempt to do.

Even a fully comprehensive answer to the first question does not preempt the second. The fact that some formulated right has all the conceptual features of a human right does not entail that it exists (can be justified as such) any more than the fact that Robinson Crusoe as described has all the conceptual features of a human being entails that there is (atemporally) such a person. Settling what human rights there are requires not merely careful conceptual explication but also substantive moral argument pro and con. It will be easier to engage in such substantive moral argument, however, once we have a shared understanding of what human rights are and hence of what the assertion of some particular human right actually amounts to, especially as regards correlative responsibilities.

A straightforward answer to the question proposes that human rights are whatever governments—individually, in domestic law, or collectively, in international law—create under this title. The expression human rights is often used in this sense by lawyers, politicians, activists, and others. Without objecting to this use in the slightest, I am here interested in human rights as moral rights. That there are such rights is a widely shared presumption, which manifests itself, for instance, in the common phrase "internationally recognized human rights." That international legal documents recognize human rights suggests that people have human rights quite apart from such recognition—already in the Nazi era, for example—and that people would continue to have human rights even if governments decided to repeal and abrogate all national and international human-rights legislation. More generally, this common phrase leaves open the possibility that, even today, some human rights may not be legally recognized as such and also the converse possibility that some legal texts may recognize as human rights what are not human rights at all. Where legal texts confer recognition correctly, they create then a second, legal right in addition to the moral one they recognize and thus present as preexisting: A government that used torture against its political opponents violated a (moral) human right of the persons it tortured—and, if it did so after March 23, 1976, it also breached its legal obligation under article 7 of the International Covenant on Civil and Political Rights, violating a legal right (or a legal human right) of the tortured persons. My attention in what follows is focused exclusively on human rights of the first kind.

How should we understand the assertion that something is a human right in this moral sense? The moral concept of a human right has six rather uncontroversial elements that any plausible understanding of human rights must incorporate. First, human rights express *ultimate* moral concerns: agents have a moral duty to respect human rights, a duty that does not derive from a more general moral duty to comply with national or international laws. (In fact, the opposite may hold: conformity with human rights is a moral requirement on any legal order whose capacity to create moral obligations depends in part on such conformity.) Second, human rights express *weighty* moral concerns, which normally override other normative considerations. Third, these moral concerns are focused on *human beings*, as all of them and they alone have human rights and the special moral status associated therewith. Fourth, with respect to these moral concerns, *all* human beings have *equal status:* They have exactly the same human rights, and the moral significance of these rights and of their fulfillment does not vary with whose human rights are at stake.[17] Fifth, human rights express moral concerns whose validity is *unrestricted,* that is, they are conceived as binding on all human agents irrespective of their particular epoch, culture, religion, moral tradition, or philosophy. Sixth, these moral concerns are *broadly sharable,* that is, capable of being understood and appreciated by persons from different epochs and cultures as well as by adherents of a variety of different religions, moral traditions, and philosophies. These last two elements of unrestrictedness and broad sharability are related in that we tend to be more confident about conceiving of a moral concern as unrestricted when this concern is not parochial to some particular epoch, culture, religion, moral tradition, or philosophy.[18]

Various understandings of human rights are consistent with these six points. Though I cannot here examine all such understandings in detail, I want briefly to present three of the more prominent ones as a backdrop to the one I will endorse. I have tried to arrange the four understandings so that their sequence can be seen as a dialectical progression.

The first understanding, U_1, conceives of human rights as moral rights that every human being has against every other human being or perhaps, more generally, against every other human agent (where this also includes collective agents, such as groups, firms, or governments).[19] Given this understanding of human rights, it matters greatly whether one then postulates human rights that impose only negative duties (to avoid depriving) or whether one instead postulates human rights that in addition impose positive duties (to protect and/or to aid).[20] A human right to freedom from assault might then give every human agent merely a weighty moral duty to refrain from assaulting any human being or also an additional weighty moral duty to help protect any human beings from assaults and their effects.

I do not deny that there are such universal moral rights and duties, but it is clear that we are not referring to them when we speak of human rights in the modern context. To see this, consider first some ordinary criminal assault. Though the victim may be badly hurt, we would not call this a human-rights violation. A police beating of a suspect in jail, on the other hand, does appear to qualify. This suggests that, to engage human rights, conduct must be in some sense official. This suggestion is confirmed, secondly, by the human rights that have actually been recognized in various international documents. Many of them do not appear to be addressed to individual agents at all in that, rather than forbearance or support of a kind that individuals could provide, they demand appropriately constrained institutional arrangements such as equality before the law (§7), a nationality (§15.1), and equal access to public service (§21.2).[21] Finally, these documents also envisage the possibility of human rights that are limited in scope to the territory of the state to which the right holder belongs, or in which she or he resides, and thus they do not impose duties upon foreigners. Examples are the right to equal access to public service in his country (§21.2) and the right to an education (§26.1).[22]

These problems with U_1 suggest another understanding, U_2, according to which human rights are moral rights that human beings have specifically against governments, understood broadly so as to include their various agencies and officials. This understanding solves the first problem with U_1 by supporting a distinction between official and nonofficial violations, between assaults committed by the police and those committed by a petty criminal or a violent husband. It solves the second problem insofar as governments are in a position to underwrite and reform the relevant institutional arrangements, at least within their own territory. And it facilitates a solution to the third problem by allowing a distinction between human rights persons have against their own government only and those they have against any government. A human right to education could be conceived as a right that every human being has against his or her own government (which thus is thought to have a weighty moral duty to ensure that each national or resident in its territory receives an appropriate education), even while a human right not to be subjected to arbitrary arrest (§9) is conceived as one that every human being has against every government (which thus is thought to have a weighty moral duty to refrain from arbitrarily arresting any human being at all).[23]

The main problem with U_2 is that it unburdens private human agents. So long as one is not a government official, one need not worry about human rights at all. In response, it might be said that in a democracy it is ultimately the people at large who, collectively, constitute the government. But this response does not help with other kinds of regimes. People who live under an undemocratic government need not worry about human rights, because it is the duty of that government alone to fulfill these rights, including the human right of its subjects to take part in government (§21.1). On this understanding, wealthy and influential nationals would have no moral duty to do anything to prevent or to mitigate human-rights violations that their nondemocratic government is committing against their compatriots or against foreigners—at least they would have no moral duty arising from the human rights of the victims. This limitation is not only morally implausible; it also goes against common parlance, as when people speak of a country's human-rights record, thereby suggesting that the government does not bear sole responsibility for human rights.

This problem is avoided by yet another understanding, U_3, according to which human rights are basic or constitutional rights as each state ought to set them forth in its fundamental legal texts and ought to make them effective through appropriate institutions and policies.[24] So understood, a human right to X might be said to have two distinct components: juridification and observance. Through its *juridification* component, a human right to X would entail that every state ought to have a right to X enshrined in its constitution (or comparable basic legal documents). A human right to X would contain, then, a moral right to effective legal rights to X, which gives all citizens of a state a weighty moral duty to help ensure that an effectively enforced and suitably broad legal (or better, constitutional) right to X exists within this state.[25] Through its *observance* component, a human right to X would give a weighty moral duty to each government and its officials to ensure that the right to X—whether it exists as a legal right or not—is observed.

Though a definite improvement over U_1 and U_2, this understanding still faces three problems. First, in regard to some human rights, the juridification component of U_3 would seem to be excessively demanding. Consider a human right to adequate nutrition (§25.1). A society may be so situated and organized that all its members have secure access to adequate nutrition, though not a legal right thereto. Would this be a human rights problem? I think not. Having the corresponding legal right in addition may be a good thing, to be sure, but it is not so important that this and every other human right must constitutively require its own juridification. Secure access is what really matters and, if secure access can be maintained through a culture of solidarity among relatives, neighbors, friends, or compatriots, say, then an additional legal right to adequate food when needed is not so important. The juridification component of U_3 is likely, then, to lead to a conception of human rights diluted by elements that are not truly essential.[26] Moreover, insistence on the juridification of human rights also provokes the familiar communitarian and East Asian criticisms, to be further discussed in section 7.

In reply to this first criticism, a proponent of U_3 might point out that poor people may have secure access to food through reliable charities that do, however, require demeaning forms of supplication. Legal rights to food would protect poor people from having to choose between hunger and humiliation.[27] This reply, however, does not block the first criticism of U_3. Suppose it is right that people must be protected from facing such a choice, and suppose people thus have not merely a human right to adequate food but a human right to adequate food without humiliation. (Since I am leaving aside here the substantive question what human rights there are, I am in no position to dispute these suppositions.) The first criticism can then still be reapplied to how U_3 would understand this stronger human right. A society may be so situated and organized that all its members have secure access to adequate nutrition without humiliation, though not a legal right thereto. Legal rights to food without humiliation are not necessary to protect people from facing a choice between hunger and humiliation. And U_3 is then too demanding by requiring legal rights to what really matters even when secure access thereto is achievable in other ways.

The remaining two problems show that U_3 is, in other ways, not demanding enough. Thus a second problem with U_3 is that, even when a human right is appropriately juridified and the corresponding legal rights are observed and reliably enforced by the government and the courts, citizens may nevertheless be unable to insist on their rights. Being illiterate or uneducated, they may not know what their legal rights are, or they may lack either the knowledge or the minimal economic independence necessary to claim these rights through the proper legal channels. In this way, a human right to freedom from inhuman and degrading treatment (§5) may remain unfulfilled for most of a society's domestic servants even if the state provides them with an effective legal path on which they could defend themselves against abuse by their employers. This problem can be avoided by interpreting "observance" in a demanding sense as requiring that human rights be made fully (not merely legally) effective to ensure secure access to their objects.[28] I use "fulfillment" for this demanding sense of observance and develop this notion further below.

The third problem with U_3 is that it excessively unburdens agents with regard to human-rights fulfillment abroad. According to U_3, our task as citizens or government officials is to ensure that human rights are juridified and observed (or fulfilled) in our own society and also observed by our government abroad. We have no human-rights based duties to promote the fulfillment of human rights in other countries or to oppose human-rights violations by foreign governments—though it may be morally praiseworthy, of course, to work on such projects.[29] But, you will ask, what is wrong with this unburdening? To what extent, and on what grounds, should we be held responsible for the underfulfillment of human rights abroad?

4 An Institutional Understanding of Human Rights Based in §28

We find the beginnings of an answer to these questions in what may well be the most surprising and potentially most consequential sentence of the entire *Universal Declaration*: "Everyone is entitled to a social and international order in which the rights and freedoms set forth in this Declaration can be fully realized" (§28). This article has a peculiar status. As its reference to "the rights and freedoms set forth in this Declaration" indicates, §28 does not add a further right to the list but rather addresses the concept of a human right by saying something about what a human rights is. It is then consistent with any substantive account of what human rights there are—even while it significantly affects the meaning of any human rights postulated in the other articles of this *Universal Declaration*. They all are to be understood as claims on the institutional order of any comprehensive social system.[30]

At this point §28 suggests a fourth, institutional understanding of human rights, U_4, according to which human rights are moral claims on any coercively imposed institutional order. This understanding can be further specified through four plausible interpretive conjectures:

1. Alternative institutional orders that do not satisfy the requirement of §28 can be ranked by how close they come to enabling the full realization of human rights. Social systems ought to be structured so that human rights can be realized in them as fully as possible.

2. How fully human rights *can* be realized in some institutional order is measured by how fully these human rights generally are, or (in the case of a hypothetical institutional order) generally would be, realized in it.

3. An institutional order *realizes* a human right insofar as (and fully if and only if) this human right is *fulfilled* for the persons upon whom this order is imposed.

4. A human right is fulfilled for some person if and only if this person enjoys *secure access to the object of this human right*. Here the *object* of a human right is whatever this human right is a right to— adequate nutrition, for example, or physical integrity. And what matters is *secure access* to such objects rather than these objects themselves, because an institutional order is not morally problematic merely because some of its participants are choosing to fast or to compete in boxing matches.

Taking these four conjectures together, I thus read §28 as holding that the moral quality, or justice, of any institutional order depends primarily on its success in affording all its participants secure access to the objects of their human rights. Any institutional order is to be assessed and reformed principally by reference to its relative impact on the realization of the human rights of those on whom it is imposed.[31] Postulating a human right to X is then tantamount to declaring that every society and comparable social system ought to be so organized that, as far as possible, all its members enjoy secure access to X.

When an institutional order avoidably fails to realize human rights, then those of its members who significantly collaborate in its impo-sition are violating a negative duty of justice. This duty should not mandate in all cases that such persons discontinue their participa-tion. It may indeed come to this in extreme cases: toward the end of Nazi rule in Germany, for instance, when citizens, as far as possible, ought to have ceased all support, including payment of taxes and performance of services useful to the state. In most cases, however, it is better for the victims of injustice if we continue participation while also working toward appropriate institutional reforms or toward shielding these victims from the harms we also help produce. The duty in question should then afford this option. It should be for-mulated as a duty not to contribute to the coercive imposition of any institutional order that avoidably fails to realize human rights, unless one also compensates for one's contribution by working toward appropriate institutional reforms or toward shielding the victims of injustice from the harms one helps produce. Pursuant to U_4, a person's human rights are then not only moral claims *on* any insti-tutional order imposed upon her, but also moral claims *against* those (especially more influential and privileged) persons who collaborate in its imposition.[32]

Given this understanding, a human right may be fulfilled for some and unfulfilled for other members of the same society. This is so because security of access to the object of some human right may vary across social groups. For example, only women may be facing a significant risk of assault, only rural dwellers may be in any real danger of hunger, only persons with a certain skin color may be excluded from the franchise. Because an institutional order ought to be such that the human rights of all its participants are fulfilled, a human right is *fully realized* by some institutional order if and only if *all* of its participants have secure access to its object.

To be sure, no society can make the objects of all human rights *absolutely* secure for all. And making them as secure as possible would constitute a ludicrous drain on societal resources for what, at the margins, would be minor increases in security. To be plausible, any conception of human rights employing the proposed concept must therefore incorporate an idea of reasonable security thresholds. Any human right of some person is fulfilled (completely) when access to its object is sufficiently secure—with the required degrees of security suitably adapted to the means and circumstances of the relevant social system. Thus, your human right to physical integrity (§3) is fulfilled by some institutional order when it is sufficiently unlikely that you suffer a violation of your physical integrity without your consent.[33] Of course, what is sufficiently unlikely, within a well-designed institutional order, may nevertheless happen. We should allow then for the possibility that a person is actually assaulted even while his human right is fulfilled (because he is sufficiently secure from assault). And, conversely, use should allow for the possibility that someone's human right is not fulfilled (because his physical integrity is endangered) even though he never actually suffers an assault.

We have seen how U_4 goes beyond U_3 by insisting that, to realize human rights, a national institutional order must secure the objects of all participants' human rights not only against abuse by their government and its officials but also against other social threats arising, for example, from death squads, criminals, domestic violence, or economic dependency. U_4 may and (I believe) should nevertheless hold that insecure access is more serious when its source is official. It is, other things being equal, more important that our laws and the agents and agencies of the state should not themselves endanger the objects of human rights than that they should protect these objects against other social dangers. The need for this differential weighing shows itself, for instance, in our attitudes toward the criminal law and the penal system.[34] The point can be communicated most quickly, perhaps, by distinguishing, in a preliminary way, six ways in which an institutional order may affect the lives of its participants. The following illustration uses six different scenarios, arranged in order of their intuitive moral significance, in which, due to the prevailing institutional order, certain innocent persons are avoidably insecure in their access to some vital nutrients V (the vitamins contained in fresh fruit, say).[35]

In scenario 1, the deficit is *officially mandated*, paradigmatically by the law: legal restrictions bar certain persons from buying foodstuffs containing V. In scenario 2, the deficit results from *legally authorized* conduct of private subjects: sellers of foodstuffs containing V lawfully refuse to sell to certain persons. In scenario 3, social institutions *foreseeably and avoidably engender* (but do not specifically require or authorize) the deficit through the conduct they stimulate: certain persons, suffering severe poverty within an ill-conceived economic order, cannot afford to buy foodstuffs containing V. In scenario 4, the deficit arises from private conduct that is *legally prohibited but barely deterred*: sellers of foodstuffs containing V illegally refuse to sell to certain persons, but enforcement is lax and penalties are mild. In scenario 5, the deficit arises from social institutions *avoidably leaving unmitigated the effects of a natural defect*: certain persons are unable to metabolize V due to a treatable genetic defect, but they avoidably lack access to the treatment that would correct their handicap. In scenario 6, finally, the deficit arises from social institutions *avoidably leaving unmitigated the effects of a self-caused deficit*: certain persons are unable to metabolize V due to a treatable self-caused disease[36] and avoidably lack access to the treatment that would correct their ailment.

Behind the moral significance we attach to these distinctions—and one could easily maintain that a human-rights standard should not be sensitive to scenario 6 (and scenario 5?) deficits at all—lies the idea that an institutional order and the political and legal organs established through it should not merely *serve* justice, but also *symbolize* it. The point is important, because it undermines the plausibility of consequentialist (e.g., utilitarian) and hypothetical-contract (e.g., Rawlsian) moral conceptions that assess alternative institutional orders from the standpoint of prudent prospective participants who, of course, have no reason to care about this distinction among sources of threats.[37] A conception of human rights should avoid the mistake of such recipient-oriented approaches. To do so it must, for each human right, distinguish and measure separately the different ways in which access to its object can be insecure; and it must then give more weight to first-class insecurities than to second-class insecurities, and so on.

5 The Global Normative Reach of Human Rights

Human rights are often said to be universal—a word also used in the title of the *Universal Declaration*. I have listed two senses in which human rights are universal among the uncontroversial elements of the concept of a human right: human rights are equally possessed by, and are also equally binding upon, each and every human being. These two features are compatible with a nationalistic interpretation of human rights, according to which any person's responsibility for the fulfillment of human rights is limited by the boundaries of his or her society.[38] Yet §28 specifically excludes this interpretation by requiring that the *international* institutional order, as well, must be hospitable to the realization of human rights. Pursuant to U_4, human rights are then universal also in the further sense of having global normative reach: human rights give persons moral claims not merely on the institutional order of their own societies, which are claims against their fellow citizens, but also on the global institutional order, which are claims against their fellow human beings. Any national *and any global* institutional order is to be assessed and reformed principally by reference to its relative impact on the realization of the human rights of those on whom it is imposed. Human-rights-based responsibilities arise from collaboration in the coercive imposition of any institutional order in which some persons avoidably lack secure access to the objects of their human rights. For persons collaborating in the coercive imposition of a global institutional order, these responsibilities extend worldwide.[39]

This view presented by U_4 must be distinguished from the more common but also less plausible position that emerges when, in the context of U_1, human rights are interpreted as entailing duties to protect—the position, namely, that we ought to defend, as best we can, the objects of the human rights of any person anywhere. This position is less demanding in that it postulates merely positive duties, whereas U_4 supports a stronger negative duty not to impose an institutional order under which human rights avoidably cannot be fully realized. In another respect, this position is also more demanding by making the global normative reach of human rights unconditional, specifically, independent of the existence and causal significance of a coercively imposed global order. By contrast, what §28 is asking of the citizens and governments of the developed states is not that we assume the role of a global police force ready to intervene to aid and protect all those whose human rights are imperiled by brutal governments or (civil) wars, but that we support institutional reforms toward a global order that would strongly support the emergence and stability of democratic, rights-respecting, peaceful regimes and would also tend to reduce radical economic deprivations and inequalities, which now engender great vulnerabilities to civil rights violations as well as massive premature mortality from malnutrition and easily preventable diseases.

Unmoved by §28, influential citizens and politicians in the wealthy countries tend to regard the massive global underfulfillment of human rights with self-satisfied detachment. They are not unaware of the basic facts presented here in section 1, but they do not see themselves as connected to, let alone responsible for, massive global poverty. They might give three reasons for their supposed innocence. First, they might say that the massive underfulfillment of human rights is caused by a variety of local factors endemic to particular developing countries and is thus quite independent of the existing global order.[40] Second, they might say that this global order is so complex that it is impossible, even with the good will of the world's rich and mighty, to reform it in a way that would reliably improve human rights fulfillment. Third, they might say that this global order is upheld by many people acting together so that the contribution of each is negligible or even naught.

The third of these reasons is a bad one. Even a very small fraction of responsibility for a very large harm can be quite large in absolute terms and would be in the case before us.[41] To be sure, nearly every privileged person might say that she bears no responsibility at all because she alone is powerless to bring about a reform of the global order. But this, too, is an implausible line of argument, entailing as it does that each participant in a massacre is innocent, provided any persons he killed would have been killed by others, had he abstained. It is true that we, as individuals, cannot single-handedly reform the global order and would find it very difficult to give up our privileged position in it so as to avoid making further contributions to its imposition. But we can clearly indicate our willingness to support institutional reforms, urge others to participate, and make efforts to facilitate cooperation. In addition, thanks to international human rights organizations like UNICEF, Oxfam, or Amnesty International, we can also help prevent or mitigate some of the harms caused by the global order, thereby making up, as it were, for our contribution to their production.

The first two reasons are harder to disprove. It is quite true that national factors (such as political and economic institutions, entrenched power structures, culture, contingencies of history, population density, climate, soil conditions, and mineral wealth) significantly affect a society's levels of poverty and human rights fulfillment. Yet, it is also true that the existing global order plays a profound role both in shaping many of these local factors and in influencing their effects. Let me illustrate this point by focusing on one consequential and reform-worthy feature of this order. Any group controlling a preponderance of the means of coercion within a country is internationally recognized as the legitimate government of this country's territory and people—regardless of how that group came to power, of how it exercises power, and of the extent to which it may be supported or opposed by the population it rules. That such a group exercising effective power receives international recognition means not merely that we are prepared to negotiate with it. It also means that we acknowledge this group's right to act for the people it rules; most significantly, that we confer upon it the privileges freely to borrow in the country's name (international borrowing privilege) as well as freely to dispose of the country's natural resources (international resource privilege).

The *international borrowing privilege* includes the power to impose internationally valid legal obligations upon the country at large. Any successor government that refuses to honor debts incurred by an ever so corrupt, brutal, undemocratic, unconstitutional, repressive, unpopular predecessor will be severely punished by the banks and governments of other countries; at minimum it will lose its own borrowing privilege by being excluded from the international financial markets. Such refusals are therefore quite rare, as governments, even when newly elected after a dramatic break with the past, are constrained to pay the debts of their ever so awful predecessors.

The international borrowing privilege has three important detrimental effects on human rights fulfillment in the developing countries. First, this privilege facilitates borrowing by destructive governments. Such governments can borrow more money and can do so more cheaply than they could do if they alone, rather than the entire country, were obliged to repay. In this way, the borrowing privilege helps such governments maintain themselves in power even against near-universal popular discontent and opposition. Second, the privilege imposes upon democratic successor regimes the often huge debts of their corrupt predecessors. It thereby saps their capacity to implement institutional reforms and other political programs, thus rendering these democratic governments less successful and less stable than they would be otherwise. Third, the international borrowing privilege provides incentives toward coup attempts: whoever succeeds in bringing a preponderance of the means of coercion under his control gets this privilege as an additional reward.

The *international resource privilege* enjoyed by a group in power is much more than our mere acquiescence in its effective control over the natural resources of the country in question. This privilege includes the power to effect legally valid transfers of ownership rights in such resources. Thus a corporation that has purchased resources from the Saudi or Suharto families, or from Mobuto or Sani Abacha, has thereby become entitled to be—and *is*—recognized anywhere in the world as the legitimate owner of these resources. This is a remarkable feature of our global order. A group that overpowers the guards and takes control of a warehouse may be able to give some of the merchandise to others, accepting money in exchange. But the fence who pays them becomes merely the possessor, not the owner, of the loot. Contrast this with a group that overpowers an elected government and takes control of a country. Such a group, too, can give away some of the country's natural resources, accepting money in exchange. In this case, however, the purchaser acquires not merely possession but all the rights and liberties of ownership, which are supposed to be—and *are*—protected and enforced by all other states' courts and police forces. The international resource privilege, then, is the power to confer globally valid legal ownership rights in the country's resources.

The international resource privilege has disastrous effects on vast numbers of people, especially in the poorest countries in which the resource sector often constitutes a large segment of the national economy. Whoever can take power in such a country by whatever means can maintain his rule, even against widespread popular opposition, by buying the arms and soldiers he needs with (funds borrowed abroad in the country's name and) revenues from the export of natural resources. This fact in turn provides a strong incentive toward the undemocratic acquisition and unresponsive exercise of political power in these countries. And the international resource privilege also gives foreigners strong incentives to corrupt the officials of such countries who, no matter how badly they rule, continue to have resources to sell and money to spend. This shows how the local causal chain (persistent poverty caused by corrupt government caused by natural resource wealth) can itself be traced back to the international resource privilege, which makes it the case that resource-rich developing countries are more likely to experience coup attempts and civil wars and more likely also to be ruled by corrupt elites, so that—despite considerable natural wealth—poverty in these countries tends to decline only slowly, if at all.[42]

It is hardly surprising that the causal role of global institutional factors is so often overlooked. We have a very powerful personal motive to want to see ourselves as unconnected to the unimaginable deprivations suffered by the global poor. This motive produces self-deception and automatic rejection of politicians, academics, and research projects that explore the wider causal context of global poverty. Moreover, we have a general cognitive tendency to overlook the causal significance of stable background factors (e.g., the role of atmospheric oxygen in the outbreak of a fire) in a diverse and changing situation. Looking at human rights fulfillment worldwide, our attention is thus drawn to local factors, which sometimes change dramatically (e.g., recently in Eastern Europe) and which vary greatly from country to country. Through an exhaustive analysis of these factors, it appears, all phenomena relevant to the realization of human rights can be explained. And yet, it is not so.

When human rights are more fully realized in one country than in another, then there must be, some difference that contributes to this discrepancy. But an explanation that merely points to this difference leaves many questions open. One question concerns the broader context determining which national factors have these effects rather than others. It is quite possible that in the context of a different global order the same national factors, or the same international differences, would have quite another impact on the realization of human rights.[43] Another question concerns the explanation of the national factors themselves. It is quite possible that, within a different global order, national factors that tend to undermine the fulfillment of human rights would occur much less often or not at all.[44] These considerations show that the global level of human rights fulfillment cannot be explained by national factors alone.

This discussion of some central features of the existing global order was meant to illustrate the following important points: (1) The fulfillment of human rights in most countries is strongly affected not merely by national factors but also by global ones. (2) Explanations in terms of national and global factors do not simply compete with each other. Only their synthesis: one explanation that integrates factors of both kinds can be a true explanation. This is so because the effects of national factors are often strongly affected by global factors (and vice versa) and because global factors strongly shape those national factors themselves (though the inverse influence is generally slight). (3) The influences emanating from global order are not necessarily the way they are, but are codetermined by reformable institutional features, such as the two privileges I have discussed.

These points can help refute the first two reasons that influential citizens and politicians in the wealthy countries might adduce in support of their innocence: the global order we uphold plays a major role in causing the massive underfulfillment of human rights today. It does so in four main ways: it crucially affects what sorts of persons shape national policy in the developing countries, what incentives these persons face, what options they have, and what impact the implementation of any of their options would have on domestic poverty and human rights fulfillment. Once the causal effects of specific global institutional arrangements are appreciated, it is not too difficult to take on the second reason by developing plausible proposals for reform—though space constraints do not allow me to do this here.[45]

Pursuant to U_4, human rights support then a severe critique of the more influential citizens and politicians in the wealthy countries. We are quite wrong to present ourselves as the most advanced in terms of human rights, and we are chiefly responsible for the fact that most human beings still lack secure access to the most vital goods.[46] And we are also the chief beneficiaries of the existing global order. This order perpetuates our control over the weaker developing countries. And it also guarantees us a reliable and cheap supply of natural resources, because we can acquire ownership rights in such resources from anyone who happens to exercise effective power and because the resource consumption of the majority of humankind is severely constrained by poverty.[47]

The discussion of the international borrowing and resource privileges thus illustrates the empirical background against which the global demand of §28 makes sense. It is the point of human rights, and of official declarations thereof, to ensure that all human beings have secure access to certain vital goods. Many persons currently lack such security.[48] We can assign responsibility for such insecurity to the governments and citizens of the countries in which it occurs; and doing so makes good sense, but leaving it at this does not make good sense. For the hope that these countries will, from the inside, democratize themselves and abolish the worst poverty and oppression is entirely naive as long as the institutional context of these countries continues to favor so strongly the emergence and endurance of brutal and corrupt elites. The primary responsibility for this institutional context, for the prevailing global order, lies with the governments and citizens of the wealthy countries, because we maintain this order, with at least latent coercion, and because we, and only we, could relatively easily reform it in the directions indicated. §28 should be read as a recognition of these points: a clear repudiation of the common and ever so dear conviction that human rights do not reach beyond national borders, that we normally have no responsibilities for the fulfillment of the human rights of foreigners (living abroad).[49]

In the world as it is, U_4 thus tends to undermine the self-satisfied detachment with which the governments and peoples of the wealthy countries tend to look down upon the sorry state of human rights in many of the so-called less developed countries. This disaster is the responsibility not only of their governments and populations, but also ours, in that we continuously impose upon them an unjust global order without working toward reforms that would facilitate the full realization of human rights.

6 The Universality of Human Rights

Having shown that it makes sense to conceive of human rights, as U_4 suggests, as having global normative reach, let us proceed to survey the advantages of this understanding. Some advantages have already been touched upon in the preceding discussion: U_4 is more suitable than U_1-U_3 for singling out the truly essential elements in human quality of life and it incorporates a more plausible assignment of responsibilities in regard to the underfulfillment of human rights. In sections 6 through 8, I lay out three further important advantages which show that U_4 can make a much greater contribution toward facilitating agreement on how to specify and to pursue the realization of human rights worldwide.

The first of these additional advantages lies in the profound implications of U_4 for the debate about the universal validity of human rights. Many people see the fact that human rights are understood as universal as a strong reason for denying them. They view human rights as an outgrowth of a provincial morality whose pretension to universal validity is yet one more variant of European imperialism. They might say: "Non-European peoples have cultural traditions of their own from which they construct their own moral conceptions, perhaps wholly without the individualistic concept of a right. If you westerners want to make a conception of human rights the centerpiece of your political morality and want to realize it in your political system, then go ahead, by all means. But leave other peoples the same freedom to define their values within the context of their own culture and national discourse."

Even if such admonitions are often put forward in bad faith,[50] they nevertheless require a reasoned response which, pursuant to U_4, can be formulated as follows. When human rights are understood as a standard for assessing only national institutional orders and governments, then it makes sense to envision a plurality of standards for societies that differ in their history, culture, population size and density, natural environment, geopolitical context, and stage of economic and technological development. But when human rights are understood also as a standard for assessing the *global* institutional order, international diversity can no longer be accommodated in this way. There can be, at any given time, only *one* global order. If it is to be possible to justify this global order to persons in all parts of the world and also to reach agreement on how it should be adjusted and reformed in the light of new experience or changed circumstances, then we must aspire to a *single, universal* standard which all persons and peoples can accept as the basis for moral judgments about the global order that constrains and conditions human life everywhere.

Consider a domestic parallel. Imagine someone setting forth a moral conception of decent family life in the hope of achieving nationwide agreement. Our first reaction might be: we do not need such agreement, nor do we need such a shared conception. We can happily live together in one society even while we differ in many of our deepest aspirations, including those about family life. Having received this response, our interlocutor says that she meant to raise a quite different issue: the social rules of our society affect family life in countless ways. A few do so directly—they define and limit the legal freedoms of spouses with regard to how they may treat each other and their children, how they may use and dispose of individually or jointly owned property, what kinds of education and medical care they may give to or withhold from their children, and so forth. Many other rules influence family life more indirectly by affecting the economic burdens of child rearing or by shaping the physical and social environment within which families exist, for instance, or by determining the extent to which women are respected as the full equals of men, can successfully participate in the economy, and can present their concerns within the political process. Since a society's social rules are subject to intelligent redesign and also exert a profound influence upon family life within this society, its citizens have a responsibility to bring their sharable values concerning family life to bear upon the design of their shared institutional order. This, concludes our interlocutor, was her point in proposing a moral conception of decent family life.

As the domestic parallel shows, attaining a common standard for assessing a shared institutional order does not presuppose thoroughgoing agreement. Thus, our interlocutor in the domestic case need not decide what kinds of relationships among spouses and children are best. She may merely advocate certain constraints, insisting, for example, that wives must be secure from coercion by their husbands, which can be achieved by promoting through the education system equal respect and equal opportunities for women, by criminalizing interspousal rape, by safeguarding the voluntariness of religious practices, and by guaranteeing an economically safe option of divorce.

The analogous point holds for human rights as a moral standard for our global order. This standard does not presuppose agreement on all or even most moral questions. It may merely demand that this global order be so designed that, as far as possible, all persons have secure access to a few goods vital to human beings. Now it is true that designing an institutional order with an eye to a few key values will have collateral effects on the prevalence of other values. A solidly Catholic (or Muslim) family life may well be harder to sustain within a society that safeguards freedom of religion than in one in which Catholicism (Islam) is the official state religion. Similarly, the choice of a global order designed to realize human rights would have a differential impact on the cultures of various societies and on the popularity of various religions and ways of life. But such collateral effects are simply unavoidable: *any* global (and national) institutional order can be criticized on the grounds that some values do not optimally thrive in it. So long as there is any global order at all, this problem will necessarily persist.

Still, the problem can be mitigated by formulating a common moral standard so that the global order it favors will allow a wide range of values to thrive locally. Human rights meet this condition because they can be fully realized in a wide range of countries that differ greatly in their culture, traditions, and national institutional order.

The crucial thought here is this: once human rights are understood as moral claims on the global order, there simply is no attractive, tolerant, and pluralistic alternative to conceiving them as valid universally. Although the world can contain societies that are structured in a variety of ways (according to diverse, even incompatible values), it cannot itself be structured in a variety of ways. If the Iranians want their society to be organized as an Islamic state and we want ours to be a secular democracy, we can both have our way.[51] But if the Iranians wanted the global order to be designed on the basis of the Koran while we want it to secure the objects of everyone's human rights, then we cannot both have our way. The global order cannot be designed so as to give all human beings the assurance that they will be able to meet their most basic needs *and* so as to give all governments maximal control over the lives and values of the peoples they rule *and* so as to ensure the fullest flourishing of Islam and so on. Among competing plans for the future of global order, *one* will necessarily win out—through reason or through force. Neutrality is not an option here. The policies of the major societies will necessarily affect the outcome. It is, for the future of humankind, the most important and most urgent task of our time to set the development of the global order upon an acceptable path. To do this together, peacefully, we need international agreement on a common moral standard for assessing the feasible alternatives. The best hope for such a common moral standard that is both plausible and capable of wide international acceptance today is a conception of human rights. At the very least, the burden now is on those who reject the very idea of human rights to formulate and justify their own alternative standard for achieving a global order acceptable to all.

7 Making Human Rights More Broadly Sharable

To serve as a common moral standard, a conception of human rights must meet the sixth condition of broad sharability. Whether it does depends not only on its content (the specific human rights it postulates) but also on the concept of a human right it employs. U_4 renders human rights significantly less vulnerable to critical doubts and hence more broadly sharable. Let me briefly indicate why this is so.

One important communitarian critique, often claimed to show that human rights are alien to communal cultures (for instance in Southeast Asia), asserts that human rights discourse leads persons to view themselves as Westerners: as atomized, autonomous, secular, and self-interested individuals ready to insist on their rights no matter what the cost may be to others or to society at large.[52]

This critique may have some plausibility when human rights are understood as demanding their own juridification as basic legal rights held by individuals (U_3). But it has much less force when, as I have proposed, we avoid any conceptual connection of human rights with legal rights. We are then open to the idea that, in various economic and cultural contexts, secure access to the objects of human rights might be established in other ways. Yes, secure access to minimally adequate nutrition can generally be maintained through legal rights to food when needed. But it can also be maintained through other legal mechanisms—ones that keep land ownership widely dispersed, ban usury or speculative hoarding of basic staples, or provide child-care, education, retraining subsidies, unemployment benefits, or start-up loans. And nonlegal practices—such as a culture of solidarity among friends, relatives, neighbors, compatriots—may also play an important role. Even those hostile to a legal-rights culture can, and often do, share the goal of realizing human rights as understood by U_4; and they may be quite willing to support a legally binding international commitment to shape national and international institutional arrangements so that all human beings can securely meet their most basic needs. We have reason then to conceive the realization of human rights in this broad way, rather than insist on conceiving it narrowly as involving individual legal rights of matching content. We may feel strongly that such matching individual legal rights ought to exist in our own culture. But there is no good reason for requiring that secure access to the objects of human rights must be maintained in the same way everywhere on earth.

One important libertarian critique, which is often claimed to show that human rights are alien to individualist (especial Anglo-American) cultures, asserts that human rights impose excessive restrictions on individual freedom by requiring all human agents to defend, as best they can, the objects of the human rights of any person anywhere (U_1). Libertarians reject such a requirement not merely because it would be excessively burdensome in a world in which the human rights of so many remain unfulfilled, but mainly because they hold that all moral duties must be *negative* ones, that is, duties to refrain from harming others in certain ways. Libertarians may acknowledge that it is morally good to protect or to aid or to benefit others, but they deny that anyone has a duty to do such things. And since they recognize no positive moral duties, libertarians also deny the existence of any moral rights to be protected, aided, or benefited.

U_4 can help accommodate this critique as well. U_4 does not assume that human agents have human-rights-based obligations merely by virtue of the fact that the human rights of some persons avoidably remain unfulfilled. U_4 envisions such obligations specifically for agents who significantly collaborate in imposing an institutional order that produces this human-rights problem. Such agents must either stop contributing to this imposition or else compensate for this contribution by working toward appropriate institutional reforms and toward shielding the victims of injustice from the harms they help produce.[53] This is a *negative* duty on a par with the libertarians' favorite duty not to defraud others by breaking a contract or promise one has made. One can avoid all obligations arising from these duties, respectively, by not taking part in the coercive imposition of an unjust institutional order and not making any contracts or promises. But if one does contribute significantly to imposing an institutional order upon others, one is obligated to help ensure that it fulfills the human rights of these others as far as possible—just as, if one does make a promise, one is obligated to keep it.

8 Reconciling Conflicting Priorities among Human Rights

The substance of a conception of human rights continues to be controversial. Prominent here is the debate between those who, like many Western governments, emphasize civil and political rights and those who, like many developing and socialist states, emphasize social, economic, and cultural rights. I have shown already how U_4 can be detached from such controversies and defended with powerful, independent arguments. I will now show how its acceptance would also greatly reduce the significance of such controversies, which have occasioned much discord in the United Nations and elsewhere. The third further advantage of U_4 is that it can facilitate agreement on the substance or content of our conception of human rights.

U_4 does not lead to the idea that civil and political rights require only restraint, while social, economic, and cultural rights also demand positive efforts and costs. Rather, it emphasizes negative duties across the board: we are not to collaborate in the coercive imposition of any institutional order that avoidably fails to realize human rights of whatever kind. Moreover, there is no systematic correlation between categories of human rights, understood pursuant to U_4, and effective institutional means for their realization, which may vary in time and place. Thus, to realize the classical civil right to freedom from inhuman and degrading treatment (§5), for instance, a state may have to do much more than create and enforce appropriate criminal statutes. It may also need to establish adequate social and economic safeguards, ensuring perhaps that domestic servants are literate, know about their rights and options, and have some economic security in case of job loss. Conversely, to realize a human right to adequate nutrition, perhaps all that is needed is an effective criminal statute against speculative hoarding of foodstuffs.

These considerations greatly narrow the philosophical gap between the friends of civil and political rights and the friends of social, economic, and cultural rights. Let me now show how they may also greatly reduce the practical significance of such controversies.

Suppose that only civil and political human rights are worthy of the name, that the social, economic and cultural rights set forth in the *Universal Declaration* (foremost the much ridiculed right to "periodic holidays with pay" of §24) should hence be repudiated. Conjoining this view with U_4 yields the moral assertion that every human being is entitled to a national and global institutional order in which civil and political human rights can be fully realized. The existing global order falls far short in this respect, and it does so largely on account of the extreme poverty and inequality it reproduces: in most developing countries, the legal rights of ordinary citizens cannot be effectively enforced. Many of these countries are so poor that they cannot afford properly trained judges and police forces in sufficient numbers; and in many of them social institutions as well as politicians, officials and government agencies are in any case (partly through foreign influences) so thoroughly corrupted that the realization of civil and political human rights is not even seriously attempted. Even in those few countries where the legal rights of ordinary citizens can be effectively enforced, too many citizens are under too much economic pressure, too dependent on others, or too uneducated to effect the enforcement of their rights. Thus, even the goal of realizing only the recognized civil and political human rights—if only they were interpreted in the light of §28—suffices to support the demand for global institutional reforms that would reduce global poverty and inequality.

Suppose that only social, economic, and cultural human rights are worthy of the name. Conjoining this view with U_4 yields the moral assertion that every human being is entitled to a national and global institutional order in which social, economic, and cultural human rights can be fully realized. The existing global order falls far short in this respect as billions live in poverty with little access to education and health care and in constant mortal danger from malnutrition and diseases that are easily controlled elsewhere. Their suffering is in large part due to the fact that the global poor live under governments that do little to alleviate their deprivations and often even contribute to them. The global poor are dispersed over some 150 countries, many of which are ruled not by general and public laws, but by powerful persons and groups (dictators, party bosses, military officers, landlords) often sponsored or assisted from abroad. In such societies, they are unable to organize themselves freely, to publicize their plight, or to work for reform through the political or legal system. Thus, even the goal of realizing only the usual social and economic human rights—if only they were interpreted in the light of §28—suffices to support the call for a global order that would strongly encourage the incorporation of effective civil and political rights into national constitutions.[54]

I certainly did not mean to contend, in this section, that it makes no difference which rights we single out as human rights. I merely wanted to show that both the philosophical and practical-political importance of the actual controversies about this question would diminish if human rights were understood pursuant to U_4: as moral claims on any coercively imposed institutional order. Even if we continue to disagree about which goods should be included in a conception of human rights, we will then—provided we really care about the realization of human rights rather than about ideological propaganda victories—work together on the same institutional reforms instead of arguing over how much praise or blame is deserved by this state or that.

9 Conclusion

In the aftermath of World War II, a fledgling United Nations issued a *Universal Declaration of Human Rights* as the preeminent moral standard for all of humankind. This declaration, in its §28, specifically suggests that the realization of human rights will crucially depend on the achievement of a just global order.[55] In the intervening half century, the dominant powers, led by the United States, have created a far more comprehensive global order that severely constrains and conditions the political and economic institutions and policies of all national societies and governments. It is hardly surprising that these powers have tried to shape this order in their own interest. They have done so quite successfully, bringing peace and unprecedented prosperity to their populations.

And yet, if we judge this global order from a less parochial moral standpoint, one that makes the fulfillment of everyone's human rights the central concern, then we must conclude that this order is still deeply flawed and quite avoidably so. The last fifty years project a strong image of brisk progress from one declaration, summit, and convention to the next. There has been significant progress in formulations and ratifications of human rights documents, in the gathering and publication of statistical information, and even in the realization of some human rights. But these fifty years have also culminated in unprecedented economic inequality between the most affluent tenth of humankind and the poorest fifth.[56] What makes this huge and steadily growing inequality a monstrosity, morally, is the fact that the global poor are also so incredibly poor in absolute terms. They lack secure access to food, safe water, clothing, shelter, basic education, and they are also highly vulnerable to being deprived of the objects of their civil and political human rights by their governments as well as by private agents. Some 18 million of them die prematurely every year.

Since features of the global order are the decisive variable for the realization of human rights today, the primary moral responsibility for the realization of human rights must rest with those who shape and impose this order, with the governments and peoples of the most powerful and affluent countries. We lay down the fundamental rules governing internal and external sovereignty, national property rights in land and resources, global trade, international financial transactions, and so on. And we enforce these rules through economic sanctions and occasional military interventions. These rules and their foreseeable effects are then our responsibility. And our failure to initiate meaningful institutional reforms that would drastically reduce global poverty is all the more appalling as the opportunity costs such reforms would impose upon ourselves have declined steeply with the end of the Cold War and the great economic and technological advances of the last decade.

Against this background I conclude, then, that the understanding of human rights and correlative human responsibilities that I have presented here in explication of §28 is more compelling than the three competing understandings and the draft *Universal Declaration of Human Responsibilities*. U_4 correctly identifies the crucial human-rights-based responsibility in this world: the responsibility of the affluent states and their citizens for the global economic and political order they impose. This order is the key obstacle to the realization of human rights. Our preeminent moral task is to reshape this order so that all human beings have secure access to the basic goods they need to be full and respected members of their communities, societies, and of the wider world.

Acknowledgments

I am indebted to Pablo De Greiff, Cecile Fabre, Andrew Nathan, Thomas Mertens, Guido Pincione, Markus Pins, and Ling Tong for their very helpful critical comments. A preliminary version of this essay, "The International Significance of Human Rights," was published in *The Journal of Ethics* 4/1 (March 2000), 45–69, and in Guido Pincione and Horacio Spector, eds.: *Rights, Equality, and Liberty* (Dordrecht: Kluwer 2000). Composition of this final version was supported by a generous grant from the Research and Writing Initiative of the Program on Global Security and Sustainability of the John D. and Catherine T. MacArthur Foundation.

Notes

1. §25, *Universal Declaration of Human Rights*, adopted and proclaimed by the General Assembly of the United Nations on December 10, 1948, as resolution 217A(III). I use the symbol "§" throughout to refer to articles of this document.

2. This information is collated in the annual *Human Development Reports* (henceforth *HDR*) produced by the United Nations Development Programme (with most data supplied by the World Bank) and published by Oxford University Press. The information I have cited is from *HDR 2000*, 30; *HDR 1999*, 22; and *HDR 1998*, 49.

3. As soldiers, prostitutes, or domestic servants, for instance, or in agriculture, construction, textile, or carpet production. The International Labor Organization (ILO) reports that "at least 120 million children between the ages of 5 and 14 work full time. The number is 250 million . . . if we include those for whom work is a secondary activity." (http://www.ilo.org/public/english/270asie/feature/child.htm). *Cf.* World Bank: *World Development Report 1999/2000* (New York: Oxford University Press 1999), 62, also available at http://www.worldbank.org/wdr/2000/fullreport.html. I will cite this report as *WDR 1999/2000*.

4. *Cf.* U.S. Department of Agriculture (USDA): *U.S. Action Plan on Food Security* (http://www.fas.usda.gov:80/icd/summit/usactplan.pdf; March 1999), iii: "Worldwide 34,000 children under age five die daily from hunger and preventable diseases." For full details, see World Health Organization (WHO): *The World Health Report 1999* (http://www.who.int/whr/1999), especially Annex Table 2, and United Nations Childrens Fund (UNICEF): *The State of the World's Children 1999* (New York: Oxford University Press 1999).

5. *HDR 1999*, 3.

6. http://www.fao.org/wfs/policy/english/96-3eng.htm.

7. "Interpretive Statement" filed by the U.S. government in reference to the first paragraph of the Rome Declaration on World Food Security (http://www.fas.usda.gov:80/icd/summit/interpre.html).

8. Nikos Alexandratos, ed.: *World Agriculture: Toward 2010, an FAO Study* (Chichester, UK: J. Wiley & Sons, and Rome: FAO, 1995).

9. USDA: *U.S. Action Plan on Food Security*, Appendix A: "As part of the *U.S. Action Plan on Food Security*, USAID commissioned a separate study of the projected cost of meeting the world Food Summit target and a strategy for reaching this goal. The study, completed in mid-1998, focused on a potential framework for ODA investments and estimated that the target could be reached with additional global ODA of $2.6 billion annually, as compared to the FAO's estimate of $6 billion annually." The hunger reduction plan announced by the 186 governments in Rome implicitly envisions well over 200 million deaths from hunger and preventable diseases during the 1997–2015 period. So one might have thought that, even if the FAO's proposed annual ODA increase of U.S.$6 billion were to reduce hunger faster than planned, this should be no cause for regret. Halving hunger in nineteen years, after all, is glacial progress. And U.S.$6 billion is a small amount for those asked to provide it: the combined annual gross national product (GNP) of the high-income countries was $22,599 billion in 1998 (*WDR 1999/2000*, 231). How important are U.S.$3.4 billion, 0.015 percent of the high-income countries' GNPs, in comparison to the tens of millions of human lives at stake?

10. At 0.10 percent of its GNP in 1998, versus 0.21 percent under Ronald Reagan in 1987/8, the United States provides the lowest level of net ODA among developed countries, which have followed the United States lead by reducing their aggregate net ODA from 0.33 percent of their combined GNPs to 0.24 percent during the same period (*HDR 2000*, 218). In 1998, United States net ODA was U.S.$8.8 billion, global net ODA was U.S.$51.9 billion (ibid.). The allocation of such funds is, moreover, governed by political considerations: only 21 percent goes to the 43 least developed countries (ibid.) and only 8.3 percent, rather than the 20 percent promised under the 20:20 compact, are spent on meeting basic needs (*HDR 2000*, 79). Thus, the 21 affluent donor states together spend U.S.$4.3 billion annually on meeting basic needs abroad—1.5 cents per day for each malnourished person. The United States has also reduced its funding of other unilateral and multilateral international antipoverty programs, the World Food Program (WFP) being the notable exception (www.brown.edu / Departments / World_Hunger_Program / hungerweb / HN / Articles/WFS/EDIT2.html). Still, "the United States is more prepared and dedicated than ever to feeding a hungry world" (Remarks of Secretary of Agriculture Dan Glickman on Behalf of the United States of America to the World Food Summit Rome; November 13, 1996; http://www.usda.gov/news/releases/1996/11/0603).

11. "Rich countries cut their tariffs by less in the Uruguay Round than poor ones did. Since then, they have found new ways to close their markets, notably by imposing anti-dumping duties on imports they deem 'unfairly cheap'. Rich countries are particularly protectionist in many of the sectors where developing countries are best able to compete, such as agriculture, textiles, and clothing. As a result, according to a new study by Thomas Hertel, of Purdue University, and Will Martin, of the World Bank, rich countries' average tariffs on manufacturing imports from poor countries are four times higher than those on imports from other rich countries. This imposes a big burden on poor countries. The United Nations Conference on Trade and Development (UNCTAD) estimates that they could export U.S.$700 billion more a year by 2005 if rich countries did more to open their markets. Poor countries are also hobbled by a lack of know-how. Many had little understanding of what they signed up to in the Uruguay Round. That ignorance is now costing them dear. Michael Finger of the World Bank and Philip Schuler of the University of Maryland estimate

that implementing commitments to improve trade procedures and establish technical and intellectual-property standards can cost more than a year's development budget for the poorest countries. Moreover, in those areas where poor countries could benefit from world trade rules, they are often unable to do so.... Of the WTO's 134 members, 29 do not even have missions at its headquarters in Geneva. Many more can barely afford to bring cases to the WTO . . ." (*The Economist*, September 25, 1999, 89). The full texts of both studies are available on the internet as, respectively, Working Paper 7 at www.agecon.purdue.edu/gtap/wkpapr/index.htm and Working Paper 2215 at http://wbln0018.worldbank.org/research/workpapers. nsf/12e6920265e1e0d3852567e50050df1f/.

12. This spike shows up in the number of people living below the international poverty line, which is described as "that income or expenditure level below which a minimum, nutritionally adequate diet plus essential non-food requirements are not affordable" (*HDR 1996*, 222). In 1997, this number was "nearly 1.3 billion" (*HDR 1999*, 22). In 1999, the World Bank reported that it "rose from 1.2 billion in 1987 to 1.5 billion today and, if recent trends persist, will reach 1.9 billion by 2015" (*WDR 1999/2000*, 25). In view of widespread protests against the prevailing global economic order, these statistics must have been politically inconvenient. So this year's reports are sporting a new methodology. The number of malnourished people as reported by the UNDP has dropped sharply: from 840 million (*HDR 1999*, 22) to 790 million (*HDR 2000*, 30). And the number of people below the international poverty line is reported to be back down to 1.2 billion (*WDR 2000/2001*, 23; *HDR 2000*, 4). Unfortunately, these dramatically improved numbers reflect not changes in the world, but changes in World Bank methodology. Heretofore, the international poverty line had been defined in terms of $30.42 PPP 1985 per person per month. (PPP stands for "purchasing power parity," so comparison is made with the purchasing power that $30.42 had in the US in 1985.) This year the international poverty line has been redefined in terms of $32.74 PPP 1993 per person per month. The old poverty line is said to be representative of the poverty lines found among thirty-three low-income countries; the new poverty line is said to be the median *of the lowest ten* of these thirty-three lines. See *WDR 2000/2001*, 17, and Shaohua Chen and Martin Ravallion: "How Did the World's Poorest Fare in the 1990s?" www.worldbank.org/research/growth/paper%20of%20the%20month_800.htm. The redefinition is implemented by the UNDP, which revised its poverty line from "$1 a day (1985 PPP $)" (*HDR 1999*, table 4) to "$1 a day (1993 PPP US$)" (*HDR 2000*, table 4) and by the World Bank (*WDR 1999/2000*, 276, versus *WDR 2000/2001*, 23). Since U.S. inflation between 1985 and 1993 was 34.3 percent, the redefinition lowers the international poverty line by roughly 20 percent, from U.S.$48.4289 PPP to U.S.$38.8122 PPP per person per month in today's (year 2000) Dollars (http://stats.bls.gov/cpihome.htm). In response to my query, the World Bank has informed me that the redefinition is justified by the slower rise in basic foodstuff prices. I must say, I find it hard to believe that $38.81 per person per month in the United States—or a quarter that amount in the typical developing country ssee the conversion rates implied in *WDR 2000/2001*, 274–275)—really suffices for "a minimum, nutritionally adequate diet plus essential non-food requirements." Be this as it may, the new calculation does provide a useful snapshot of current global income inequality: Those in the poorest fifth fall on average 30 percent below the $38.81 PPP international poverty line (Chen and Ravallion, Hon Did the World's Poorest Fare, tables 2 and 4—calculated by dividing the poverty gap index by the headcount index). They have then an average annual income of U.S.$326 PPP or, at market exchange rates, about U.S.$82 annually per person. The collective annual income of these 1.2 billion people is then about U.S.$98 billion or 1/300 of the $30

Human Rights and Human Responsibilities

trillion global social product. It is thus possible to double, even triple, the incomes of the poorest fifth, to eradicate global poverty, at barely noticeable cost to the affluent countries and their citizens.

13. See *Ethics and International Affairs* 12 (1998), 195–199. The full text, with an accompanying report, is also available at http://www.asiawide.or.jp/iac/UDHR/EngDecl1.htm. The InterAction Council was founded in 1983 by the late Takeo Fukuda, former Prime Minister of Japan. Other prominent politicians associated with it include Helmut Schmidt (Germany) Malcolm Frasier (Australia), Lord James Callaghan (United Kingdom), Jimmy Carter (USA), Valéry Giscard d'Estaing (France), Mikhail S. Gorbachev (Russia), Lee Kuan Yew (Singapore), Kiichi Miyazawa (Japan), Shimon Peres (Israel), Henry A. Kissinger (USA), and Robert S. McNamara (USA). Among the "high-level experts" consulted in drafting the declaration are Hans Küng (Tübingen University) and Richard Rorty (Stanford Humanities Center).

14. With the end of the Cold War, military expenditures by the affluent countries of the Organization for Economic Co-operation and Development (OECD) declined from 4.1 percent of their combined gross domestic product (GDP) in 1985 to 2.2 percent in 1998 (*HDR 1998*, 197, and *HDR 2000*, 217). As the combined GDP of the OECD countries is currently around U.S.$23 trillion (*HDR 2000*, 209), the peace dividend for the OECD countries can be estimated to be 1.9 percent of this or U.S.$420 billion.

15. Immanuel Kant: *Grundlegung zur Metaphysik der Sitten* (1784), in *Preußische Akademieausgabe*, vol. IV (Berlin: Georg Reimer 1911), 430n.

16. In addition, the negative version of the Golden Rule is subject to numerous well-known further problems. On its face, it would seem to rule out many ordinarily accepted activities, such as one person entering into competition with another (for customers, a job, a house, a spouse, or whatever), an officer sending a soldier on a dangerous mission, a lawyer asking a witness embarrassing questions, and so on. This problem is aggravated by the Draft Declaration's insistence (in Article 13) that general ethical standards, such as the Golden Rule, must take precedence over specific ethical standards appropriate in particular contexts (e.g., business, military, or law).

17. This second component of equality is compatible with the view that the weight agents ought to give to the human rights of others varies with their relation to them—that agents have stronger moral reasons to secure human rights in their own country, for example, than abroad—as long as this is not seen as being the result of a difference in the moral significance of these rights, impersonally considered. (One can believe that the flourishing of all children is equally important and yet be committed to showing greater concern for the flourishing of one's own children than for the flourishing of other children.)

18. These six central elements are discussed in greater detail in the first two sections of my essay "How Should Human Rights be Conceived?" *Jahrbuch für Recht und Ethik* 3 (1995), 103–120, reprinted in Patrick Hayden, ed.: *The Philosophy of Human Rights: Readings in Context* (St. Paul: Paragon House Publishers 2001). If we can agree that these are indeed elements of the moral concept of human rights, then each human right will have these six features. The converse, however, does not hold true, as alternative conceptions of human rights go beyond the shared core in two ways: (a) by

Thomas Pogge

further specifying the concept of human rights through additional elements and (b) by selectively postulating a list of particular human rights (*cf.* second paragraph of this section).

19. Here is an example of U_1: "A human right, then, will be a right whose beneficiaries are all humans and whose obligors are all humans in a position to effect the right"—David Luban: "Just War and Human Rights" in Charles Beitz et al., eds.: *International Ethics* (Princeton: Princeton University Press 1985), 209.

20. The first of these possibilities is exemplified by Robert Nozick: *Anarchy, State and Utopia* (New York: Basic Books 1974), the second by Henry Shue: *Basic Rights* (Princeton: Princeton University Press 1996 [11980]). Nozick and Shue prefer to write of, respectively, *fundamental* and *basic* rights. U_1 leads to views like theirs but phrased in terms of *human* rights.

21. By drawing on the *Universal Declaration of Human Rights* for examples and illustrations, I am not implying that all the rights it lists are human rights or that its list is complete. Rather, I am using these rights as evidence for how the concept of a human right has been understood, on the assumption that any plausible understanding of human rights must be critically developed out of this established and customary notion.

22. The right to equal pay for equal work (§23.2) appears intended to be doubly limited in scope. Equality needs to be achieved only within each state, not internationally—equal work need not be paid the same in Bangladesh as in Switzerland. And the duty to help maintain such equality within each country is confined to its citizens—we have no duty to help implement the equal pay principle in foreign countries. Of course, a defender of U_1 could respond that the international human rights documents are mistaken on this point: Every human agent has a moral responsibility to promote the fulfillment of every human right of every human being.

23. This distinction will not be clear-cut because some human rights may have components that differ in scope. Pursuant to U_2, the human right not to be subjected to torture (§5), for example, would presumably be interpreted as giving each government negative duties not to use torture as well as positive duties to prevent torture. The negative duties would most plausibly be construed as being equal in content and strength toward all human beings: a government must not order or authorize the torture of any human being at all. But not so for positive duties: a government has much stronger duties to prevent the torture of persons within the territory it can effectively control than to prevent the torture of persons elsewhere.

24. See, for example, Jürgen Habermas: "Kants Idee des ewigen Friedens—aus dem historischen Abstand von 200 Jahren," *Kritische Justiz* 28 (1995) 3, 293–319. He claims that "the concept of human rights is not of moral origin, but . . . *by nature* juridical" (310) and that human rights "belong, through their structure, to a scheme of positive and coercive law which supports justiciable individual right claims. Hence it belongs to the meaning of human rights that they demand for themselves the status of constitutional rights" (312; my translations, italics in the original). Though Alexy explicitly refers to human rights as moral rights, he holds an otherwise similar position that equates the institutionalization of human rights with their transformation into positive law. See Robert Alexy: "Die Institutionalisierung der Menschenrechte im demokratischen Verfassungsstaat," in Stefan Gosepath and Georg Lohmann, eds.: *Die Philosophie der Menschenrechte* (Frankfurt: Suhrkamp 1997), 244–264.

25. The expression "suitably broad" alludes to how U_2 had solved the third problem with U_1. Some human rights—such as the human right not to be subjected to arbitrary arrest (§9)—are meant to protect every human being regardless of location or citizenship. Such human rights would be only partially juridified through a constitutional right that prohibits the government's arbitrary arrest merely of its own citizens or residents but not the arbitrary arrest of foreigners. The juridification component of a human right not to be subjected to arbitrary arrest would then give a weighty moral duty to all citizens of every state to help ensure that their state affords all human beings a legal right not to be arbitrarily arrested by its government.

26. This is not to deny that some human rights are difficult or impossible to fulfill without corresponding legal or even constitutional protections. This seems manifestly true, for instance, of a human right to an effective remedy by the competent national tribunals for acts violating fundamental rights granted by the constitution or by law (§8). It is also hard to imagine a society under modern conditions whose members are secure in their property or have secure access to freedom of expression even while no legal right thereto exists. I assume below that secure access to the objects of civil and political human rights generally requires corresponding legal protections.

27. I am grateful to Pablo De Greiff for suggesting that I address this reply.

28. As the examples indicate, my notion of *secure access* involves a knowledge condition: a person has secure access to the object of a human right only when she is not prevented by social obstacles from acquiring the knowledge and know-how necessary to secure this object for herself.

29. In response to this objection, U_3 might be amended to say that human rights require their *supranational* juridification as well. Habermas appears to leave room for this amendment when he writes: "in spite of their *claim* to universal validity, these rights have thus far managed to achieve an unambiguous positive form only within the national legal orders of democratic states. Beyond that, they possess only a weak force in international law and still await institutionalization within the framework of a cosmopolitan order that is only now beginning to take shape" (Habermas, op.cit., 312). Again, I am grateful to Pablo de Greiff for this point.

30. My reading of §28 emphasizes its statement that all human beings have a claim that any institutional order imposed upon them be one in which their postulated rights and freedoms can be fully realized. §28 could be read as making the additional statement that human beings have a claim that such an order be newly established in any (state-of-nature or "failed state") contexts in which no effective institutional order exists. I do not, however, read §28 as including this additional statement.

31. "*Relative* impact," because a comparative judgment is needed about how much more or less fully human rights are realized in this institutional order than they would be realized in its feasible alternatives.

32. This understanding of human rights is laid out more extensively in my "How Should Human Rights be Conceived?" (note 19). That earlier essay applied the idea only to the case of national institutional schemes, while the present one applies it also to the global institutional order.

33. The task of specifying, for the object of each particular human right, acceptable probabilities for threats from various (official and nonofficial) sources belongs to the second, substantive component of a conception of human rights, which is not discussed in the present essay.

34. We do not believe that the police should be authorized to beat up suspects in its custody, say, if such authorization (by deterring criminal beatings) reduces the number of beatings overall.

35. Other things must be presumed to be equal here. Deficits become less weighty, morally, as we go through the list. But greater low-weight deficits can still outweigh smaller high-weight deficits.

36. This might have been caused, for instance, by their maintaining a long-term smoking habit in full knowledge of the medical dangers associated therewith.

37. My critique of such recipient-oriented moral conceptions is presented more fully in my essays "Three Problems with Contractarian-Consequentialist Ways of Assessing Social Institutions," *Social Philosophy and Policy* 12 (1995), 241–266, and "Gleiche Freiheit für alle?" in Otfried Höffe, ed.: *John Rawls: Eine Theorie der Gerechtigkeit* (Berlin: Akademie Verlag 1998), 149–168.

38. See note 18.

39. On the stronger reading of §28 (*cf.* note 31), human agents would also have a duty to *establish* a global institutional order that fulfills human rights even if no such order presently exists. It is doubtful, however, whether this duty could, in such a context, be considered to be a negative one. Kant suggests how it might be: "A human being (or a people) in a mere state of nature robs me of this assurance and injures me through this very state in which he coexists with me—not actively (facto), but through the lawlessness of his state (statu iniusto) through which I am under permanent threat from him—and I may compel him either to enter with me into a common juridical state or to retreat from my vicinity." Immanuel Kant: "Zum ewigen Frieden" (1795), in *Preußische Akademieausgabe*, vol. VIII (Berlin: de Gruyter 1923), 349n (my translation).

40. Typical here is John Rawls: *The Law of Peoples* (Cambridge, MA: Harvard University Press 1999), 108: "the causes of the wealth of a people and the forms it takes lie in their political culture and in the religious, philosophical, and moral traditions that support the basic structure of their political and social institutions, as well as in the industriousness and cooperative talents of its members, all supported by their political virtues. . . . Crucial also is the country's population policy."

41. See Derek Parfit: *Reasons and Persons* (Oxford: Oxford University Press 1984), chapter 3, entitled "Five Mistakes in Moral Mathematics." Even if each privileged person typically bears only one billionth of the moral responsibility for the avoidable underfulfillment of human rights caused by the existing global order, each of us would still be responsible for significant harms (see note 3 above and accompanying text).

42. This is confirmed by the—otherwise startling—empirical finding of a *negative* correlation between developing countries' resource endowments and their rates of

economic growth, exemplified by the relatively low growth rates, over the past forty years, of resource-rich Nigeria, Kenya, Angola, Mozambique, Zaire, Venezuela, Brazil, Saudi Arabia, Burma, and the Philippines. *Cf.* Ricky Lam and Leonard Wantchekon: "Dictatorships as a Political Dutch Disease," working paper (Yale University, January 19, 1999), 35: "a one percentage increase in the size of the natural resource sector generates a decrease by half a percentage point in the probability of survival of democratic regimes." The paper specifically supports the hypothesis that the causal connection between resource wealth and poor economic growth (the so-called "Dutch disease)" is mediated through reduced chances for democracy: "all petrostates or resource-dependent countries in Africa fail to initiate meaningful political reforms. . . . besides South Africa, transition to democracy has been successful only in resource-poor countries" (ibid. 31). Cf. also Leonard Wantchekon: "Why Do Resource Dependent Countries Have Authoritarian Governments?," working paper (Yale University, December 12, 1999, www.yale.edu/leitner/pdf/1999-11.pdf).

43. An analogous point plays a major role in debates about the significance of genetic vis-à-vis environmental factors: Factors that are quite unimportant for explaining the observed *variation* of a trait (e.g., height, IQ, cancer) in some population may be very important for explaining this trait's *overall level* (frequency) in the same population. Suppose that, in some province, the observed variation in female adult height (54–60 inches) is almost entirely due to hereditary factors. It is still quite possible that the height differentials among these woman are minor compared to how much taller they all would be (67–74 inches) if it had not been the case that, when they were growing up, food was scarce and boys were preferred over girls in its distribution. Or suppose that we can know quite accurately, on the basis of genetic information, who is likely to get cancer and who is not. It is still quite possible that, in a healthy environment, cancer would hardly occur at all.

44. This point is frequently overlooked in the manner exemplified by Rawls (*cf.* note 41). His superficial explanation is not so much false as incomplete. As soon as one asks (as Rawls does not), *why* so many less developed countries (LDCs) have oppressive governments and corrupt elites, one will unavoidably hit upon global factors—such as the ones I have discussed: Local elites can afford to be oppressive and corrupt, because, with money and weapons from abroad, they can stay in power even without popular support. And they are so often oppressive and corrupt, because it is, in light of the prevailing extreme international inequalities, far more lucrative for them to cater to the interests of foreign governments and firms rather than those of their impoverished compatriots. Examples abound: there are plenty of LDC governments that came to power and/or stay in power only thanks to foreign support. And there are plenty of LDC politicians and bureaucrats who, induced or even bribed by foreigners, work against the interests of their people: *for* the development of a tourist-friendly sex industry (whose forced exploitation of children and women they tolerate and profit from); *for* the importation of unneeded, obsolete, or overpriced products at public expense; *for* the permission to import hazardous products, wastes, or productive facilities; *against* laws protecting employees or the environment, etc. It is perfectly unrealistic to believe that corruption and oppression in the LDCs, which Rawls rightly deplores, can be abolished without a significant reduction in international inequality.

45. For a somewhat more extensive discussion with additional data and reform proposals, see my "The Influence of Global Institutions on the Prospects for Genuine Democracy in the Less Developed Countries" in *Ratio Juris* 14/3 (2001).

46. Participants in an institutional order will be differentially responsible for its moral quality: influential and privileged participants should be willing to contribute more to the maintenance of a just, or the reform of an unjust institutional order. Moreover, we must here distinguish responsibility from guilt and blame. Our substantial causal contribution to the imposition of an unjust institutional order means that we share moral responsibility for this imposition and the avoidable harms it entails. It does not follow from this that we are also guilty or blameworthy on account of our conduct. For there might be applicable excuses such as, for instance, factual or moral error or ignorance.

47. All this does not diminish in any way the responsibility of repressive and corrupt rulers in the developing countries, who also strongly support, and greatly benefit from, the international borrowing and resource privileges. These two groups should be seen as a symbiotic unit, a global elite who are together imposing a mutually agreeable institutional order that allows them to exploit the natural wealth of this planet at the expense of the excluded majority of humankind.

48. This is so no matter which of the available substantive accounts of human rights one might endorse.

49. For a different argument, which attacks the same conviction by appeal to the inherently regrettable incentives it provides, see my "Loopholes in Moralities," *Journal of Philosophy* 89 (1992), 79–98.

50. For example, by representatives of Western governments and corporations who benefit from or support sweat shops, child prostitution, or torture in developing countries and seek to defend their involvement in such practices against moral criticism from other Westerners.

51. Mutual toleration with regard to this question is at least *possible*. This is not to say that we *ought* to tolerate the national institutional order of any other country no matter how unjust it may be.

52. This criticism has been voiced by Singapore's patriarch Lee Kuan Yew, by Mary Ann Glendon: *Rights Talk: The Impoverishment of Political Discourse* (New York: The Free Press 1991), and by many others as well.

53. We might try to initiate appropriate changes in our global order, for example, by publicizing its nature and effects and by formulating feasible paths of reform. And we might help preempt or undo some of the harms through volunteer work or donations to effective relief organizations. How much should one contribute to such reform and protection efforts? In proportion to one's affluence and influence, at least as much as would suffice for the full realization of human rights if most similarly situated others followed suit. Thus, if 1 percent of the income of the most affluent tenth of humankind would suffice to eradicate world hunger within a few years, then we should give at least 1 percent of our incomes to fight hunger. For an extensive discussion of the fair distribution of demands, see Liam Murphy: *Moral Demands in Nonideal Theory* (New York: Oxford University Press 2000).

54. A global order could give such encouragement through centrally determined economic (trade, loans, aid) and diplomatic privileges and penalties. Stronger sanctions, like embargoes and military interventions, should probably be triggered only in cases of extreme oppression. Some of the governments that profess allegiance

solely to social, economic, and cultural human rights maintain that certain prominent (legal) civil and political rights are currently unnecessary in their country,
unhelpful, or even counterproductive (distracting and expensive). But most of these
governments would, I believe, concede that more extensive civil and political rights
would often be helpful elsewhere or at other times. The Chinese government, for
example, might maintain that instituting more extensive civil and political rights in
China today would not work to the benefit of the Chinese poor, for whom the Party
and the government are already doing all they can. But the same government might
acknowledge that there are other regions today—Africa, perhaps, or Latin America,
Eastern Europe, the former Soviet Union, Indonesia—where more extensive civil and
political rights would help the poor and ethnic minorities to fend for themselves.
Unofficially, some of its members would perhaps also acknowledge that the Chinese
famine of 1959–61, whose staggering death toll of nearly 30 million has only recently
become widely known, could not have occurred in a country with independent mass
media and a competitive political system. Compare once more an analogous domestic case. A decent police officer, who cares deeply about the suffering caused by
crime, may see no good reason why she and her fellow officers at her station should
not do everything they can to nail a suspect they know to be guilty, without regard
to procedural niceties. But would she also advocate a civil order in which the police
in general can operate without procedural encumbrances? She must surely understand that not all officers would always use their greater powers in a decent, fair, and
judicious fashion, and also that some persons with criminal intentions would then
have much greater incentives to try to join the police force. This example shows how
one may consistently believe of certain safeguards that their observance should be
strongly encouraged by social institutions and that they are unnecessary or even
counterproductive in this or that particular case.

55. This explanatory insight is interestingly anticipated in the seventh proposition
of Immanuel Kant's essay "Idee zu einer allgemeinen Geschichte in weltbürgerlicher
Absicht" (1784), in *Preußische Akademieausgabe*, vol. VIII (Berlin: de Gruyter 1923),
24: "The problem of establishing a perfect civil constitution is subordinate to the
problem of law-governed external relations among states and cannot be solved
without the latter [problem]" (my translation).

56. See note 13.

6

On Legitimation through Human Rights

Jürgen Habermas

In this essay I use the term "legitimation" (and the associated term "legitimacy") in a doubly restricted sense: I am referring, first, to the legitimation of political systems and, second, only to the legitimation of constitutional democracies. I begin by recalling a proposal I have made for reconstructing the internal relation between democracy and human rights.[1] I then briefly examine a few of the aspects under which this Western style of legitimation is criticized today—whether in the discourse among Western theorists or in the discourses between others cultures and the West.

I   The Procedural Justification of Constitutional Democracy

Let me begin by explicating the concept of political legitimation. Social orders in which authority is organized through a state—orders that can, for example, be distinguished from tribal societies—experience a need for legitimation that is already implicit in the concept of political power. Because the medium of state power is constituted in forms of law, political orders draw their recognition from the legitimacy claim of law. That is, law requires more than mere acceptance; besides demanding that its addressees give it de facto recognition, the law claims *to deserve* their recognition. Consequently, all the public justifications and constructions meant to redeem this claim to be worthy of recognition belong to the legitimation of a government organized in the form of law.

Jürgen Habermas

This holds for all governments. Modern states are characterized by the fact that political power is constituted in the form of positive law, which is to say enacted and coercive law. Because the question regarding the mode of political legitimation is bound up with this legal form, I would like first to delineate modern law by describing its structure and mode of validity. Only then can I discuss the kind of legitimation associated with such law.

(1)   Individual rights make up the core of modern legal orders. By opening up the legal space for pursuing personal preferences, individual rights release the entitled person from moral precepts and other prescriptions in a carefully circumscribed manner. Within the boundaries of what is legally permitted no one is legally obligated to publicly justify her action. With the introduction of individual liberties, modern law—in contrast to traditional legal orders—validates the Hobbesian principle that whatever is not explicitly prohibited is permitted. As a result, law and morality split into two.[2] Whereas morality primarily tells us what our obligations are, law has a structure that gives primacy to entitlements. Whereas moral rights are derived from reciprocal duties, legal duties stem from the legal constraints on individual liberties. This conceptual privileging of rights over duties is implicit in the modern concepts of the legal person and the legal community. The moral universe, which is *unlimited* in social space and historical time, includes *all natural persons* with all the complexities of their life histories. By contrast, a legal community, which has a spatiotemporal location, protects the integrity of its members only insofar as they acquire the artificial status of bearers of individual rights.

This structure is reflected by the law's peculiar mode of validity. In the legal mode of validity, we find the facticity of the state's enforcement and implementation of law intertwined with the legitimacy of the purportedly rational procedure of lawmaking. Modern law leaves its addressees free to approach the law in either of two ways. They can consider norms merely as factual constraints on their freedom and take a strategic approach to the calculable consequences of possible rule violations, or they can comply with regulation "out of respect for the law." Kant already expressed this point with his concept of legality, highlighting the connection between these two moments without which legal obedience cannot be reasonably expected of morally responsible persons. Legal norms must be so fashioned that they can be viewed simultaneously in two different ways, as laws that coerce and as laws of freedom. It must at least be possible to obey laws not because they are compulsory but because they are legitimate. The validity of a legal norm means that the state guarantees both legitimate lawmaking and de facto enforcement. The state must ensure both of these: on the one hand, the legality of behavior in the sense of an average compliance that is, if necessary, enforced through penalties; on the other hand, a legitimacy of legal rules that always makes it possible to comply with a norm out of respect for the law.

For the legitimacy of the legal order, however, another formal characteristic is especially important, namely the positivity of enacted law. How can we ground the legitimacy of rules that are always able to be changed by the political legislator? Constitutional norms too are changeable; even the basic norms that the constitution itself has declared nonamendable share, along with all positive law, the fate that they can be abrogated, say, after a change of regime. As long as one was able to fall back on a religiously or metaphysically grounded natural law, the whirlpool of temporality enveloping positive law could be held in check by morality. Even temporalized positive law was at first supposed to remain subordinate to, and be permanently oriented by, the eternally valid moral law, which was conceived of as a "higher law." But in pluralistic societies such integrating world-views and collectively binding ethical systems have disintegrated.

Political theory has given a twofold answer to the question of legitimacy: popular sovereignty and human rights. The principle of popular sovereignty lays down a procedure that, because of its democratic features, justifies the presumption of legitimate outcomes. This principle is expressed in the rights of communication and participation that secure the public autonomy of politically enfranchised citizens. The classical human rights, by contrast, ground an inherently legitimate rule of law. These rights guarantee the life and private liberty—that is, scope for the pursuit of personal life plans—of citizens. Popular sovereignty and human rights provide the two normative perspectives from which an enacted, changeable law is supposed to be legitimated as a means to secure both the private and civic autonomy of the individual.

(2)   Political philosophy, however, has never really been able to strike a balance between popular sovereignty and human rights, or between the "freedom of the ancients" and the "freedom of the moderns." *Republicanism*, which goes back to Aristotle and the political humanism of the Renaissance, has always given the public autonomy of citizens priority over the prepolitical liberties of private persons. *Liberalism*, which goes back to John Locke, has invoked (at least since the nineteenth century) the danger of tyrannical majorities and postulated the priority of human rights. According to republicanism, human rights owed their legitimacy to the ethical self-understanding and sovereign self-determination achieved by a political community. In liberalism, such rights were supposed to provide inherently legitimate barriers that prevented the sovereign will of the people from encroaching on inviolable spheres of individual freedom. In opposition to the complementary one-sidedness of these two traditions, one must insist that the idea of human rights—Kant's fundamental right to equal individual liberties—must neither be merely imposed on the sovereign legislator as an external barrier nor be instrumentalized as a functional requisite for democratic self-determination.[3]

To express this intuition properly, in what follows I start with the question: What basic rights must free and equal citizens mutually accord one another if they want to regulate their common life legitimately by means of positive law? This idea of a constitution-making practice links the expression of popular sovereignty with the creation of a system of rights. Here I assume a principle that I cannot discuss in detail, namely, that a law may claim legitimacy only if all those possibly affected could consent to it after participating in rational discourses. As participants in "discourses," we want to arrive at shared opinions by mutually convincing one another about some issue through arguments, whereas in "bargaining" we strive for a balance of different interests. (One should note, however, that the fairness of bargained agreements depends in turn on discursively justified procedures of compromise formation.) Now, if discourses (and bargaining processes) are the place where a reasonable political will can develop, then the presumption of legitimate outcomes, which the democratic procedure is supposed to justify, ultimately rests on an elaborate communicative arrangement: the forms of communication necessary for a reasonable will-formation of the political lawgiver, the conditions that ensure legitimacy, must be legally institutionalized.

The desired internal relation between human rights and popular sovereignty consists in this: human rights institutionalize the communicative conditions for a reasonable political will-formation. Rights, which make the exercise of popular sovereignty *possible*, cannot be imposed on this practice like external constraints. To be sure, this claim is *immediately* plausible only for political rights, that is, the rights of communication and participation; it is not so obvious for the classical human rights that guarantee the citizen's private autonomy. The human rights that guarantee everyone a comprehensive legal protection and an equal opportunity to pursue their private life plans clearly have an intrinsic value. They are not reducible to their instrumental value for democratic will-formation.

At the same time, we must not forget that the medium through which citizens exercise their political autonomy is not a matter of choice. Citizens participate in legislation only as *legal* subjects; it is no longer in their power to decide which language they will make use of. Hence the legal code as such must already be available before the communicative presuppositions of a discursive will-formation can be institutionalized in the form of civil rights. To establish this legal code, however, it is necessary to create the status of legal persons who as bearers of individual rights belong to a voluntary association of citizens and can, when necessary, effectively claim their rights. There is no law without the private autonomy of legal persons in general. Consequently, without the classical liberty rights, in particular the basic right to equal individual liberties, there also would not be any medium in which to legally institutionalize the conditions under which citizens could participate in the practice of self-determination.

This shows how private and public autonomy reciprocally presuppose each other. The internal relation between democracy and the rule of law consists of this: on the one hand, citizens can make appropriate use of their public autonomy only if, on the basis of their equally protected private autonomy, they are sufficiently independent; on the other hand, they can realize equality in the enjoyment of their private autonomy only if they make appropriate use of their political autonomy as citizens. Consequently, liberal and political basic rights are inseparable. The image of kernel and husk is misleading—as though there were a core area of elementary liberty rights that would have priority over rights of communication and participation.[4] For the Western style of legitimation, the cooriginality of liberty rights and the rights of citizens is essential.

II The Self-Criticism of the West

Human rights are Janus-faced, looking simultaneously toward morality and the law. Their moral content notwithstanding, they have the form of legal rights. *Like* moral norms, they refer to every creature "that bears a human countenance," but *as* legal norms they protect individual persons only insofar as the latter belong to a particular legal community—usually the citizens of a nation-state. Thus a peculiar tension arises between the universal meaning of human rights and the local conditions of their realization: they *should* have unlimited validity for all persons, but how is that to be achieved? On the one hand, one can imagine the global expansion of human rights in such a way that all existing states are transformed—not just in name only—into constitutional democracies, while each individual receives the right to a nationality of his or her choice. We are a long way from achieving this goal. An alternative route would emerge if each individual attained the effective enjoyment of human rights immediately, as a world citizen. In this sense, Article 28 of the United Nations Declaration of Human Rights refers to a global order "in which the rights and liberties set forth in this Declaration are completely realized." But even the goal of an actually institutionalized cosmopolitan legal order lies in the distant future.

In the transition from nation-states to a cosmopolitan order, it is hard to say which poses the greater danger: the disappearing world of sovereign subjects of international law, who lost their innocence long ago, or the ambiguous mishmash of supranational institutions and conferences, which can grant a dubious legitimation but which depend as always on the good will of powerful states and alliances.[5] In this labile situation, human rights provide the sole recognized basis of legitimation for the politics of the international community; nearly every state has by now accepted, at least on paper, the United Nations Declaration of Human Rights. Nevertheless, the general validity, content, and ranking of human rights are as contested as ever. Indeed, the human rights discourse that has been argued on normative terms is plagued by the fundamental doubt about whether the form of legitimation that has arisen in the West can also hold up as plausible within the frameworks of other cultures. The most radical critics are Western intellectuals themselves. They maintain that the universal validity claimed for human rights merely hides a perfidious claim to power on the part of the West.

This is no accident. To gain some distance from one's own traditions and to broaden limited perspectives is one of the advantages of occidental rationalism. The European history of the interpretation and realization of human rights is the history of such a *decentering* of our way of viewing things. So-called equal rights have only been gradually extended to oppressed, marginalized, and excluded groups. Only after tough political struggles have workers, women, Jews, Romany, gays, and political refugees been recognized as "human beings" with a claim to fully equal treatment. The important thing now is that the individual advances in emancipation reveal in hindsight the ideological function that human rights had also fulfilled *up to that time*. That is, the egalitarian claim to universal validity and inclusion had also always served to mask the de facto unequal treatment of those who were silently excluded. This observation has aroused the suspicion that human rights might be reducible to this ideological function. Have they not always served to shield a false universality—an imaginary humanity—behind which an imperialistic West could conceal its own ways and interests? Following Martin Heidegger and Carl Schmitt, Western intellectuals have read this hermeneutic of suspicion in two ways, as a critique of reason and as a critique of power.

According to the first reading, the idea of human rights is the expression of a specifically Western notion of reason that has its origins in Platonism. Spurred by an "abstractive fallacy," this notion leaps beyond the boundaries of its original context of emergence, thus exceeding the merely local validity of its alleged universality. The critique of reason contends that every tradition, world-view, or culture has inscribed its own—indeed incommensurable—standards for what is true and false. But this leveling critique fails to notice the peculiar self-referential character of the discourse of modernity. The discourse of human rights is also set up to provide *every* voice with a hearing. Consequently, this discourse itself sets forth the standards in whose light the latent violations of its own claims can be discovered and corrected. Lutz Wingert has called this the "detective aspect" of human rights discourses: human rights, which demand the inclusion of the other, function at the same time as sensors for exclusionary practices exercised in their name.[6]

The variants of the critique of power proceed somewhat more awkwardly. They too deny the claim to universal validity by referring to the genetic priority of a suppressed particularity. But this time a reductionistic feint suffices. The normative language of law can supposedly reflect nothing else but the factual claims to power of political self-assertion; according to this view, consequently, universal legal claims always conceal the particular will of a specific collectivity to have its own way. But the critics of power forget that the more fortunate nations learned in the eighteenth century how sheer power can be domesticated by legitimate law. "He who says 'humanity' is lying"—this familiar piece of German ideology only betrays a lack of historical experience.[7]

III   The Discourse between the West and Other Cultures: "Asiatic Values"

Western intellectuals should not confuse their discourse over their own Eurocentric biases with the debates in which members of other cultures engage them. True, in the cross-cultural discourse we also encounter arguments that the spokespersons of other cultures have borrowed from European critics to show that the validity of human rights remains imprisoned, despite everything, in the original European context. But those non-Western critics, whose self-consciousness comes from their own traditions, certainly do not reject human rights lock, stock, and barrel. The reason is that other cultures and world religions are now also exposed to the challenges of social modernity, just as Europe was in its day, when it in some sense "discovered" or "invented" human rights and constitutional democracy.

In what follows I will take the apologetic role of a Western participant in a cross-cultural discussion of human rights. My working hypothesis is that those standards stem less from the particular cultural background of Western civilization than from the attempt to answer specific challenges posed by a social modernity that has in the meantime covered the globe. Whether we evaluate this modern starting point one way or another, it confronts us today with a fact that leaves us no choice and thus neither requires, nor is capable of, a retrospective justification. The contest over the adequate interpretation of human rights has to do not with the desirability of the "modern condition" but with an interpretation of human rights that does justice to the modern world from the viewpoints of other cultures as well as our own. The controversy turns above all on the individualism and secular character of human rights that are centered in the concept of autonomy.

For the purposes of clarity I base my metacritical remarks on a description that provides a frank expression of the Western standards of legitimacy. The above reconstruction of the relation between liberty rights and the rights of citizens starts from a situation in which we assume that free and equal citizens take counsel together on how they can regulate their common life not only by means of positive law but also legitimately. I recall in advance three implications of this proposal, which are relevant for the further course of the argument:

First, this model begins with the horizontal relationships that citizens have with one another. Only in a second step, and thus only on an established rights basis, does the model introduce the relationships that citizens have to the functionally necessary state apparatus. This allows us to avoid the liberal fixation on the question of how one controls the state's monopoly on force. Although the liberal question is understandable from the perspective of European history, it shoves the more innocuous question about the solidaristic justification of a political community into the background.

Second, in the model I propose, the starting question assumes that we can take the medium of enacted, coercible law more or less at face value as effective and unproblematic. Unlike classical contract theory, the proposed model does not treat the creation of an association of legal persons, defined as bearers of individual rights, as a decision in need of normative justification. A functional account suffices as justification, because complex societies, whether Asian or European, appear to have no functional equivalent for the integrative achievements of law. This kind of artificially created norm, at once compulsory and freedom guaranteeing, has also proven its worth for producing an abstract form of civic solidarity among strangers who want to remain strangers.

Finally, the model of constitution making is understood in such a way that human rights are not pregiven moral truths to be *discovered* but rather are *constructions*. Unlike moral rights, it is rather clear that legal rights must not remain politically nonbinding. As individual, or "subjective," rights, human rights have an inherently juridical nature and are conceptually oriented toward positive enactment by legislative bodies.

These reflections change nothing about the individualistic style and secular basis of legal systems based on human rights; indeed, they emphasize the centrality accorded to autonomy. At the same time, however, they cast a different light on the criticisms one hears in the cross-cultural discourse, which target both aspects of Western legal systems.

As became evident at the Vienna Conference on Human Rights, a debate has gotten underway since the 1991 report of the Singapore regime on "shared values" and the 1993 Bangkok Declaration jointly signed by Singapore, Malaysia, Taiwan, and China. In this debate the strategic statements of government representatives are in part allied with, and in part clash with, the contributions of oppositional and independent intellectuals. The objections are essentially directed against the individualistic character of human rights. The critique, which invokes the indigenous "values" of Far Eastern cultures shaped by Confucianism, moves along three lines. Specifically, the critics (1) question the principled priority of rights over duties, (2) appeal to a particular communitarian "hierarchy" of human rights, and (3) lament the negative effects that an individualistic legal order has on the social cohesion of the community.

(1)   The core of the debate lies in the thesis that the ancient cultures of Asia (as well as the tribal cultures of Africa[8]) accord priority to the community over the individual and do not recognize a sharp separation between law and ethics. The political community is traditionally integrated more by duties than by rights. The political ethic recognizes no individual rights, but only rights that are conferred on individuals. For this reason, the individualistic legal understanding of the West is supposedly incompatible with the community-based ethos that is deeply anchored in a particular tradition and that requires individual conformity and subordination.[9]

It seems to me that the debate takes a false turn with this reference to cultural differences. In fact, one can infer the function of modern law from its form. Individual rights provide a kind of protective belt for the individual's private conduct of life in two ways: rights protect the conscientious pursuit of an ethical life project just as much as they secure an orientation toward personal preferences free of moral scrutiny. This legal form is tailored for the functional demands of modern economic societies, which rely on the decentralized decisions of numerous independent actors. Asiatic societies, however, also deploy positive law as a steering medium in the framework of a globalized system of market relations. They do so for the same functional reasons that once allowed this form of law to prevail in the Occident over the older guild-based forms of social integration. Legal certainty, for example, is one of the necessary conditions for a commerce based on predictability, accountability, and good faith protections. Consequently, the decisive alternatives lie not at the cultural but at the socioeconomic level. Asiatic societies cannot participate in capitalistic modernization without taking advantage of the achievements of an individualistic legal order. One cannot desire the one and reject the other. From the perspective of Asian countries, the question is not whether human rights, as part of an individualistic legal order, are compatible with the transmission of one's own culture. Rather, the question is whether the traditional forms of political and societal integration can be reasserted against—or must instead be adapted to—the hard-to-resist imperatives of an economic modernization that has won approval on the whole.

(2) These reservations about European individualism are often expressed not for normative reasons but with a strategic intention. This intention can be recognized insofar as the arguments are connected with the political justification of the more or less "soft" authoritarianism that characterizes the dictatorships of developing nations. This is especially true of the dispute over the hierarchy of human rights. The governments of Singapore, Malaysia, Taiwan, and China appeal to a "priority" of social and cultural basic rights in an effort to justify the violations against basic legal and political rights of which the West accuses them. These dictatorships consider themselves authorized by the "right to social development"—apparently understood as a collective right—to postpone the realization of liberal rights and rights of political participation until their countries have attained a level of economic development that allows them to satisfy the basic material needs of the population equally. For a population in misery, they claim, legal equality and freedom of opinion are not so relevant as the propect of better living conditions.

One cannot convert functional arguments into normative ones this easily. True, some conditions are more beneficial than others for the long-term implementation of human rights. But that does not justify an authoritarian model of development, according to which the freedom of the individual is subordinated to the "good of the community" as it is paternalistically apprehended and defined. In reality, these governments do not defend individual rights at all, but rather a paternalistic care meant to allow them to restrict rights that in the West have been considered the most basic (the rights to life and bodily integrity, the rights to comprehensive legal protection and equal treatment, to religious freedom, freedom of association, free speech, and so forth). From a normative standpoint, according "priority" to social and cultural basic rights does not make sense for the simple reason that such rights only serve to secure the "fair value" (Rawls) of liberal and political basic rights, that is, the factual presuppositions for the equal opportunity to exercise individual rights.[10]

(3)   The two arguments above are often linked with a critique of the suspected effects of an individualistic legal order, which appears to endanger the integrity of the naturally emergent living systems of family, neighborhoods, and politics. According to this critique, a legal order that equips persons with actionable individual rights is set up for conflict and thus at odds with the orientation of the indigenous culture toward consensus. It helps if we distinguish the principled reading of this criticism from a political reading.

From the principled point of view, the reservations about the individualistic style of European human rights are backed by the justified critique of an understanding of rights that stems from the Lockean tradition and that has been revived today by neoliberalism. This possessive individualism misses the idea that actionable individual rights can only be derived from the preexisting, indeed intersubjectively recognized norms of a legal community. It is true that individual rights are part of the equipment of legal persons; but the status of legal persons as rights bearers develops only in the context of a legal community that is premised on the mutual recognition of its freely associated members. Consequently, the understanding of human rights must jettison the metaphysical assumption of an individual who would exist prior to all socialization and would, as it were, come into the world already equipped with innate rights. Dropping this "Western" thesis, however, also makes its "Eastern" antithesis unnecessary—that the claims of the legal community have priority over individual legal claims. The choice between "individualist" and "collectivist" approaches disappears once we approach fundamental legal concepts with an eye toward the dialectical *unity* of individuation and socialization processes. Because even legal persons are individuated only on the path to socialization, the integrity of individual persons can be protected only together with the free access to those interpersonal relationships and cultural traditions in which they can maintain their identities. Without this kind of "communitarianism," a properly understood individualism remains incomplete.

In contrast to the principled critique, the political objection to the disintegrating effects of modern law is rather weak. The processes of economic and social modernization, which are both accelerated and violent in the developing nations, must not be confused with the legal forms in which social disintegration, exploitation, and the abuse of administrative power occur. The only means of countering the factual oppression exercised by the dictatorships of developing nations is a juridification of politics. The integration problems that every highly complex society has to master can be solved by means of modern law, however, only if *legitimate* law helps to generate that abstract form of civic solidarity that stands and falls with the realization of basic rights.[11]

IV The Challenge of Fundamentalism

The attack on the individualism of human rights targets one aspect of the underlying concept of autonomy, namely the liberties that are guaranteed to private citizens vis-à-vis the state and third parties. But citizens are autonomous in a political sense only when they give themselves their laws. The model of a constitutional assembly points toward a constructivist conception of basic rights. Kant conceived autonomy as the capacity to bind one's own will by normative insights that result from the public use of reason. This idea of self-legislation also inspires the procedure of democratic will-formation that makes it possible to base political authority on a mode of legitimation that is neutral toward world-views. As a result, a religious or metaphysical justification of human rights becomes superfluous. To this extent, the secularization of politics is simply the flip-side of the political autonomy of citizens.

The European conception of human rights is open to attack by the spokespersons of other cultures not only because the concept of autonomy gives human rights an individualistic character, but also because autonomy implies a secularized political authority uncoupled from religious and cosmological world-views. In the view of Islamic, Christian, or Jewish fundamentalists, their own truth claim is absolute in the sense that it deserves to be enforced even by means of political power, if necessary. This outlook has consequences for the exclusive character of the polity; legitimations based on religions or world-views of this sort are incompatible with the inclusion of equally entitled nonbelievers or persons of other persuasions.

A profane legitimation through human rights, however, and thus the uncoupling of politics from divine authority, poses a provocative challenge not only for fundamentalists. Indian intellectuals, such as Ashis Nandy, have also written "antisecularization manifestos."[12] They expect the mutual toleration and cross-fertilization of Islamic and Hindu religious cultures to develop more from a reciprocal inter-penetration of the modes of religious perception of both cultures than from the neutrality of the state toward world-views. They are skeptical about an official politics of neutrality that merely neutral-izes the public meaning of religion. Such considerations, however, combine the *normative* question—how one can find a shared basis for a just political life in common—with an *empirical* question. The differentiation of a religious sphere separate from the state may in fact weaken the influence of privatized "gods and demons." But the principle of toleration itself is not directed against the authenticity and truth claims of religious confessions and forms of life; rather, its sole purpose is to enable their equally entitled coexistence within the same political community.

The central issue in the controversy cannot be described as a dispute over the relevance that different cultures each give to reli-gion. The conception of human rights was the answer to a problem that once confronted Europeans—when they had to overcome the political consequences of confessional fragmentation—and now confronts other cultures in a similar fashion. The conflict of cultures takes place today in the framework of a world society in which the collective actors must, regardless of their different cultural traditions, agree for better or worse on norms of coexistence. The autarkic iso-lation against external influences is no longer an option in today's world.

The pluralism of world-views, however, is also breaking out inside societies that are still conditioned by strong traditions. Even in societies that, culturally speaking, are comparatively homogeneous, a reflexive reformulation of the prevailing dogmatic traditions is increasingly harder to avoid.[13] The awareness is growing, first of all among the intellectuals, that one's own religious truths must be brought into conformity with publicly recognized secular knowledge and defended before other religious truth claims in the same universe of discourse. Like Christianity since the Reformation, traditional world-views are thus being transformed into "reasonable comprehensive doctrines" under the reflexive pressure generated by modern life circumstances. This is how Rawls designates an ethical world-view and self-understanding that has become reflexive, open to reasonable disagreement with other belief systems but also able to reach an understanding with them on the rules of equal coexistence.[14]

My apologetic reflections present the Western mode of legitimation as an answer to general challenges that are no longer simply problems just for Western civilization. Naturally, this does not mean that the answer found by the West is the only one or even the best one. To this extent, the current debate provides us with an opportunity to become aware of our own blind spots. However, hermeneutical reflection on the starting point of a human rights discourse among participants from different cultures draws our attention to normative contents that are present in the tacit presuppositions of *any* discourse whose goal is mutual understanding. That is, independently of their cultural backgrounds all the participants intuitively know quite well that a consensus based on conviction cannot come about as long as symmetry relations do not exist among the participants—relations of mutual recognition, reciprocal perspective-taking, a shared willingness to consider one's own tradition with the eyes of the stranger and to learn from one another, and so forth. On this basis, we can criticize not only selective readings, tendentious interpretations, and narrow-minded applications of human rights, but also that shameless instrumentalization of human rights that conceals particular interests behind a universalistic mask—a deception that misleads one to the false assumption that the meaning of human rights is exhausted by their misuse.

Acknowledgments

An earlier version of this essay was read at the Conference on Globalization held at Saint Louis University, October 18–19, 1996.

Translated by William Rehg

Notes

1. Jürgen Habermas, *Between Facts and Norms: Contributions to a Discourse Theory of Law and Democracy*, trans. William Rehg (Cambridge: MIT Press, 1996), chapter 3.

2. Ingeborg Maus, "Die Trennung von Recht und Moral als Begrenzung des Rechts," in Maus, *Zur Aufklärung der Demokratietheorie* (Frankfurt: Suhrkamp, 1992), 308–336.

3. On the following, see also Jürgen Habermas, "On the Internal Relation between the Rule of Law and Democracy," in Habermas, *The Inclusion of the Other: Studies in Political Theory*, eds. Ciaran Cronin and Pablo De Greiff (Cambridge: MIT Press, 1998). Here I cannot go into the sympathetic critique of Ingeborg Maus, "Freiheitsrechte und Volkssouveränität," *Rechtstheorie* 26 (1995): 507–562.

4. R. Herzog, "Die Rechte des Menschen," *Die Zeit*, September 6, 1996, however, correctly distinguishes the justification of human rights from their implementation.

5. Ingeborg Maus, "Weltfrieden, Menschenrechte und Volkssouveränität: Das Projekt Immanuel Kants und die Globalisierungskonzepte der Gegenwart," ms. 1996.

6. Lutz Wingert, "Türöffner zu geschlossenen Gesellschaften," *Frankfurter Rundschau*, August 6, 1995.

7. For a comprehensive critique of Carl Schmitt's legal theory, see Ingeborg Maus, *Bürgerliche Rechtstheorie und Faschismus: Zur sozialen Function und aktuellen Wirkung der Theorie Carl Schmitts*, 2nd ed. (Munich: W. Fink, 1980).

8. Compare the parallel position of the Nigerian political scientist Claude Ake, "The African Context of Human Rights," *Africa Today* 34 (1987): 5: "The idea of human rights, or legal rights in general, presupposes a society which is atomized and individualistic, a society of endemic conflict. It presupposes a society of people conscious of their separateness and their particular interests and anxious to realize them. . . . We put less emphasis on the individual and more on the collectivity, we do not allow that the individual has any claims which may override that of the society. We assume harmony, not divergence of interests, competition and conflict; we are more inclined to think of our obligations to other members of our society rather than of our claims against them."

9. Yash Ghai, "Human Rights and Governance: The Asia Debate," *Center for Asian Pacific Affairs*, November 1994, 1–19.

10. See my exchange with Günther Frankenberg in Habermas, "Reply to Symposium Participants," *Cardozo Law Review* 17 (1996): 1542–1545.

11. Cf. Ghai, "Human Rights and Governance," 10: "Governments have destroyed many communities in the name of development or state stability, and the consistent refusal of most of them to recognize that there are indigenous peoples among their population who have a right to preserve their traditional culture, economy and beliefs, is but a demonstration of their lack of commitment to the real community. The vitality of the community comes from the exercise of rights to organize, meet, debate, and protest, dismissed as 'liberal' rights by these governments."

12. Partha Chatterjee, "Secularism and Toleration," *Economic and Political Weekly*, July 9, 1994, 1768–1776; Rajeev Bhargave, "Giving Secularism Its Due," *Economic and Political Weekly*, July 9, 1994, 1784–1791.

13. H. Hoibraaten, "Secular Society," in *Islamic Law Reform and Human Rights*, eds. T. Lindholm and K. Vogt (Oslo, 1993), 231–257.

14. John Rawls, *Political Liberalism* (New York: Columbia University Press, 1993).

III

Transnational Politics and National Identities

7

The European Nation-State and the Pressures of Globalization

Jürgen Habermas

"The all-important question today," states the introduction to a book entitled *Global Dynamics and Local Environments*, "is whether, beyond the limits of the nation-state, at the supranational and global levels, capitalism's potential for playing ecological, social, and cultural havoc can be brought back under control."[1] The market's capacity to steer the economy and bring new information to light is beyond question. But markets only respond to messages coded in the language of prices. They are insensible to their own external effects, those they produce in *other* domains. This gives the liberal sociologist Richard Münch reason to fear that we will be faced with the depletion of nonrenewable resources, cultural alienation on a mass scale, and social explosions unless we succeed in *politically* fencing in markets that are, as it were, running away from enfeebled and overburdened nation-states.

It is true that states in advanced capitalist societies have stepped up, rather than defused, capitalism's capacity to commit ecological mayhem in the postwar period, and that they have built up social security systems with the help of welfare-state bureaucracies hardly given to encouraging their clients to take charge of their own lives. Yet, in the third quarter of this century, the welfare state succeeded in substantially offsetting the socially undesirable consequences of a highly productive economic system in Europe and other OECD states. For the first time in its history, capitalism did not thwart fulfillment of the republican promise to include all citizens as equals before the law; it made it possible. For the democratic constitutional state also guarantees equality before the law, in the sense that all citizens are to have an equal opportunity to exercise their rights. John Rawls, the most influential theoretician of political liberalism writing today, speaks in this connection of the "fair value" of equitably distributed rights. Confronted with the homeless, whose numbers are silently increasing before our eyes, we are reminded of Anatole France's bon mot: the right to "spend the night sleeping out under a bridge" should not be the only one everyone enjoys.

If we read our constitutions in this material sense, as texts about achieving social justice, then the idea of citizens prescribing laws for themselves—according to which those subject to the law should regard themselves as the ones who make the law—takes on *political* dimension: that of a society that deliberately *acts upon itself.* In constructing the welfare state in postwar Europe, politicians of all stripes were guided by this dynamic conception of the democratic process. Today, we are becoming aware that this idea has so far been realized only in the framework of the nation-state. But if the nation-state is reaching the limits of its capacities in the changed context defined by global society and the global economy, then two things stand and fall with this form of social organization: the political domestication of a capitalism unleashed on a planetary scale, and the unique example of a broad democracy that works at least reasonably well. Can this form of the democratic self-transformation of modern societies be extended beyond national borders?

I propose to examine this question in three stages. We need first to see how the nation-state and democracy are interconnected, and to identify the source of the pressures to which this unique symbiosis is currently being subjected. I shall then briefly describe, in the light of this analysis, four political responses to the challenges raised by the postnational constellation; these responses also set the parameters of the ongoing debate about a "Third Way." Finally, using this debate as a springboard, I shall map out an offensive position on the future of the European Union. If, in discussing their future, the generally privileged citizens of this region wish to take the viewpoints of other countries and continents into account, they will have to deepen the European Union along federative lines so as to create, as citizens of the world, the requisite conditions for a global domestic politics.

The Challenges Facing Democracy and the Nation-State

The trends that are today attracting general attention under the catch-all rubric "globalization" are transforming a historical constellation characterized by the fact that state, society, and economy are, coextensive within the same national boundaries. The *international* economic system, in which states draw the borderline between the domestic economy and foreign trade relations, is being metamorphosed into a *transnational* economy in the wake of the globalization of markets. Especially relevant here are the acceleration of worldwide capital flows and the imperative assessment of national economic conditions by globally interlinked capital markets. These factors explain why states no longer constitute nodes endowing the worldwide network of commercial relations with the structure of interstate or international relations.[2] Today, it is states that are embedded within markets rather than national economies embedded within the boundaries of states.

Needless to say, the ongoing erosion of borders is not just characteristic of the economy. The study of "global transformation" recently published by David Held and his collaborators contains, over and above chapters on world trade, capital markets, and multinational corporations—whose production networks span the planet—chapters on global domestic politics, peace-keeping and organized violence, the new media and communications networks, burgeoning migratory movements, hybrid cultural forms, and so on. The "disenclavement" of society, culture, and the economy, which is proceeding apace, is impinging on the fundamental conditions of existence of the European state system, which was erected on a territorial basis beginning in the seventeenth century and still positions the most important collective actors on the political stage. But the postnational constellation is putting an end to this situation, in which politics and the legal system intermesh in constructive ways with economic circuits and national traditions within the borders of territorial states. The trends summed up in the word "globalization" are not only jeopardizing, internally, the comparatively homogeneous makeup of national populations—the prepolitical basis for the integration of citizens into the nation-state—by prompting immigration and cultural stratification; even more tellingly, a state that is increasingly entangled in the interdependencies between the global economy and global society is seeing its autonomy, capacity for action, and democratic substance diminish.[3]

Leaving aside empirical limitations on state sovereignty, which continue to exist at the formal level,[4] I shall here limit myself to considering three aspects of the erosion of the nation-state's prerogatives: (1) the decline in the state's capacities for control; (2) growing deficits in the legitimation of decision-making processes; and (3) an increasing inability to perform the kinds of steering and organizational functions that help secure legitimacy.

Weakening of the Nation-State

(i) The loss of autonomy means, among other things, that a state can no longer count on its own forces to provide its citizens with adequate protection from the external effects of decisions taken by other actors, or from the knock-on effects of processes originating beyond its borders. In question here are, on the one hand, "spontaneous border violations" such as pollution, organized crime, arms trafficking, epidemics, security risks associated with large-scale technology, and so on, and, on the other, the reluctantly tolerated consequences of other states' calculated policies, which affect people who did not help formulate them no less than people who did—think, for example, of the risks caused by nuclear reactors that are built beyond a state's borders and fail to meet its own safety standards.

(ii) Deficits in democratic legitimation arise whenever the set of those involved in making democratic decisions fails to coincide with the set of those affected by them. Democratic legitimation is also sapped, less obviously but more durably, whenever the growing need for coordination, due to increasing interdependence, is met by interstate agreements. The fact that nation-states are institutionally embedded in a network of transnational agreements and organizations creates equivalents, in certain policy areas, for prerogatives forfeited at the national level.[5] But the more matters that are settled through interstate negotiation, and the more important these matters are, the more political decisions are withdrawn from the arenas of democratic opinion-formation and will-formation—which are exclusively national arenas. In the European Union (EU), the largely bureaucratic decision-making process of the experts in Brussels offers an example of the type of democratic deficit caused by the shift away from national decision-making bodies to interstate committees of government representatives.[6]

(iii) The debate focuses, however, on the restriction of those capacities for intervention that the nation-state has heretofore mobilized to carry out legitimating social policies. With the widening gap between nation-states' territorially limited room for action on the one hand and global markets and accelerated capital flows on the other, the "functional self-sufficiency of the domestic economy" is going by the board: "functional self-sufficiency should not be equated with autarky. . . . [It] does not imply that a nation must possess a 'full range' of products, but only those complementary factors—above all, capital and organization—which the labor-supply available in a society needs in order to produce."[7] Footloose capital that is, as it were, exempt from the obligation to stay at home in its search for investment opportunities and speculative profits can threaten to exercise its exit option whenever a government puts burdensome constraints on the conditions for domestic investment in the attempt to protect social standards, maintain job security, or preserve its own ability to manage demand.

Thus national governments are losing the power to mobilize all the available steering mechanisms of domestic economies, stimulate growth, and so secure vital bases for their legitimation. Demand-management policies have counterproductive external consequences on the workings of the national economy—as was the case in the 1980s under the first Mitterrand government—because international stock exchanges have now taken over the function of assessing national economic policies. In many European countries, the fact that markets have supplanted politics is reflected in the vicious circle of soaring unemployment, strained social security systems, and shrinking national insurance contributions. The state is on the horns of a dilemma: the greater the need to replenish exhausted state budgets by raising taxes on movable property and enacting measures to boost growth, the harder it becomes to do so within the confines of the nation-state.

The Parameters of a Discussion

There are two blanket responses to this challenge and two rather more nuanced ones. The polarization between the two camps that advance blanket arguments (i) for or (ii) against globalization and deterritorialization has led to a search for a "third way" in a (iii) somewhat defensive or (iv) somewhat offensive variant.

(i) Support for globalization is based on the neoliberal orthodoxy that has ushered in the shift toward the supply-side economic policies of the past few decades. Partisans of globalization advocate unconditional subordination of the state to the imperatives of market-led integration of a global society; they plead for an "entrepreneurial state" that would abandon the project of decommodifying labor power or even protecting environmental resources. Ratcheted into the transnational economic system, the state would give citizens access to the negative freedoms of global competition, while essentially restricting itself to providing, in business-like fashion, infrastructures that foster entrepreneurial activity and make local production sites attractive from the standpoint of profitability. I cannot discuss here the assumptions informing neoliberal models, or the venerable doctrinal quarrel over the relationship between social justice and market efficiency.[8] Two objections, however, are thrown up by the premises of neoliberal theory itself.

Let us assume that a fully liberalized world economy, characterized by the unfettered mobility of all the factors of production (including labor power), will eventually begin operating smoothly under the conditions projected by advocates of globalization: a world of harmoniously equilibrated production sites and—the grand aim—a symmetrical division of labor. Even if there are grounds for this assumption, it implies acceptance, on the national and international plane, of a transitional period that would see not only a drastic increase in social inequalities and social fragmentation, but the deterioration of moral standards and cultural infrastructures as well. This leads us to ask how long it will take to cross the "valley of tears" and what sacrifices will have to be made en route. How many people will be marginalized and then left by the wayside before the goal is reached? How many monuments of world culture will fall victim to "creative destruction" and be forever lost?

The question as to what the future holds for democracy is no less a cause for concern. For, to the extent that the nation-state is shorn of functions and margins of maneuver for which no equivalents emerge on the supranational level, the democratic procedures and institutional arrangements that enable the associated citizens of a state to change the conditions they live under will inevitably be drained of their real content. Wolfgang Streeck calls this the "declining purchasing power of the ballot."[9]

From Territoriality to Xenophobia

(ii) In reaction to the erosion of democracy and the power of the nation-state, a coalition has been put together by those resisting the potential or actual social decline of the victims of structural change and the disabling of the democratic state and its citizens. But its energetic desire to stop the sluices ultimately betrays this "party of territoriality" (as Charles Maier puts it) into contesting the egalitarian and universalist bases of democracy itself. At a minimum, protectionist sentiment is grist for the mill of ethnocentric rejection of diversity, xenophobic rejection of the other, and antimodernist rejection of complex social conditions. Such sentiment is directed against anyone or anything that crosses national borders: the arms-smugglers and drug-dealers or mafiosi who threaten domestic security, the American movies and flood of information that threaten national cultures, or the immigrant workers and refugees who, like foreign capital, threaten living standards.

Even giving due consideration to the rational kernel of these defensive reactions, it is easy to see why the nation-state cannot recover the strength it once had by simply battening down the hatches. The liberalization of the global economy, which began after World War II and temporarily took the form of an embedded liberalism resting on a system of fixed exchange rates, has been sharply accelerated since the demise of the Bretton Woods system. But this acceleration was not inevitable. The systemic constraints that are today imposed by the imperatives of a free-trade system that was powerfully undergirded with the creation of the World Trade Organization (WTO) are the fruits of political voluntarism. Although the United States forced the pace of the various General Agreement on Tariffs and Trade (GATT) rounds, GATT did not involve unilaterally imposed decisions but rather cumulative negotiated agreements, each with its particular history; these agreements were coordinated in concessive negotiations between a large number of individual governments. And because it is this kind of negative integration of many independent actors that has given rise to the globalized marketplace, projects to restore the status quo ante by *unilaterally* revoking the functioning system that has emerged from a *concerted* decision stand no chance of success; any such attempts must expect to meet with sanctions.

The stand-off in the debate between the "parties" of globalization and territoriality has sparked attempts to find a "third way." They branch off in two directions, toward a more or less defensive and a more or less offensive variant. One sets out from the premise that, if the forces of global capitalism now that they have been unleashed can no longer be domesticated, their impact *can* be cushioned at the national level. The other pins its hopes on the transformative power of a supranational politics that will gradually catch up with runaway markets.

(iii) The defensive variant has it that it is too late to reverse the subordination of politics to the requirements of a global society unified by the market. Nevertheless, the argument goes, the nation-state should not merely play a reactive role, with an eye to creating favorable conditions for valorizing investment capital; it should also participate actively in all attempts to provide citizens the skills they need to compete. The new social policy is no less universalistic in its orientation than the old. However, it is intended not to protect people from the typical risks of working life, but, first and foremost, to supply them with the entrepreneurial skills of "achievers," capable of looking after themselves. The well-known adage about "helping people to help themselves" is thus given an economistic slant: it now conjures up a kind of fitness training that should enable everyone to assume personal responsibility and take initiatives that will allow them to hold their own in the marketplace—not to end up as the kind of "failure" who has to turn to the state for help. "Social democrats have to shift the relationship between risk and security involved in the welfare state, to develop a society of 'responsible risk-takers' in the spheres of government, business enterprise and labour markets. . . . Equality must contribute to diversity, not stand in its way."[10] This is, of course, only one aspect of the program; it is, however, pivotal.

The Ethical Triumph of Neoliberalism

What bothers "old" socialists about the prospect held out by "New Labor" or the "New Center" is not only its normative chutzpah, but also the debatable empirical assumption that jobs, even when they do not take the form of traditional work relationships, remain the "key variable in social integration."[11] In view of the secular tendency of technical progress to reduce labor time and increase productivity, and the simultaneous rise in the demand for jobs (which comes from women, above all), the opposite assumption—that we are witnessing the "end of a society based on full employment"—is not entirely far-fetched. If we are to give up the political goal of full employment, however, then we will either have to scrap the social standards of distributive justice or else consider fresh alternatives that will put considerable strain on national investment climates. Given the conditions prevailing in today's global economy, it is scarcely possible to implement cost-neutral projects to share the shrinking volume of available work, promote capital ownership among broad layers of the population, or institute a basic minimum wage uncoupled from real earnings and pegged above current welfare levels.

In normative terms, advocates of this Third Way fall in with the line of a liberalism that regards social equality solely from the standpoint of input, making it a mere matter of equal opportunity. This borrowed *moral* element aside, however, public perception of the difference between Thatcher and Blair is blurred above all because the "Newest Left" has accommodated the *ethical* conceptions of neoliberalism.[12] I have in mind its willingness to be drawn into the ethos of a "lifestyle attuned to the world market,"[13] which expects every citizen to obtain the education he or she needs to become "an entrepreneur managing his or her own human capital."[14]

(iv) Those unwilling to cross this divide may wish to consider a second, offensive variant of the Third Way. The perspective it offers turns on the notion that politics should take precedence over the logic of the market: "To what extent the logic of the market system should be 'turned loose,' where and in what framework the market should 'rule'—these are ultimately questions that, in a modem society, it should be left to deliberative politics to decide."[15] This sounds like voluntarism; indeed, it is, for the time being, merely a normative proposal that, if what has been said so far holds, cannot be put into practice in a national context. The attempt to resolve the dilemma between disarming welfare-state democracy or rearming the nation-state, however, leads us to look to larger political units and transnational systems that could compensate for the nation-state's functional losses in a way that need not snap the chain of democratic legitimation. The EU naturally comes to mind as an example of a democracy functioning beyond the limits of the nation-state. The creation of larger political entities does not by itself alter the process of competition between local production sites, that is, it does not challenge the primacy of market-led integration per se.

Politics will succeed in "catching up" with globalized markets only if it eventually becomes possible to create an infrastructure capable of sustaining a global domestic politics without uncoupling it from democratic processes of legitimation.[16] The notion that politics can "catch up" with markets by "growing up in their wake" is, of course, not meant to evoke the image of a struggle for power between political and economic actors. Indeed, the problematic consequences of a politics that equates society as a whole with market structures find their explanation in the fact that money cannot be indefinitely substituted for political power. The criteria for the legitimate uses of power differ from those used to measure economic success; for example, markets, unlike polities, cannot be democratized. A more appropriate image here would be that of competition between different media. The politics that sets up markets is self-referential, to the extent that every step toward market deregulation entails a simultaneous disqualification or self-restriction of political authority qua medium for enacting binding collective decisions. A "catch-up" politics inverts this process; it is reflexive politics in its positive rather than negative version.

Europe and the World

If we observe, from this vantage point, the way the EU has evolved to date, we find ourselves confronting a paradox. The creation of new political institutions—the Brussels authorities, the European Court of Justice, and the European Central Bank—by no means implies that politics has taken on greater importance. Monetary union represents the last step in a process that, notwithstanding Schumann's, de Gasperi's, and Adenauer's original program, can, in retrospect, be soberly described as "intergovernmental market-creation."[17] The EU today constitutes a broad continental region that, horizontally, has become a tightly meshed net thanks to the market, but vertically it is subject to rather weak political regulation by indirectly legitimated authorities. As member-states have transferred sovereignty over their monies to the Central Bank, and thus surrendered the ability to steer their national economies by adjusting exchange rates, the heightened competition we are likely to see within the single currency zone will give rise to problems of new dimensions.

The hitherto nationally structured European economies have reached different levels of development and are marked by different economic styles. Until a unified economy emerges from this heterogeneous mix, the interaction between Europe's individual economic zones, which are still inserted into different political systems, will generate friction. This holds, to begin with, for weaker economies, which will have to compensate for their competitive disadvantage through wage cutting; the stronger economies, for their part, fear wage dumping. An inauspicious scenario is being written for the existing social security systems, already bones of contention: they remain under national jurisdiction and have very different structures. While some countries fear the loss of advantages derived from lower costs, others fear downward adjustment. Europe is being confronted with an alternative: it can either relieve these pressures by way of the market—via competition between different centers of economic activity and different social protection policies—or resolve them by political means, through an attempt to bring about "harmonization" and gradual mutual adjustment of welfare, labor market, and tax policies. The basic question is whether the institutional status quo, in which states balance out conflicting national interests in interstate negotiation, is to be defended even at the price of a race to the bottom, or whether the EU should evolve beyond its present form of interstate alliance toward true federation. Only in the latter case could it summon up the political strength to decide to apply *corrective* measures to markets and set up *redistributive* regulatory mechanisms.

The Camps on Europe

Within the parameters of the current debate about globalization, the choice between these alternatives is an easy one for both neoliberals and nationalists. While desperate "Euroskeptics" are banking on protectionism and exclusion, all the more so now that monetary union has gone into effect, "Market Europeans" are satisfied with monetary union, which completes the European domestic market. Opposed to both these camps, "Eurofederalists" are striving to transform the existing international accords into a political constitution that would provide the decisions of the European Commission, Council of Ministers, and Court of Justice with their own basis for legitimacy. Those who adopt a *cosmopolitan* stance take their distance from all three positions. They regard a federal European state as a starting point for developing a network of transnational regimes that can, even in the absence of a world government, conduct something like a global domestic policy.

However, the central opposition between Eurofederalists and Market Europeans is complicated by the fact that the latter have concluded a tacit alliance with erstwhile Euroskeptics seeking a Third Way based on the existing monetary union. Blair and Schröder are, it would appear, no longer all too far removed from Tietmeyer.

The Market Europeans would like to preserve the European status quo because it seals the subordination of the fragmented nation-states to market-led integration. Thus, a spokesman for the Deutsche Bank can only regard the debate over the alternative "state alliance" or "federal state" as "academic": "In the context of the integration of economic zones, any distinction between civic and economic activity ultimately disappears. Indeed, effacing such a distinction is the main goal being pursued via the ongoing processes of integration."[18] From this vantage point, competition in Europe is supposed to "lift the taboo" protecting national assets like the public credit sector or state social insurance schemes, which it will then gradually liquidate. To be sure, the position of the Market Europeans rests on an assumption shared by those social-democratic partisans of the nation-state who now want to carve out a Third Way: "In the age of globalization, it is impossible to remove restrictions on state power; [globalization] ...demands above all that we reinforce the autonomous, liberal forces in civil society," namely, "people's individual initiative and sense of personal responsibility."[19] This common premise explains the turnaround in alliances. Erstwhile Euroskeptics today support Market Europeans in their defense of the European status quo, even if their motives and goals differ. They do not want to dismantle welfare policies, but prefer to redirect them toward investment in human capital—and, let us add, they do not quite wish to see all social "shock absorbers" placed in private hands.

Thus the debate between neoliberals and Eurofederalists becomes caught up with the one between defensive and offensive variants of the Third Way that is smoldering in the social-democratic camp between, let us say, Schröder and Lafontaine. This conflict touches on more than just the question of whether the EU can, by harmonizing divergent national fiscal, social, and economic policies, win back the leeway that nation-states have lost. After all, the European economic zone is still relatively insulated from global competition, thanks to a tightly woven regional network of trade relations and direct investments. The debate between Euroskeptics and Eurofedersalists hinges above all on whether the EU, despite the diversity of its member-states, with their many different peoples, languages, and cultures, can ever acquire the character of an authentic state, or must rather remain the prisoner of neocorporatist systems of negotiation.[20] Eurofederalists strive to enhance the governability of the EU, so as to make it possible to implement pan-European policies and regulations that will oblige member-states to coordinate their actions, even when the measures involved have a redistributive effect. From the Eurofederalist point of view, any extension of the EU's capacity for political action must go hand-in-hand with a broadening of the base for its legitimation.

Extending Solidarity

It is beyond dispute that the sine qua non for democratic will-formation on a pan-European scale, of the kind that can legitimate and sustain positively coordinated redistribution policies, is greater solidarity at the base. Social solidarity has hitherto been limited to the nation-state; it must be widened to embrace all citizens of the EU, so that, for example, Swedes and Portuguese will be ready to stand by one another. Only then can they reasonably be expected to consent to a roughly equal minimum wage or, more generally, to the creation of identical conditions for forging individual life plans, which, to be sure, will continue to display national features. Skeptics are doubtful; they argue that nothing exists resembling a European "people" capable of constituting a European state.[21] Peoples come into being, however, only with their state constitutions. Democracy itself is a juridically mediated form of political integration. Of course, democracy depends, in its turn, on the existence of a political culture shared by all citizens. But there is no call for defeatism, if one bears in mind that, in the nineteenth-century European states, national consciousness and social solidarity were only gradually produced, with the help of national historiography, mass communications, and universal conscription. If that artificial form of "solidarity among strangers" came about thanks to a historically momentous effort of abstraction from local dynastic consciousness to a consciousness that was national and democratic, then why should it be impossible to extend this learning process beyond national borders?

Major hurdles undoubtedly remain. A constitution will not be enough. It can only initiate the democratic processes in which it must then take root. Since agreements between member-states will remain a factor even in a politically constituted EU, a federal European state will, in any case, be of a different caliber than national federal states; it cannot simply copy their legitimation processes.[22] A European party system will come about only to the extent that the existing parties, in national arenas at first, debate the future of Europe, discovering in the process interests that transcend borders. This discussion must be synchronized throughout Europe in interlinked national public spheres; that is, the same issues must be discussed at the same time, so as to foster the emergence of a European civil society with its interest groups, nongovernmental organizations, civic initiatives, and so forth. But transnational mass media can establish a polyglot communicative context only if the national school systems see to it that Europeans have a common grounding in foreign languages. If that happens, the cultural legacies of a common European history, radiating outward from their scattered national centers, will gradually be brought back together in a common political culture.

In conclusion, a word about the prospects for world citizenship that such a process implies. With its broadened economic base, a federal European state would benefit from economies of scale that, ideally, would give it certain advantages in the arena of global competition. But, if the federative project aimed only to field another global player with the clout of the United States, it would remain particularistic, merely endowing what asylum seekers have come to know as "Fortress Europe" with a new—that is, an economic—dimension. Neoliberals might even counter by beating the drums for the "morality of the market," vaunting the "unprejudiced verdicts" of a world market that has, after all, already given the emerging economies a chance to exploit their relative cost advantages, relying on their own forces to close a gap that well-meaning development programs have proven incapable of overcoming. I need not say anything about the social costs implied by the dynamics of such development.[23] But it is hard to gainsay the argument that supranational groupings that become political entities capable of action on a global scale are morally unobjectionable only if this first step—the one leading to their creation—is followed by a second. This prompts us to ask whether the small group of actors capable of political action on the scale of the planet can, within the framework of a reformed international organization, develop the present loosely woven net of transnational regimes and then use it so as to enable a global domestic politics to emerge in the absence of a global government.[24] A politics of that kind would have to be conducted with a view to bringing about harmonization, not *Gleichschaltung*. The long-term aim would have to be the gradual elimination of the social divisions and stratification of world society without prejudice to cultural specificity.

Acknowledgments

This essay originally appeared in *Blatter für deutsche und internationale Politik*, April 1999, 425–436. The translation first appeared in *New Left Review* 235 (1999), 46–59.

Translated by G. M. Goshgarian

Notes

1. R. Münch, *Globale Dynamik—Lokale Lebenswelten* (Frankfurt: Suhrkamp, 1998).

2. R. Cox, "Economic Globalization and the Limits to Liberal Democracy," in A. McGrew, ed., *The Transformation of Democracy* (Cambridge: Polity Press, 1997), 49–72.

3. L. Brock, "Die Grenzen der Demokratie: Selbstbestimmung im Kontext des globalen Strukturwandels," in B. Kohler-Koch, ed., *Regieren in entgrenzten Räumen*, *PVS*, special issue 29, 1998, 271–292.

4. D. Held, *Democracy and the Global Order* (Stanford: Stanford University Press, 1995), 99ff.

5. M. Zürn, "Gesellschaftliche Denationalisierung und Regieren in der OECD-Welt," in Kohler-Koch, ed., *Regieren in entgrenzten Räumen*, 91–120.

6. Invoking the veto power held by all participants in intergovernmental negotiations, W. Scharpf maintains that the results of such negotiations "[find] their basis for legitimation in the rule that all participants must consent to decisions and that none will if, on balance, he would fare more poorly if he did than if the negotiations failed." W. Scharpf, "Demokratie in der transnationalen Politik," in U. Beck, ed., *Politik der Globalisierung* (Frankfurt: Suhrkamp, 1998), 237. This argument takes into account neither the derivative nor the diminished character of such legitimation, that is, neither the fact that supranational agreements are not subject to pressures for legitimation to the same extent that domestic decisions are, nor the fact that the institutionalized process of will formation at the level of the nation-state is also guided by intersubjectively recognized norms and values and does not come down to a process of pure compromise, in other words, to rational choice trade-offs between the interested parties. By the same token, the deliberative politics of citizens and their representatives cannot be reduced to the expertise of specialists. See the justification of "European Committee-ology" advanced by C. Joerges and J. Neyer, "Von intergouvernermentalem Verhandeln zur deliberativen Politik," in Kohler-Koch, ed., *Regieren in entgrenzten Räumen*, 207–234.

7. W. Streeck, ed., *Internationale Wirtschaft, nationale Demokratie* (Frankfurt: Campus, 1998), 19f.

8. J. Habermas, *Die postnationale Konstellation* (Frankfurt: Suhrkamp, 1998), 140ff.

9. Streeck, ed., *Internationale Wirtschaft*, 38.

10. A. Giddens, *The Third Way* (Cambridge: Polity Press, 1999), 100. See also J. Cohen and J. Rogers, "Can Egalitarianism Survive Internationalisation?" in Streeck, ed., *Internationale Wirtschaft*, 175–194.

11. Zukunftskommission der Friedrich-Ebert-Stiftung, ed., *Wirtschaftliche Leistungsfähigkeit, sozialer Zusammenhalt und ökologische Nachhaltigkeit* (Bonn, 1998), 225ff.

12. On this terminology, see J. Habermas, "Von pragmatischen, ethischen und moralischen Gebrauch der Vernunft," in Habermas, *Erläuterungen zur Diskursethik* (Frankfurt: Suhrkamp, 1990), 100ff.

13. T. Maak and Y. Lunau, eds., *Weltwirtschaftsethik* (Bern: P. Haupt, 1998), 24.

14. U. Thielemann, "Globale Konkurrenz, Sozialstandards und der Zwang zum Unternehmertum," in Maak and Lunau, eds., *Weltwirtschaftsethik*, 231.

15. P. Ulrich, *Integrative Wirtschaftsethik* (Bern: P. Haupt, 1997), 334.

16. E. Richter, "Demokratie und Globalisierung," in A. Klein and R. Schmalz-Bruns, eds., *Politische Beteiligung und Bürgerengagement in Deutschland* (Baden-Baden: Nomos, 1997), 173–120.

17. W. Streeck, "Vom Binnenmarkt zum Bundesstaat?" in S. Leibfried and P. Pierson, eds., *Standort Europ* (Frankfurt, 1998), 369–421.

18. R. E. Breuer, "Offene Bürgergesellschaft in der globalisierten Weltwirtschaft," *Frankfurter Allgemeine Zeitung*, 4 January 1999, p. 9.

19. Ibid.

20. C. Offe, "Demokratie und Wohlfahrtsstaat: Eine europäische Regimeform unter dem Stress der europäischen Integation," in Streeck, ed., *Internationale Wirtschaft*, 99–136.

21. D. Grimm, *Braucht Europa eine Verfassung?* (Munich: Siemens Stiftung, 1995); see also J. Habermas, *The Inclusion of the Other* (Cambridge, MA: MIT Press, 1998), 155–161.

22. K. Eder, K. U. Hellmann, and H. J. Trenz, "Regieren in Europa jenseits öffentlicher Legitimation?" in Kohler-Koch, ed., *Regieren in entgrenzten Räumen*, 321–344.

23. See the introduction and the essays in part 4 of Maak and Lunau, eds., *Weltwirtschaftsethik.*

24. Habermas, *Die postnationale Konstellation*, 156ff.

8

On Reconciling Cosmopolitan Unity and National Diversity

Thomas McCarthy

Few ideas are as important to the history of modern democracy as that of the nation as a political community. And yet, by comparison to its companion idea of political community based upon the agreement of free and equal individuals, it remained until recently a marginal concern of liberal political theory. The aftermath of decolonization and the breakup of the Soviet empire, among other things, have changed that and brought it finally to the center of theoretical attention. And once there, the deep-seated tensions in theory between nationalism and liberalism have proved to be as hard to overlook as their all too familiar tensions in practice.

Thus many liberal political theorists have taken to framing their inquiries into nationalism by asking whether there is a conception of nationhood that is compatible with basic liberal principles. Can the values of nation and culture be combined with those of freedom and equality within the basic structure of the democratic constitutional nation-state? One fault line that has attracted its share of attention divides liberal universalism from nationalist particularism. That division becomes all the more salient when the topic of cosmopolitanism comes up—as it does more and more frequently, partly in reaction to horrors perpetrated under the banner of ethnonationalism. The framing question then is whether there is a conception of nationhood that is compatible with cosmopolitanism when the latter is understood as the establishment of a basic structure of cosmopolitical justice under a global rule of law.

Immanuel Kant was among the first to understand cosmopolitanism in these terms, and his attempt to reconcile it with nationalism, most famously in his essay on "Perpetual Peace," has remained among the most influential. Kant was writing during the birth of the modern nation-state from the American and French Revolutions. Political theorists addressing these issues today can look back on a 200 year history of the nation-state and ahead to the anticipated consequences of the accelerated globalization processes now underway. The work of Jürgen Habermas is particularly interesting in this regard, for he explicitly takes up Kant's reading of history "with a cosmopolitan intent," complicates it with lessons drawn from the intervening two centuries of experience with the nation-state, and projects it into a hoped-for cosmopolitan future. In this essay, after framing the problem of reconciling nationalism and cosmopolitanism in a certain way (I), I want to take a new look at how Kant tried and failed to resolve it (II), and then to examine Habermas's recent efforts to update the Kantian project (III). In the final section (IV), I will consider some doubts about that project raised by Charles Taylor in his defense of "alternative modernities."

I

From the time of the French Revolution to the present, through successive waves of nation-state formation in the nineteenth and twentieth centuries, a distinctively modern form of political community has gradually prevailed over all competitors.[1] Within the boundaries of preexisting territorial states and through the formation of new states, amidst the disintegration of empires and the dismantling of colonialism, it has become the characteristic modern expression of shared political identity. The idea of the nation as political community was present not only at the birth of modern democracy, when "we the people" became the bearers of sovereignty, but also through the wars of national liberation and the struggles for national self-determination that shaped the twentieth century. The development of the nation-state system that now covers the globe is, of course, a complex and variegated story, whose proper telling requires extensive historical and comparative analysis. Here I am interested, however, only in the core idea of linking political communities to communities of origin. In this sense, the basic principle of nationalism, in its strictest form, demands that every nation have its own state; and the basic right of nationalism, in its strictest form, is the right of every people to political self-determination.

Taken in this strict sense, nationalism as a normative doctrine today raises specters of ethnic cleansing, forced resettlement, massive repression, and the like. Nation-states require territories within whose boundaries they have a monopoly on force. But the earth is entirely covered by already existing states, which are less than 200 in number, while the identifiable ethnic groups that might conceivably invoke the nationalist principle and the nationalist right number some 5,000.[2] Moreover, the globe is not divided into ethnically homogeneous regions that might become independent states; ethnic intermingling is almost everywhere the rule. So taking ethnonationalism as the basic principle of state formation is, in the world we now inhabit, a recipe for bloody disaster. This should be kept in mind when considering nationalism's claimed superiority as regards sensitivity to and accommodation of difference. A global mosaic of politically organized, ethnically homogeneous enclaves is about as unaccommodating, not to mention unrealistic, a scheme as could be imagined. So we have to turn to less extreme conceptions of nationalism if we want to get at the unresolved theoretical issues.

It is now generally recognized that national identities are neither natural nor prepolitical. They are socioculturally constructed— "imagined communities" as Benedict Anderson has it, or "imagined commonalities" as Max Weber had it—and they typically serve political purposes, as vehicles of emancipation or aggression, for instance, or of political unification and economic modernization. To be sure, they are usually constructed as quasi-natural, precisely as the prepolitical basis of and justification for the national political communities embracing them. Thus national consciousness typically includes a belief by members of the national community that they share some distinct subset of such "objective" features as common descent, language, culture, homeland, customs, traditions, religion, history, destiny, or the like. But these commonalities are as often fictive as real. The classical nation-states were never as homogeneous in these respects as members characteristically took them to be, and contemporary nation-states are even less so. As historians have documented, the process of nation building typically involved the work of intellectuals and writers, scholars and publicists, historians and artists using media of mass communication to forge a national consciousness and generate a common allegiance, first among the professional classes and then through them among the masses. Correspondingly, standard languages were typically not a ground but a goal of nation building processes. In short, nations were not found but created (not *ex nihilo*, of course); and they were created in response to historical contingencies and for political purposes. This is especially clear in the case of states that emerged from former colonies within territorial boundaries that cut across traditional ethnic groupings and homelands. But it is true, in varying degrees, of the classical nation-states as well.

The constructed character of national identity makes it notoriously susceptible to being instrumentalized for political purposes, good or bad. Raising national consciousness in the liberation struggles of oppressed groups usually counts as the former, fanning nationalist xenophobia for aggressive or expansive purposes as the latter. Historical sociologists and sociological historians often maintain that nation-building fulfilled essential functions in processes of modern state formation—functions of cultural and linguistic unification, for instance, or of economic and political modernization—and in particular that it was an important catalyst in the spread of republican government. Some argue, even, that for many purposes there were no functional alternatives to nationalism, and thus that it was an indispensable element in social, cultural, political, and economic modernization processes. In the same vein, theorists of contemporary politics sometimes claim that political integration in complex societies is not possible in the absence of strong national identification, that a purely "constitutional" or "civic" patriotism is no adequate substitute for loyalties rooted in culture, history, religion, or the like. This is said to be true even, or rather especially, of liberal democratic societies.

The arguments here are familiar from the recent liberal-communitarian debates in political theory. One basic issue is whether a citizenship of individual liberties and a politics of interest aggregation are a functionally and normatively adequate basis for democratic societies, or whether citizenship has rather to be tied to community and politics to common values if we are to have the solidarity and stability that democratic societies require.

Another important line of argument for the indispensability of nationalism intersects the main line of normative political theory in the modern period. There is, the argument goes, a huge gap in classical social contract theories: they provide no convincing normative delimitation of the "multitude of men" (Hobbes) or "number of men" (Locke) who are to be parties to the contract, that is, no normative account of just who must consent to the terms of association and why just them, though it appears generally to be assumed that the parties share a language and culture.[3] Nationalism claims to fill this normative-theoretical gap rather than leaving the matter, as liberal theorists in effect have, to the contingencies of history, which means in practice to shifting constellations of power. On this view, the boundaries of the nation should be the boundaries of the state.

Against these functional and normative arguments, a growing number of theorists have been arguing that the traditional nation-state system of national and international organization has outlived its usefulness, that it has become dysfunctional and thus must be superseded. The path to a postnational system is variously conceived, but in all the different scenarios the inexorable thrust of globalization plays a significant role. Globalization of capital and labor markets, of production and consumption, of communication and information, of technological and cultural flows is already posing problems that can not be resolved within the borders of individual states or with the traditional means of interstate treaties. Just as the problems that accompanied the rise of capitalism in modern Europe created a need for delocalizing law and politics which led eventually to the formation of the nation-state, the globalization of capitalism, and of everything that goes with it, is creating a growing need for denationalizing—in the sense of supranationalizing—law and politics. Many fear that if legal and political institutions do not expand to global proportions so as to keep up with the economy, we will be left with a more or less self-regulating capitalism that simply "creates a world in its own image," as national governments become less and less able to sustain the social-welfare arrangements with which they have heretofore sought to "domesticate" capitalism within their borders.[4]

In this conjuncture, the task of a political theory committed to principles of freedom and equality under the rule of law is to think beyond the present, to elaborate normative models—or, if you like, utopian projections—of a world order that could measure up to such principles, that is, in which they would no longer be institutionalized, however imperfectly, only at the national level and below. To borrow a term from Rawls, political theorists should attempt to sketch the "basic structure" of a system of cosmopolitcal justice that could serve as a point of normative orientation and guide to political practice. They should strive to overcome the deep-seated inclination to think largely within the taken-for-granted confines of the nation-state and seek to conceptualize transnational structures for guaranteeing individual rights, securing democratic accountability, and ensuring fair distribution on a global scale.

The local "inside" is now increasingly linked with the global "outside"; but it is not only this aspect of globalization that sets the idea of the ethnocultural nation-state at odds with reality. The vast movements and minglings of populations around the world have a parallel effect: the "inside" is also increasingly diverse. And there appears to be no halting this diversification short of violence, coercion, and repression. The growing heterogeneity of most populations makes any model of political community based on ethnocultural homogeneity or on forced assimilation to a hegemonic culture increasingly unsuitable as a normative model. The political-theoretical challenge it raises is, rather, to think unity in diversity, to conceptualize forms of political integration that are sensitive to, compatible with, and accommodating of varieties of difference. Reconciling national diversity with cosmopolitan unity is one component of a response.

This brings us back to the tensions between liberalism and nationalism, between voluntary membership and ascriptive membership, between citizens with legally defined basic rights and conationals with culturally defined shared features. It is clear that any attempt at reconciliation will have to involve transformation. In particular, if we are trying to conceptualize a *liberal* nationalism, in the broadest sense, then it will have to be compatible with the universal content of the basic rights of citizens under the rule of law. To be sure, these basic or "human" rights are given particular and various expressions in different constitutional traditions. But it belongs to their very meaning that they claim a universal validity transcending any particular legal system—precisely the surplus of meaning characteristic of normative or "regulative" (Kant) ideas. Liberal theorists have always known this and thus have felt obliged to explain, again and again, why it was that women, slaves, the unpropertied and uneducated, and virtually the entire non-Western world could not in practice be granted the fundamental rights that in theory belonged to "all men."[5]

If nationalism has to be transformed to be compatible with liberal universalism, what of liberal universalism? What changes must it undergo to be compatible even with a transformed nationalism? That will become clearer as we proceed, but even at the start, it is evident that it will have to accommodate somehow the cultural differences that nationalism stresses and liberalism has, until quite recently, largely ignored. For it is clear that a theory of justice that respects individuals' rights to define and pursue happiness in their own ways should, in particular, take into consideration their desires to continue living with others distinct forms of life—to go on speaking the languages, adhering to the customs, passing on the traditions, practicing the religions, and so forth, which inform who they are and who they want to be as individuals and as communities.

The formation of an independent state is by no means the only way of safeguarding the integrity of a valued form of life. In addition to antidiscrimination legal protections and voluntary cultural associations, there is a wide range of political-organizational possibilities for securing some measure of autonomy short of sovereign statehood: consociation, federal union, loose confederation, functional decentralization, devolution, special representation or veto rights, special language or land rights, and so on. Given the demographics of the planet, it appears evident that a vast array of such arrangements would be necessary even to begin to accommodate existing diversity in any cosmopolitical legal and political order. The one arrangement that would have to go is precisely the absolutely sovereign nation-state—which does not mean that the nation-state must simply disappear. For the present, it appears, any viable scheme of cosmopolitan unity will have to preserve while transforming it. To borrow a term from Hegel, the nation-state must be *aufgehoben*.

On the other hand, a liberal cosmopolitanism could not countenance granting communal rights for the sake of protecting cultures that deny individual rights. More specifically, if culturally diverse nations are the rule, then cultural pluralism has to be integral to national self-understanding. And this suggests that ethnic nationalism will have to give way increasingly to civic nationalism. The latter is, to be sure, a more abstract form of integration; but allegiance to a national community was itself already more abstract than the local ties it transcended. And, as we saw, the nation, however powerful the "we-consciousness" it generated, is not a natural but a constructed object of group loyalty. There appears to be no reason in principle, then, why it cannot itself be transformed so as to be compatible with a liberal cosmopolitanism. A look at Kant and Habermas will help us get clearer on the conceptual issues involved.

II

Kant has long been a favorite target of those opposed to abstract universalism in political theory generally and to undifferentiated cosmopolitanism in international affairs particularly.[6] And indeed his moral ideal of a kingdom of ends, as a systematic union of rational beings under laws they give to themselves, seems to warrant that characterization and that critique. But Kant's moral theory is not his political theory.[7] And a closer look at his specifically political writings, especially at his essay on "Perpetual Peace"—perhaps the single most influential discussion of cosmopolitanism by a major philosopher— shows that first and very widespread impression to be mistaken. Kant was indeed a cosmopolitan thinker; but he was also concerned to reconcile his universalistic aspirations with the diversity of national cultures, of which he had a wider knowledge than most of his contemporaries. Kant did, after all, lecture on anthropology and geography at Königsberg University for more than thirty years; he was, in fact, the first to do so. Thus it was quite in keeping with his interests when in 1785, one year after his "Idea for a Universal History with a Cosmopolitan Purpose" had appeared, he published a two-part review of Herder's "Ideas on the Philosophy of History of Mankind," that early harbinger of nationalist thinking.[8]

In his *Anthropology from a Pragmatic Point of View*, Kant defined "people" and "nation" as follows: "By the word 'people' [*Volk*] we mean a multitude of men assembled within a tract of land insofar as they comprise a whole. That multitude, or part thereof, which recognizes itself as united into a civil whole by its common descent [*Abstammung*] is called a nation [*Nation*]" (AP, 174). This mix of subjective ("recognizes itself"), objective ("common descent"), and political ("united into a civil whole") elements is not unlike that involved in the contemporary conception of the nation-state discussed in part I above. And indeed, in *The Metaphysics of Morals* Kant tells us that the term *Völkerrecht* refers to a kind of *Staatenrecht*, to the right of peoples organized as states, that is to say, to the right of nation-states.[9] There are other elements, however, having to do with race and ethnicity that clearly mark his views as belonging to a particular time and place. Thus in the *Anthropology* he goes on to characterize peoples in terms of a mix of biological and cultural factors. The inborn [*angeboren*] character of a people is a function of its racial makeup; it is "in the blood."[10] Its acquired [*erworben*] character develops out of the former through culture, especially language and religion.[11]

Human biological-cultural diversity thus belongs to the natural history of the human species, which in Kant's philosophy of history means that "nature wills" it, which for him is also to say that it is part of the providential ordering of things. More specifically, on Kant's reading of history, the separation, competition, and conflict among peoples are central ingredients in the dynamics of cultural progress. But they bring hostility and war as well, or rather as the other side of the very same developmental process. And it is here that Kant locates his reconciling project: as moral beings we must hope that "as culture grows and men gradually move towards greater agreement over their principles, [this diversity] will lead to mutual understanding and peace. And unlike that universal despotism which saps all men's energies and ends in the graveyard of freedom, this peace is created and guaranteed by an equilibrium of forces and a most vigorous rivalry" (PP, 114). To understand Kant's cosmopolitanism, we have to understand this conception of unity in difference. The main elements can be read off the lines just cited: belief in political-cultural progress and convergence; rejection of a centralized global state; retention of national difference and even national "rivalry" amidst global unity. These same elements can already be found in the conception of cosmopolitan unity advanced in "Idea for a Universal History with a Cosmopolitan Purpose" in 1784, some ten years before "Perpetual Peace." They remained more or less constant thereafter, but their relative weights and precise configuration underwent subtle changes. In a word, while a federal union of distinct peoples under a global rule of law remained the rational ideal, its distance from the real was increasingly emphasized and the more practicable goal of a loose confederation of sovereign states took center stage.

For Kant the ideal form of systematic union among rational beings with diverse, often conflicting interests is civil union under a rule of law that permits the greatest individual freedom compatible with a like freedom for all under general laws. Accordingly, "the highest task which nature has set mankind," as he puts it in "Idea for a Universal History," is that of "establishing a perfectly just civil constitution," which, by placing enforceable limits on the "continual antagonism" among men, makes it possible for the freedom of one to coexist with a like freedom for all others.[12] By the same logic, the coexistence of the freedom of one independent state with a like freedom for all others is possible only under a rule of public coercive law governing relations between them. Thus, practical reason requires not only that individuals abandon the lawless state of nature and enter into a law-governed commonwealth, but also that individual nations, in their external relations, "abandon a lawless state of savagery and enter into a federation of peoples in which every state, even the smallest, could expect to derive its security and right . . .

from a united power and the law-governed decisions of a united will" (UH, 47).

At the global level too natural rivalries and antagonisms are to be constrained by a rule of law deriving from a united will and backed by a united power. Kant is well aware of the ridicule to which earlier cosmopolitical schemes, notably those of the Abbé St. Pierre and Rousseau, were subjected, but he contends that constant war and its accompanying evils irresistibly push us in that direction. "They compel our species to discover a law of equilibrium to regulate the— in itself salutary—opposition of many states to one another, which springs from their freedom. Men are compelled to reinforce this law by introducing a system of united power, hence a cosmopolitan condition of general political security [*"einen weltbürgerlichen Zustand der öffentlichen Staatssicherheit"*].[13] This cosmopolitan condition or "perfect civil union of mankind" is the "highest purpose of nature" and the most encompassing idea of political-practical reason, for the approximate realization of which we may hope and must strive.[14]

If we move now from the "Idea for a Universal History" of 1784 to Kant's 1793 essay "On the Common Saying: 'This May Be True in Theory, But It Does Not Apply in Practice,'" the central elements of his cosmopolitan conception remain essentially the same, though his upholding of the ideal in the face of a recalcitrant reality already evinces a note, if not of desperation, at least of reservation. He repeats the claim that war and its attendant distress will eventually force people to do for reasons of self-interest what practical reason anyway prescribes, that is, "to enter into a cosmopolitan constitution [*weltbürgerliche Verfassung*]" (TP, 90). But he immediately adds that "if such a condition of universal peace is in turn even more dangerous to freedom, for, as has occurred more than once with states that have grown too large, it may lead to a most fearful despotism, distress must force men into a condition that is not a cosmopolitan commonwealth under a single ruler, but a lawful condition of federation under a commonly agreed upon international law [*Völkerrecht*]" (TP, 90).

The threat of despotism attaches, it appears, to the form of cosmopolitan unity marked by a single global state, under a single ruler, of whom all human beings are subjects. As we shall see, such a fusing or melting together [*zusammenschmelzen*] of distinct peoples is the very source of danger that Kant will later cite in "Perpetual Peace" against the idea of a universal monarchy. But whereas there it will provide grounds for espousing the very weak "substitute" of a voluntary league of nations, in this essay the alternative espoused is the still very strong idea of a federation of nation states under a rule of international law, which, he elaborates, is "backed by power" and "to which every state must submit" (TP, 92). Against the latter, Kant concedes, political realists may still object that independent states will never freely submit to such coercive laws [*Zwangsgesetzen*], and thus that the proposal for a "universal state of nations" [*allgemeinen Völkerstaat*], however fine it sounds in theory, does not apply in practice. It is just another "childish, "academic" idea.[15] Nevertheless, it is here that Kant takes his stand: "For my own part, I put my trust in the theory of what the relationship between men and states ought to be according to the principle of right." In his view, individuals and states should act in such a way "that a universal state of nations may thereby be ushered in"; accordingly, "we should thus assume that it is possible (*in praxi*), that there can be such a thing" (TP, 92).

Over the next two years, perhaps partly in reaction to the course and consequences of the French Revolution, which he followed very closely,[16] Kant shifted his emphasis in the direction of the realities of practice, endorsing in "Perpetual Peace" the more "practicable" or "achievable" [*ausführbar*] goal of a voluntary federation or league of sovereign nation states [*Völkerbund*] under an international law [*Völkerrecht*] that was *not* public coercive law backed by the united power of a universal state of nations, though he still maintained that the latter was what was called for by reason:

There is only one rational way in which states coexisting with other states can emerge from the lawless condition of pure warfare. Just like individuals, they must renounce their savage and lawless freedom, adapt themselves to public coercive laws, and thus form a state of nations (*civitas gentium*) which would necessarily continue to grow until it embraced all the peoples of the earth. But since this is not the will of nations, according to their conception of international law (so that they reject *in hypothesi* what is true *in thesi*), the positive idea of a world republic cannot be realized. If all is not to be lost, this can at best find a negative substitute in the shape of an enduring and gradually expanding federation to prevent war. The latter may check the current of man's inclination to defy the law and antagonize his fellows, although there will always be the risk of it bursting forth anew (PP, 105).

Thus, the "positive idea" of establishing a universal and lasting peace is the idea of a "world republic" the member states of which are themselves republics: a world republic of national republics. The public coercive law of this world republic would regulate external relations among states, among individuals who are citizens of different states, and among individuals and states of which they are not citizens.[17] This type of law is variously referred to by Kant as *Völkerstaatsrecht*, the right of a state of nations, and *Weltbürgerrecht*, the right of world citizens.[18] Whatever its precise form, for Kant only this type of global public law completes our emergence from the state of nature in which rights and possessions are merely "provisional" rather than "peremptory" or "conclusive" [*peremtorisch*]. Prior to its establishment, "any rights of nations and any external possessions states acquire or retain by war are merely provisional. Only in a universal union of states, analogous to that by which a people become a state, can rights come to hold conclusively and a true condition of peace come about."[19] Nevertheless, as indicated in a passage cited above, Kant concedes that in the given circumstances global public coercive law is unachievable. Not only are individual states unwilling to give up their unlimited sovereignty, but there are intrinsic difficulties in administering global justice owing to the vastness of the earth's surface and the variety of its inhabitants.

At this point in Kant's argument, many commentators head in the wrong direction by taking his admonitions against a world state in the form of a universal monarchy for a rejection of world government in any form.[20] Kant's language is occasionally less clear on this than it could be.[21] But there is overwhelming textual evidence for distinguishing his conception of a "world republic," which he consistently upholds as the most encompassing idea of political-practical reason, from the conception of a "universal monarchy" or any other form of world state that might result from one power subjugating all the others. It is the latter which he characterizes as a "soulless despotism" that would inevitably give rise to widespread resistance and ultimately lapse into anarchy" (PP, 113). For our purposes here, it is interesting to note that one basic complaint he voices against it is the *Zusammenschmeltzung* of diverse peoples.[22]

Any viable conception of global unity has to be compatible with national diversity, for "nature wills" this diversity and "uses two means to separate peoples and prevent their intermingling [*Vermischung*], the variety of languages and of religions" (PP, 113). At the same time, however, nature (or providence) also wills that the war and violence resulting from this separation be overcome by global peace. For one thing, cultural development leads to a growing agreement on basic principles and an expansion of mutual understanding (PP, 114). For another, nature unites peoples by means of their mutual self-interest, especially in the economic sphere. "For the spirit of commerce [*Handelsgeist*] sooner or later takes hold of every people and it cannot exist side by side with war. Of all the powers (or means) at the disposal of the state, the power of money is probably the most reliable; so states find themselves compelled to promote the noble cause of peace, though not from motives of morality" (PP, 114).

Kant concedes that the idea of global civil unity amidst national cultural diversity is unachievable or unworkable [*unausführbar*] in the circumstances of the time; it can at most be approximated or approached [*annähern*]. And he judges the degree of approximation possible under the given conditions to be the rather limited one of a voluntary, revocable league or federation of nations [*Völkerbund*] with the sole purpose of preserving the peace.[23] The correspondingly weak conception of international law or the law of peoples [*Völkerrecht*] he joins to it remained in central respects the predominant one well into the twentieth century, a century of global slaughter without equal. Conceding unlimited sovereignty to independent states and presenting no effective barrier to their use of arms in pursuing what they take to be their vital interests, that arrangement has proved incapable of checking the resort to violence and to the threat of violence in international affairs, incapable, that is, of fulfilling the purpose Kant intended for it. It is, in short, no longer—if it ever was—a practically adequate approximation to the idea of legal pacifism.

On the other hand, there are features even of Kant's weaker version of a peaceful world order that strike us still today as rather strong requirements, particularly the First Definitive Article, which requires that "the civil constitution of every state shall be republican" (PP, 99). On his understanding of the term, a "republican" constitution is founded on the freedom of members as human beings, their equality as subjects, and their independence as citizens.[24] It encompasses the rule of law, representative government, and the separation of powers. It expressly does not include either substantive equality[25] or universal suffrage.[26]

Thus, Kant's "practicable" scheme for global peace combines international law [*Völkerrecht: ius gentium*] that is based on a voluntary league of nations with state law [*Staats(bürger)recht: ius civitatis*] that is republican without being democratic or egalitarian. There is also a third principal component, namely cosmopolitan law [*Weltbürgerrecht: ius cosmopoliticum*], which, in the context of this more practicable scheme, is reduced to "the conditions of universal hospitality," that is, "the right of a stranger not to be treated with hostility when he arrives on someone else's territory."[27] This last, Kant maintains, is the minimum required to enable inhabitants of one society to attempt to enter into relations with those of another, and thus to foster the sorts of mutual relations among peoples that may "bring the human race nearer and nearer to a cosmopolitan constitution," that is, to a "public human right in general."[28]

This conception of cosmopolitan law is said in *The Metaphysics of Morals* to be rooted in the finitude of the earth that is our common home: "Nature has enclosed all [nations] together within determinate limits by the spherical shape of the place they live in . . . [T]hey stand in a community of possible physical interaction (*commercium*), that is, in a thoroughgoing relation of each to all the others of offering to engage in interaction [*Verkehr*] with any other, and each has right to make this attempt . . . [which,] since it concerns the possible union of all nations with a view to certain universal laws for their possible interaction, can be called cosmopolitan right (*ius cosmopoliticum*)."[29] Some of the most serious violations of the conditions of hospitality in his time, Kant repeatedly inveighs, are the conquest and colonization that mark the relations of "the civilized states of our continent" to the rest of the world.[30] Thus, while himself proposing a racial theory of ethnic difference and cultural hierarchy, Kant vigorously condemns the colonizing efforts that quite often appeal to such theories for justification!

The view of global peace advanced two years later in Kant's most systematic work of *Rechtstheorie*, part I of *The Metaphysics of Morals*, is substantially the same as that elaborated in "Perpetual Peace." Thus his tripartite division of public right in section 43 mirrors that noted in the earlier essay: *Staatsrecht, Völkerrecht, Weltbürgerrecht*, only this last is now characterized as "ineluctably" resulting from the first two, being in essence a kind of *Völkerstaatsrecht*.[31] And the internal relation among them is characterized in the strongest terms: "So if the principle of outer freedom limited by law is lacking in any one of these three possible forms of rightful condition, the framework of all the others is unavoidably undermined and must finally collapse" (MM, 89). In a word, there is no final exit from the condition of nature to the condition of right until a state of nations under the rule of cosmopolitan law is established. This last, then, is "the entire final end of the doctrine of right within the limits of reason alone" (MM, 123). Without it, the law of peoples remains merely provisional (MM, 119).

Here, too, however, Kant concedes the impracticability under present conditions of instituting a *Völkerstaatsrecht* based on a world republic and proposes to substitute a *Völkerrecht* based on a league of nations, once again restricting *Weltbürgerrecht* to the right of hospitality. "A federation of nations in accordance with the idea of an original social contract is necessary, not in order to meddle in one another's internal disagreements, but to protect against attacks from without. This alliance must, however, involve no sovereign authority (as in a civil constitution), but only an association (federation); it must be an alliance that can be renounced at any time . . ."[32] Since a "universal union of states," in which alone "right [can] come to hold conclusively and a true condition of peace come about," is an "unachievable idea," the basic principles of right require only that we strive to fashion alliances among states that more and more closely approximate it.[33] In the circumstances of late eighteenth-century Europe, the closest practicable approximation is, in Kant's view, the league of nations described above. He hastens to add, however, this concession does not absolve moral-political agents from persistently "working toward the kind of constitution that seems to us most conducive to perpetual peace, say, a republicanism of all states together and separately . . . [E]ven if the complete realization of this objective always remains a pious wish, still we are certainly not deceiving ourselves in adopting the maxim of working incessantly towards it" (MM, 123).

If Kantian cosmopolitanism is to be of service to the project of conceptual reconciliation proposed in part I, it will have to be altered in important respects. To mention only the most obvious:

1. Kant's quasi-naturalistic account of "peoples" as the prepolitical bases of political communities has to be revised in line with our heightened awareness of the historically contingent, politically motivated, and socioculturally constructed character of representations of race, ethnicity, and nationality.[34]

2. Correspondingly, Kant's understanding of nations as, at least to a considerable degree, racially, ethnically, and culturally homogeneous has to be revised to allow for the internal heterogeneity of political communities. This means not only dropping his claim that through racial and cultural differences "nature" prevents the "intermingling" [Vermischung] of peoples,[35] but also making conceptual room in his constitutional republicanism for the pluralism that has become a hallmark of democratic politics.

3. Kant's eighteenth-century understanding of republican government has to be revised to incorporate the basic democratic and social reforms achieved through political struggle in the nineteenth and twentieth centuries.

4. The Enlightenment universalism underlying Kant's construction of the cosmopolitan ideal has to be replaced by a multicultural universalism more sensitive to the dialectic of the general and the particular.

The unprecedented slaughter of the twentieth century has made a mockery even of Kant's wavering faith in the capacity of traditional international law and interstate treaties to preserve global peace. The principal theoretical alternative to these failed measures remains some form of legal pacificism, that is, of the global rule of law. Kant's own account of *Völkerstaatsrecht* and *Weltbürgerrecht* is far too sketchy to serve as anything more than a starting point for developing that alternative. In this respect, as in the others mentioned, Habermas's "discourse theory of law and democracy," which he presents as a reworking of Kant's basic approach "with the benefit of two hundred years' hindsight," can take us a few steps further in the task of conceptual reconciliation.

III

Critics typically situate Habermas's approach to law and politics at one extreme of the universalism-particularism spectrum: it is taken to be the very archetype of abstract, difference-leveling universalism. This assessment is usually arrived at in one short stroke by extrapolating from his moral universalism. But that is no less an oversimplification than was the corresponding extrapolation from Kant's moral ideal of a kingdom of ends, which, as we saw, ignored the principled differentiation between law and morality he had elaborated in *The Metaphysics of Morals*. For the past decade at least, Habermas has been similarly concerned with spelling out the differences between these two domains of "practical reason."[36] From his discourse-theoretical perspective, one of the major differences that emerges is the variety of types of reasons relevant to the legitimation of positive law. Not only moral arguments figure in legal and political discourse, but also a balancing interests and a weighing of pragmatic and of what he calls "ethical political" considerations as well. It is this last type of consideration that is most interesting for our purposes, as Habermas uses the term "ethical" here in somewhat the way Hegel used *sittlich* and *Sittlichkeit*, to represent cultures and forms of life from a normative and evaluative perspective.

Thus Habermas's discussion of "ethical-political" justifications in law and politics is, roughly speaking, a discussion of the ways in which the values, goods, and identities embedded in different cultural contexts figure into legal and political discourse. Here are two characteristic passages: "In contrast to morality, law does not regulate interaction contexts in general but serves as a medium for the self-organization of legal communities that maintain themselves in their social environments under particular historical conditions. As a result . . . laws also give expression to the particular wills of members of a particular community" (FN, 151ff.). "In justifying legal norms we must use the entire breadth of practical reason. However, these further [i.e., other than moral, TMc] reasons have a relative validity, one that depends on the context . . . The corresponding reasons count as valid relative to the historical, culturally molded identity of the legal community, and hence relative to the value orientations, goals, and interest positions of its members . . . [T]he facticity of the existing context cannot be eliminated" (FN, 156).

It is not only statutory law that is pervaded with particularity in these respects: constitutional undertakings to spell out the basic principles of government and the basic rights of citizens ineluctably also express the particular cultural backgrounds and historical circumstances of founding generations. Though Habermas expressly regards "the system of basic rights" as a normative (or "regulative") idea that should guide every legitimate constitution-framing process (FN, chapter 3), he is equally clear that any actually existing system of rights is, and can only be, a situated interpretation of that idea. "The system of rights is not given to the framers of a constitution in advance as a natural law. These rights first enter into consciousness in a particular constitutional interpretation. . . . No one can credit herself with access to the system of rights in the singular, independent of the interpretations she already has historically available. 'The' system of rights does not exist in transcendental purity" (FN, 128ff.). Surveying the history of democratic constitutional law over the past two centuries, the theorist can at most attempt a critical, systematic reconstruction of the basic intuitions underlying it. Of course, to accommodate even the existing range of legitimate variation, any such reconstruction will of necessity be highly abstract, as is indeed the case with Habermas's own.

Getting clear about the content of basic constitutional norms is only the beginning of the story, for "every constitution is a living project that can endure only as an ongoing interpretation continually carried forth at all levels of the production of law" (FN, 129). Thus, historically and culturally situated interpretation should not be seen as an unfortunate but unavoidable fall from transcendental grace, but as the very medium for developing "constitutional projects," which are by their very nature always unfinished and ongoing. "[T]he constitutional state does not represent a finished structure but a delicate and sensitive—above all fallible and revisable—enterprise, whose purpose is to realize the system of rights anew in changing circumstances, that is, to interpret the system of rights better, to institutionalize it more appropriately, and to draw out its contents more radically" (FN, 384).

Even these few sketchy remarks on Habermas's legal and political theory should make clear that for him the rule of law in the democratic constitutional state is not a fixed essence but an idea that has to be actualized in and through being variously interpreted and embodied in historically and culturally distinct constitutional projects. This suggests that there should be space in his conception of cosmopolitical justice for distinct political cultures and indeed there is. His version of civic patriotism, which he calls "constitutional patriotism," is construed broadly as allegiance to a particular constitutional tradition, that is, to a particular, ongoing, historical project of creating and renewing an association of free and equal citizens under the rule of laws they make for themselves. Each democratically constituted nation of citizens will understand and carry out that project from perspectives opened by its own traditions and circumstances. If that self-understanding is itself to include space for a pluralism of world-views and forms of life, as Habermas insists it must, then constitutional patriotism cannot be wedded to monocultural or hegemonic-cultural interpretations of basic rights and principles to the exclusion, repression, or marginalization of minority-cultural perspectives.[37]

In a move reminiscent of Rawls's introduction of the idea of an "overlapping consensus" on basic political values amidst a persistent pluralism of "comprehensive doctrines" about the meaning and value of human life, Habermas, employing sociological terminology, proposes a "decoupling" of political integration from the various forms of subgroup and subcultural integration among the population of a democratic constitutional state. "In multicultural societies . . . coexistence with equal rights for these forms of life requires the mutual recognition of the different cultural memberships: all persons must also be recognized as members of ethical communities integrated around different conceptions of the good. Hence the ethical integration of groups and subcultures with their own collective identities must be uncoupled from the abstract political integration that includes all citizens equally" (SR, 224ff.).

Rawls's proposal has given rise to vociferous debate, as have other proposals for conceptualizing legal-political neutrality in increasingly multicultural societies. Habermas can hardly hope to avoid such controversies. If his approach is to have a chance of surviving them, he will, to start with, have to understand "decoupling" in process terms, as an ongoing accomplishment of something that is never fully realized. As Charles Taylor, Will Kymlicka, and others have convincingly argued, there can be no culturally neutral system of law and politics, no privatization of culture analogous to the privatization of religion, and thus no strict separation of culture and state. Official languages, school curricula, national holidays, and the like are only the most obvious expressions of a public culture that is never perfectly neutral with respect to the diverse cultural backgrounds of members. And as we saw, Habermas himself maintains that political goals, policies, and programs are inevitably permeated by cultural values and goods, and that putting them into effect just as inevitably has cultural consequences. This suggests that "decoupling" may be the wrong notion for what we want here.

If we understand the core of a constitutional tradition dynamically and dialogically as an ongoing, legally institutionalized conversation about basic rights and principles, procedures and practices, values and institutions, then we can allow for a conflict of interpretations about them and for a multiplicity of situated perspectives upon them. Insofar as these interpretations purport to be of the same constitutional tradition, and insofar as their proponents are and want to remain members of the same political community, the ongoing accomplishment of a working consensus on fundamental legal and political norms appears to be a basic requirement of public discourse in official and unofficial public spheres. A central element of such a working consensus would be sufficiently widespread agreement about the institutions and procedures through which persistent reasonable disagreements may be legitimately settled, at least for the time being.

This is, in fact, close to the conception that Habermas actually defends. "The political integration of citizens ensures loyalty to the common political culture. The latter is rooted in an interpretation of constitutional principles from the perspective of the nation's historical experience. To this extent, that interpretation cannot be ethically neutral. Perhaps one would do better to speak of a common horizon of interpretation within which current issues give rise to public debates about the citizens' self-understanding. . . . But the debates are always about the best interpretation of the same constitutional rights and principles. These form the fixed point of reference for any constitutional patriotism . . ." (SR, 225). Even this common horizon of interpretation is in flux, however, as it too reflects participants' situated understandings, which are themselves continually shifting.

Habermas remarks on this in connection with immigration. In his view, while it is not legitimate for a democratic constitutional state to require "ethical-cultural integration" of immigrants, that is to say, assimilation to the dominant culture in the broad sense, it is, he maintains, legitimate to require political integration, that is, assent to the principles of the constitution within the scope of interpretation set by the political culture of the country (SR, 228). But he immediately concedes that the latter is itself subject to contestation and alteration from the new perspectives brought to the political public sphere through immigration. "[T]he legitimately asserted identity of the political community will by no means be preserved from alterations *indefinitely* in the wake of waves of immigration. Because immigrants cannot be compelled to surrender their own traditions, as other forms of life become established the horizon within which citizens henceforth interpret their common constitutional principles may also expand. . . . [A] change in the cultural composition of the active citizenry changes the context to which the ethical-political self-understanding of the nation as a whole refers" (SR, 229).

Despite this recognition of the "ethical permeation" of law and politics at every level, Habermas continues to speak of the "neutrality" of the law vis-à-vis internal ethical differentiations. Like "decou-pling," "neutrality" is, in my view, not the best choice of terminology for what is at issue, which is rather impartiality or fairness in the sense of equality of respect, treatment, and opportunity to participate in the political process. What Habermas is concerned to preclude, above all, is that a majority culture "usurp state prerogatives at the expense of the equal rights of other cultural forms of life" (SR, 225). And that case would, I think, better be made by extending to cul-tural membership the types of arguments historically advanced to address systematic inequalities of social position.

In any case, it is evident that Habermas's conception of a multi-plicity of political-cultural realizations of the "same" system of rights is already sketched from a cosmopolitan point of view akin to Kant's. For Kant, the cosmopolitan civil condition, as a regulative idea, was characterized by a multiplicity of republics under a rule of law reg-ulating relations among them and guaranteeing the rights of indi-viduals as world citizens. Habermas's version of cosmopolitanism may be read as updating this idea, first, to take account of the internal relation between the rule of law and democracy—so that Kant's republics become democratic constitutional states—and, second, as we saw, to make room for an irreducible plurality of forms of life. But he also wants, third, to build into his version a strong egalitar-ian component—so that the democratic constitutional project is understood as that of realizing an association of free and equal citi-zens under the rule of laws they can all reasonably consent to. There is, as we know, an unavoidable dialectic of *de jure* and *de facto* legal and substantive equality that has played itself through successive waves of critical social and political theory. Class, gender, race, eth-nicity, sexuality, and the like mark respects in which existing forms of equality under law have been revealed to sanction gross inequali-ties in life circumstances and positions of power.

Habermas's contribution to this ongoing discussion turns on his account of the internal relation between "private and public auton-omy," or, to put it another way, on his attempt to connect internally the basic values of liberalism individualism and civic republicanism. Against a purely liberal-individualist conception of equal rights, he argues that "in the final analysis, private legal persons cannot even attain the enjoyment of equal individual liberties unless they themselves, by jointly exercising their autonomy as citizens, arrive at a clear understanding about what interests and criteria are justified and in what respects equal things will be treated equally and unequal things unequally in any particular case" (SR, 208).

Understood in this way, the ongoing project of realizing a system of equal rights must be sensitive to any systematic causes of substantive inequality. And that, according to Habermas, requires a democratic politics, for there is no other nonpaternalistic way of deciding what the prerequisites are for the equal opportunity actually to exercise legally granted rights. In other words, the basic liberal ideas of equal respect, equal consideration, equal treatment, and the like cannot be specified in the abstract, once and for all, but only concretely, in the ongoing discourses of democratic public life. "It must therefore be decided from case to case whether and in which respects factual (or material) equality is required for the legal equality of citizens who are both privately and publicly autonomous. The proceduralist paradigm gives normative emphasis precisely to the double reference that the relation between legal and factual equality has to private and public autonomy. And it privileges all the arenas where disputes over the essentially contestable criteria of equal treatment must be discursively carried out" (FN, 415).

In shifting from the national to the cosmopolitan perspective, it is impossible to overlook the relative paucity of transnational arenas of this type. Insisting, as Habermas does, on the internal connection between individual rights and democratic politics implies that there could be no adequate institutionalization of human rights on a global scale without a corresponding institutionalization of transnational forms of democratic participation and accountability. Inasmuch as individual liberties, democratic procedures, and redistributive mechanisms are interdependent aspects of cosmopolitical justice, as he understands it, no one can be adequately realized without the others. This, of course, renders his cosmopolitan ideal more ambitious in theory and more difficult in practice than Kant's. And it makes all the more palpable the existing gap between a political integration that is largely restricted to the national level and an economic integration that is increasingly global. If that gap is not closed, there is a danger that the structure of mass-democratic, welfare-state integration that has predominated at the national level since World War II will itself disintegrate; for the constellation of individual freedom, democratic government, and social security that generally sustains it is being increasingly undermined by processes and problems to which the individual nation state can no longer adequately respond. In Habermas's phrase, "Under the conditions of a globalized economy, 'Keynesianism in one country' no longer functions."[38]

In addition to the daunting practical problems that attend the establishment of a basic structure of cosmopolitical justice as Habermas conceives it, there are a number of important theoretical issues his conception raises, of which I shall mention only the following:

1. Habermas's conception of civil union amidst cultural diversity takes "constitutional patriotism" to be the political-cultural glue holding multicultural polities together. This obviously raises feasibility questions as to whether allegiance to legal-political institutions, practices, ideas, values, traditions, and the like can function as the core of social integration in modern societies, whether it can provide sufficient "glue" to keep together the socially differentiated, culturally heterogeneous, and ideologically fragmented populations that characterize them. But it also raises conceptual questions concerning the very idea of "decoupling" a shared civic culture from culture(s) more broadly. I have already touched upon some of them above and will here add only the following consideration. Habermas's discussion of political-cultural neutrality (or impartiality) vis-à-vis a multiplicity of subcultures tends to focus on the contrast of civic with ethnic culture, for one of his chief aims is to disentangle state from nation. Other aspects of the politics-culture nexus tend to be neglected, at least in the context of this discussion. In *The Structural Transformation of the Public Sphere* and *The Theory of Communicative Action,* however, some of these other aspects figured prominently.[39]

There, the interpenetration of public-political and public-cultural spheres was an important theme: the analytic distinctions between them did not occlude their real interconnections. In particular, the powerful connections of political culture to popular culture, which increasingly means mass-mediated culture, was identified as a key issue for contemporary democratic theory and practice. Supposing that mass-mediated popular culture is a permanent feature of modern society, what implications does that have for shaping and sustaining a sense of national belonging? How is this likely to be affected by the transnationalization of the culture industry? To what extent and in what ways is political culture transmitted and political integration achieved in and through mass-mediated popular culture? And if the answers are "considerably" and "many," what are the consequences for Habermas's distinction between assimilating to a particular political culture and assimilating to a hegemonic national culture?

2. Similar questions can be posed at the global level as well as questions peculiar to it. Habermas's cosmopolitan scheme turns on the idea of realizing the "same" system of rights in a diversity of political-cultural settings, and that immediately raises issues concerning the transcultural notion of rights invoked here, the nature of their transcultural justification, the sense in which the "same" rights can be said to animate the rather different political-cultural traditions that embody them, and so on. In brief, how could a transnational legal-political consensus regarding the basic structure of cosmopolitcal justice be achieved across the wide range of political-cultural diversity?

3. To deal with this issue, Rawls introduces the idea of an "overlapping consensus" on a law of peoples among political societies marked by widely different political cultures—liberal and nonliberal, democratic and nondemocratic, egalitarian and hierarchical, secular and religious.[40] Habermas's cosmopolitan ideal does not allow for the same broad scope of variation among political cultures. He defends a more "comprehensive" version of a rights-based theory of justice. This has the advantage of reducing the need for citizens to develop the starkly split political/nonpolitical mentalities that Rawls's scheme requires. But it makes cosmopolitan justice turn on institutionalizing at a global level a version of the same system of rights that is variously institutionalized in national constitutional traditions. Thus it

requires a far greater degree of convergence among political cultures than does Rawls's scheme: for cosmopolitan constitutionalism to be fully realized, all subglobal political systems would themselves have to become rights-based. Nationally, as well as sub-, supra-, and transnationally, what Kant called "civil union" would comprise a diversity of historically and culturally situated projects of realizing the same system of basic human rights. Kant's world republic of national republics is reenvisioned as a global constitutional union of constitutional democracies. What warrants this stress on human rights in connection with cosmopolitanism?

4. Habermas, like Kant, is committed to some form of at least legal- and political-cultural convergence, such that "as culture grows and men generally move toward greater agreement over their principles, they lead to mutual understanding and peace."[41] In *Communication and the Evolution of Society* and *The Theory of Communicative Action* Habermas propounds the broader account of cultural and societal development as "rationalization" that underlies this political-theoretical commitment.[42] But in the present context, he argues simply that the conditions of modernity leave individual states with no other practicable option but to modernize their relations both internally and externally. This is, of course, a disputable claim, even if we restrict it's ambit to the legal-political domain. Couldn't we conceive of "alternative modernities"? Charles Taylor thinks so; and in the final section I want to air some of the issues raised here by examining his instructive differences with Habermas on that question.

IV

As Habermas is well aware, "the general validity, content, and ranking of human rights are as contested as ever. Indeed, the human rights discourse that has been argued on normative terms is plagued by the fundamental doubt about whether the form of legitimation that has arisen in the West can also hold up as plausible within the frameworks of other cultures."[43] The liberation struggles of the past 150 years, especially of the last few decades, have again and again revealed the ideological functions that established understandings of human rights have served. That much is clear. But is the meaning of human rights exhausted by such ideological functions? Or is there a normative surplus of meaning that can be rescued by critically rethinking them and offering alternative accounts of their practical implications in given circumstances? One argument that speaks for the latter option is that many of the most telling critiques of established rights regimes have themselves been mounted precisely as critical rights discourses of various sorts. In the contemporary world social, political, and cultural criticism would be severely incapacitated if such discourses were unavailable.

In any case, rethinking human rights is the route Habermas chooses, not only for normative but also for historical and sociological reasons:

> My working hypothesis is that [human rights] standards stem less from the particular cultural background of Western civilization than from the attempt to answer specific challenges posed by a social modernity that has in the meantime covered the globe. Whether we evaluate this modern starting point one way or another, it confronts us today with a fact that leaves us no choice and thus neither requires, nor is capable of, a retrospective justification. The contest over the adequate interpretation of human rights has to do not with the desirability of the "modern condition" but with an interpretation of human rights that does justice to the modern world from the viewpoints of other cultures as well as our own. (HR, 205)

To the obvious question of whether there could be such an interpretation, one can at present respond only that that remains to be seen. Writing expressly as "a Western participant in a cross-cultural discussion of human rights," Habermas has tried to rethink some of the aspects of the Western rights tradition that have proved most objectionable to non-Western participants. In that spirit, he has drawn upon his theory of communicative action to denaturalize and deindividualize the notion of rights and to disentangle it from the matrix of possessive individualism in which it has been ensnarled since Locke.[44]

Further, through accentuating elements of the republican tradition of democratic thought, he has sought to restore the balance between individual and community and to resist the liberal displacement of the search for the common good by the aggregation of individual interests. Together with his attention to the inequities produced by uncontrolled market processes and his concern to accommodate cultural diversity, these changes certainly present a version of human rights less starkly at odds with traditionally "communitarian" styles of thought. But the differences that remain are considerable. Though human rights are viewed as socially constituted, they are still borne by individual legal persons; and though rights-bearing subjects are seen as socioculturally embedded, personal and political autonomy retain their normative status. Moreover, the "decoupling" of political integration from overarching views of the meaning and value of human life remains a basic requirement. For many, such differences would be sufficient to make a conception of human rights incorporating them unacceptable.

This consideration serves as the starting point of Charles Taylor's recent reflections on the possibility of "a world consensus on human rights."[45] His line of reasoning is particularly interesting in our present context because he agrees with Habermas about having to start from the fact of global modernity and about the need that creates for agreement on norms of coexistence across different cultural traditions; but he disagrees with him on the type of agreement we should expect. Examining their differences will allow us to bring the issue of transcultural human rights into somewhat sharper focus and to connect it with another question, namely the extent to which there can be "functional equivalents" for modern law and thus "alternative modernities" in legal and political culture.

Like Habermas, Taylor regards at least some aspects of modernity as irresistible. "From one point of view, modernity is like a wave, flowing over and engulfing one traditional culture after another. If we understand by modernity, inter alia, the developments discussed above—the emergence of a market-industrial economy, of a bureaucratically organized state, of modes of popular rule—then its progress is, indeed, wavelike. The first two changes, if not the third, are in a sense irresistible. Whoever fails to take them or some good functional equivalent on will fall so far behind in the power stakes as to be taken over and forced to undergo these changes anyway . . . [They] confer tremendous power on the societies adopting them" (NM, 43ff.). But while these sorts of institutional changes are unavoidable, their cultural accompaniments in the West are not.

Some alterations or others of traditional cultures will be necessary, but there is a good deal more latitude here than with economic and administrative structures. "[A] successful transition involves a people finding resources in their traditional culture to take on the new practices. In this sense modernity is not a single wave. It would be better to speak of alternative modernities, as the cultures that emerge in the world to carry the institutional changes turn out to differ in important ways from each other . . . What they are looking for is a creative adaptation, drawing on the cultural resources of their tradition, . . . [which] by definition has to be different from culture to culture" (NM, 44).

A crucial question for our purposes is where modern law, with its conception of basic human rights, belongs. Taylor assigns it an ambivalent position, partly institutional, partly cultural, by distinguishing between norms of action and their justifications. It is only with the former that we can reasonably expect convergence; the latter may and should vary with alternative modernities. This move enables him to adopt a position on human rights that, while appealing to Rawls's notion of overlapping consensus, is in some respects more universalistic than the one Rawls himself adopts in "The Law of Peoples." Taylor writes:

> What would it mean to come to a genuine, unforced international consensus on human rights? I suppose it would be something like what John Rawls describes in his *Political Liberalism* as an "overlapping consensus." That is, different groups, countries, religious communities, civilizations, while holding incompatible fundamental views on theology, metaphysics, human nature, and so on, would come to agreement on certain norms that ought to govern human behavior. Each would have its own way of justifying this from out of its profound background conception. We would agree on the norms, while disagreeing on why they were the right norms. And we would be content to live in this consensus, undisturbed by the differences of profound underlying belief. (WC, 15)

Taylor then goes on to draw a further distinction between norms of action and the "legal forms" in which they are inscribed, and assigns the latter to the variable part of modernity as well. What this means in connection with human rights is that neither "rights talk" nor "rights forms" are necessary accompaniments of a modern economy and state.

As to the talk, Taylor notes that the language of rights has its roots in Western culture; although the norms expressed in it do turn up in other cultures, they are not expressed in rights language; nor are the justifications offered for them based in views of humans and societies that privilege individual liberty and legitimation by consent. As to the forms, the Western rights tradition ensures immunities and liberties in the peculiar form of "subjective rights," which not only reverses the traditional ethical priority of duties over rights but also understands the latter as somehow possessed by individuals. This understanding is itself embedded in the philosophical justifications mentioned above. So Western legal philosophy and Western legal forms are tightly interconnected; but according to Taylor, neither is inextricably tied to the basic norms that are expressed and inscribed in them. Hence, while some of the norms are integral to modernity, their philosophical justifications and institutional forms may vary from culture to culture.

Thus, the inquiry into the possibility of a world consensus on human rights can now be pointed in a specific direction: "what variations can we imagine in philosophical justifications or in legal forms that would still be compatible with meaningful universal consensus on what really matters to us, the enforceable norms?" (WC, 18). What Taylor hopes to encounter along this route is "a convergence on certain norms of action, however they may be entrenched in law," together with "a profound sense of difference, of unfamiliarity, in the ideals, the notions of human excellence, the rhetorical tropes and reference points by which these norms have become objects of deep agreement for us" (WC, 20). Further along the same path he sees "a process of mutual learning," leading to a "fusion of horizons" through which "the moral universe of the other becomes less strange" (WC, 20).

This adaptation of Rawls's idea of an overlapping consensus stands or falls with the independent variability of legal norms, forms, and justifications. If it turned out that what is required by modern economies and modern states are not only the norms but the forms, that is, certain ways of entrenching the norms in law, the range of alternative modernities would be more constrained than Taylor takes it to be. That is precisely what Habermas maintains to be the case.

One of the central sociological lines of argument in *Between Facts and Norms* is that modern law must have most of the formal properties it has to fulfill the functions it fulfills: there are no functional alternatives to its formality, positivity, reflexivity, individuality, actionability and the like.

The fact that modern law is based upon individual rights and liberties releases legal persons from moral obligations in certain spheres of action and gives them latitude, within legally defined limits, to act upon their own choices free from interference by the state or by third parties—as is required in decentralized market societies. If these rights and liberties are to have the protection of the law, they must be connected with actionable claims, such that subjects who consider their rights to have been violated may have recourse to legal remedies. At the same time, as membership in the legal communities of diverse modern societies can less and less be defined by gender, race, religion, ethnicity, and the like, it comes to be more and more abstractly defined by the equal rights and responsibilities of citizens as legal subjects.

The fact that positive law issues from the changeable decisions of a legislator loosens its ties with traditional morality and makes it suitable as a means of organizing and steering complex modern societies. This requires that the enactment, administration, and application of the law themselves be legally institutionalized; law becomes reflexive. And since modern law, as a positive, reflexive, and therefore fungible "steering medium," can no longer be legitimated solely by appeal to inherited beliefs and practices, there is a need for new forms of legitimation. That need is compounded by the facts that cultural pluralism limits the authority of any one tradition and that rights-based conceptions of citizenship increase the pressure for political participation. In the long run, it is not clear that there are functional alternatives to democratic forms of popular rule in modern societies. One could go on in this vein. The general line of argument is that the functions and forms of modern law are tailored to one another. Because no contemporary society, whatever its cultural traditions, can do without the former, none can do without some version of the latter.

As Habermas notes: "the decisive alternatives lie not at the cultural but at the socioeconomic level. . . . [T]he question is not whether human rights, as part of an individualistic legal order, are compatible with the transmission of one's own culture. Rather, the question is whether traditional forms of political and societal integration can be reasserted against, or must instead be adapted to, global economic modernization" (HR, 207–208). If the latter proves to be the case, then we would expect the transition to modernity to involve cultural changes more extensive than those Taylor envisages, for, as he himself remarks, legal form and legal culture are closely intertwined. To the extent that individuals are guaranteed spheres of choice free from collectively binding beliefs and values, that citizenship qualifications are made independent of religious profession or cultural membership, that legislation is legitimated by its democratic provenance, and so forth, to that extent legal and political culture is being differentiated from traditional world-views and forms of life. What further cultural changes are likely to be associated with that differentiation and its consequences is a disputed question.

Taylor is right, I think, to pose the question of alternative modernities in the way he does: given that some degree of convergence in economic, governmental, and legal institutions and practices appear to be an unavoidable feature of a globalized modernity, what kinds and degrees of divergence remain possible and desirable? In particular, how much room do such modernizing tendencies leave for deep cultural differences? Taylor is also right, in my view, to emphasize that different starting points for the transition to modernity are likely to lead to different outcomes, and thus that new forms of modern society are likely to evince new forms of difference. This is already true of European modernity: Swedish society is not the same as French or Italian society, let alone American society. And yet they are too much the same to satisfy Taylor's interest in alternative modernities, for he envisions much broader and deeper differences in ideas and beliefs, outlooks and attitudes, values and identities, institutions, and practices.

Above all, Taylor is interested in the differences among largely implicit, embodied, cultural understandings of self, society, nature, and the good. Thus, what he is most concerned to refute is the claim that that there is only one viable modern constellation of such background understandings, the one that came to dominate in the West, which he understands as the claim that modern cultures can be expected sooner or later to share atomistic-individualistic understandings of self, instrumentalist conceptions of agency, contractualist understandings of society, the fact-value split, naturalism, scientism, secularism, and so on.[46] And what he is most concerned to defend is the possibility and desirability of alternative spiritual and moral ideals, visions of the good, and forms of self-identification. That is to say, what moves him is resistance to the idea that modernity will force all cultures to become like ours.

To the question of how much and what kinds of difference we have good empirical and theoretical reasons to expect, there is clearly no generally accepted answer. But one might well conjecture that it is more than most modernization theorists have predicted but less than Taylor hopes for. He concedes that market economies and bureaucratic states are inescapable features of modern societies, and that with them come certain legal norms and spheres of instrumental action as well as increased industrialization, mobility, and urbanization. He also mentions science and technology as something all modern societies have to take on as well as general education and mass literacy. We might add to these the concomitant legal forms I mentioned above together with the legal cultures that support them.

One might further add a host of changes that Taylor presumably would also regard as irresistible for modern societies: the decline of the agricultural mode of life that has defined most of humanity for much of our recorded history; the functional differentiation and specialization of occupational and professional life; a diversity of lifestyles, outlooks, and attitudes; a pluralism of belief systems, value commitments, and forms of personal and group identity; a steady growth of knowledge understood as fallible and susceptible to criticism and revision; the dissolution of patriarchal, racist, and ethnocentric stereotyping and role-casting, as of all other "natural," "God-given," or time-honored hierarchies of that sort; the inclusion, as equals, of all inhabitants of a territory in its legal and political community; the spread of mass media and of mass-mediated popular culture; the existence of public political spheres that allow for open exchange and debate; and, of course, an ever-deeper immersion in transnational flows of capital, commodities, technology, information, communication, and culture. One could go on, but these few remarks are enough to suggest that the scope of deep divergence is somewhat more constricted than Taylor lets on, especially if we take into account the very dense internal relations and causal connections between the aforementioned changes and the cultural elements, particularly the background understandings, that Taylor sometimes appears to regard as swinging free of them.

These considerations are not meant to detract from the legitimacy or significance of Taylor's concern with identifying possibilities of divergence within convergence. Nor are they intended to controvert his claim that the extent of divergence can and likely will be greater than that countenanced in most classical and contemporary theories of modernization. And they do not profess to provide a theoretical argument for the superficiality or marginality of the differences, as compared to the similarities, among possible alternative modernities. In a word, their main purpose is not the negative one of placing a priori limits on societal and cultural variation but the positive one of showing that the idea of a global rule of law is not as hopelessly impracticable as it might appear if we attended only to cultural differences. The degree to which there is a credible case for different modern societies coming together appears to me to be sufficient to ground a "rational hope," as Kant would say, for the degree of legal- and political-cultural convergence required for some form of transnational agreement on what Habermas calls "the basic system of human rights."

How much or how little cultural convergence of other sorts will accompany it is an open question. I do think, however, that Taylor tends to overestimate the extent to which cultural differences are likely to survive societal change. To mention just one basic dimension of change: the implicit, embodied, background understandings of gender identity, difference, roles, relations, and hierarchy characteristic of traditional (and, of course, modern) patriarchal cultures are, in the long run, incompatible with the changes in legal and political culture mentioned above. Moreover, as any anthropologist or sociologist can attest, significant changes in this dimension of cultural self-understanding inevitably bring with it significant changes in any number of others. And though the new forms of gender relations that develop are not likely to be the same from culture to culture, insofar as they are tied to legal and political equality they will likely be much more similar than they have been.[47]

Spiritual descendents of Herder might see the sorts of cultural convergence I have described as tragic loss. Spiritual descendents of Kant will see some of them at least as signaling the "move toward greater agreement on principles ... [that] leads to mutual understanding and peace," of which he wrote at the birth of the modern era.

Notes

1. Among the works I have found helpful on the points raised in this section are: Benedict Anderson, *Imagined Communities* (London: Verso, 1983); Ernest Gellner, *Nations and Nationalism* (Ithaca: Cornell University Press, 1983); Liah Greenfeld, *Nationalism: Five Roads to Modernity* (Cambridge: Harvard University Press, 1992); Jürgen Habermas, *The Inclusion of the Other*, C. Cronin and P. De Greiff, eds. (Cambridge: MIT Press, 1998); E. J. Hobsbawm, *Nations and Nationalism since 1780* (Cambridge: Cambridge University Press, 1990); J. Hutchinson and A. D. Smith, eds., *Nationalism* (Oxford: Oxford University Press, 1994); R. McKim and J. McMahon, eds., *The Morality of Nationalism* (Oxford: Oxford University Press, 1997); David Miller, *On Nationality* (Oxford: Oxford University Press, 1995); and Yael Tamir, *Liberal Nationalism* (Princeton: Princeton University Press, 1993).

2. I take these estimates from Will Kymlicka, *Multicultural Citizenship* (Oxford: Oxford University Press, 1995), 1. He notes his own sources for them on 196, n.1.

3. This theoretical gap is the subject of Vernon Van Dyke's "The Individual, the State, and Ethnic Communities," in W. Kymlicka, ed., *The Rights of Minority Cultures* (Oxford: Oxford University Press, 1995), 31–56. As Van Dyke notes, there are important exceptions within the tradition of liberal political theory, for instance John Stuart Mill, who held that the boundaries of the state and of the nation should in general coincide (35).

4. This is, for instance, a chief concern of Eric Hobsbawm in his history of the "short twentieth century," *The Age of Extremes* (New York: Vintage, 1996), and of Habermas in *The Inclusion of the Other*.

5. See the interesting discussion of this in Charles W. Mills, *The Racial Contract* (Ithaca: Cornell University Press, 1997).

6. For this account of Kant's views on cosmopolitanism and nationalism I will be drawing on the following works [with bracketed abbreviations for citations]: (1784)

On Reconciling Cosmopolitan Unity and National Diversity

"Idea for a Universal History with a Cosmopolitan Purpose" [UH], in H. Reiss, ed., *Kant: Political Writings*, trans. H. B. Nisbet (Cambridge: Cambridge University Press, 1991), 41–53; (1793) "On the Common Saying: 'This May Be True in Theory, but It Does Not Apply in Practice" [TP], in Reiss, ed., *Kant: Political Writings*, 61–92; (1795) "Perpetual Peace: A Philosophical Sketch" [PP], in Reiss, ed., *Kant: Political Writings*, 93–130; (1797) *The Metaphysics of Morals* [MM], ed. and trans. M. Gregor (Cambridge: Cambridge University Press, 1966); (1797) *Anthropology from a Pragmatic Point of View* [AP], trans. M. Gregor (The Hague: Martinus Nijhoff, 1974). I will alter the translations, usually without making special note of the fact, when that is required for consistency or transparency.

7. Their distinctness is his rationale for separating the *Rechtslehre* from the *Tugendlehre* in *The Metaphysics of Morals*.

8. "Reviews of Herder's *Ideas on the Philosophy of History of Mankind*," in Reiss, ed., *Kant: Political Writings*, 201–220.

9. MM, 114. See also PP, 102, where the discussion of *Völkerrecht* in the Second Definitive Article is said to apply to *"Völker als Staaten."*

10. AP, 174, 184. For a critical account of Kant's unfortunate views on race, see Emmanuel Chukwudi Eze, "The Color of Reason: The Idea of 'Race' in Kant's Anthropology," in Eze, ed., *Postcolonial African Philosophy* (Oxford: Blackwell, 1997), 103–140. Eze makes a convincing case for the significance of race in Kant's thinking about human nature, culture, and history as well as for the claim that Kant constructed one of the more elaborate theories of race and philosophical justifications of racial hierarchy of his time. His argument for the claim that Kant's racial theories are transcendentally grounded and thus are inseparable from his transcendental philosophy and his humanist project more generally is, in my view, less conclusive.

11. AP, 174f. and PP, 113f. The relative influence of biology, i.e., race, and of culture is different for different peoples; see AP, 176ff.

12. UH, 45f. Kant immediately concedes that "a perfect solution is impossible," for, as he famously puts it, "Nothing straight can be constructed from such crooked timber as that which man is made of." But we can and must continually strive to "approximate to this idea" (UH, 46f.).

13. UH, 49. The term rendered as "cosmopolitan," *weltbürgerlichen*, will later be used to designate a specific type of transnational law. In this 1784 essay the institutional form of the "cosmopolitan condition" is characterized as a "federation of peoples" *[Völkerbund]*, which clearly refers here to a federal union with a "united power." As we shall see, in the 1790s the corresponding institutional form is designated as a *Völkerstaat* or "state of nations," while *Völkerbund* is reserved for the more "practicable" arrangement of a voluntary and revocable league of nations.

14. UH, 51. Note that the cosmopolitan—*weltbürgerliche*—condition is the civil—*bürgerliche*—union of the *Welt*, i.e., of humanity.

15. TP, 92. Kant's use of the term *Zwangsgesetzen* shows that the federation he has in mind is not the loose, voluntary federation he later proposes in "Perpetual Peace." The same thing is indicated by his use of *Völkerstaat* to characterize it: the federation of peoples envisaged here is a state of nations under international laws backed by the state.

16. The Treaty of Basel was concluded between France and Prussia early in 1795; "Perpetual Peace" appeared later that year.

17. Compare *The Metaphysics of Morals*, 114.

18. Thus in "Perpetual Peace" he characterizes a global civil constitution as one "based on *Weltbürgerrecht*, in so far as individuals and states, coexisting in an external relationship of mutual influences, may be regarded as citizens of a universal state of humankind (*ius cosmopoliticum*)." And in *The Metaphysics of Morals*, 114, he refers to this type of law as "*Völkerstaatsrecht or Weltbürgerrecht*" (my emphasis).

19. MM, 119. Cf. the discussion of provisional and conclusive acquisition in relation to the "civil condition" at MM, 51–53, which ends with the thought that until this condition "extends to the entire human race," acquisition will remain provisional.

20. Sharon Byrd presents a good discussion of this point in "The State as a 'Moral Person'," in *Proceedings of the Eighth International Kant Congress*, vol. I, part I, sections 1–2, ed. H. Robinson (Milwaukee: Marquette University Press, 1995), 171–189. She lists some of those who have gotten it wrong in n.57, 186f. To that list can be added the names of John Rawls, "The Law of Peoples," in *On Human Rights*, S. Shute and S. Hurley, eds. (New York: Basic Books, 1993), 41–82, at 54f., and Jürgen Habermas, "Kant's Idea of Perpetual Peace, with the Benefit of Two Hundred Years' Hindsight," in *Perpetual Peace. Essays on Kant's Cosmopolitan Ideal*, J. Bohman and M. Lutz-Bachmann, eds. (Cambridge: The MIT Press, 1997), 113–154, at 119 and 128.

21. See especially the oft-cited passage in "Perpetual Peace," 102, which is not only ambiguous in the original German but too freely translated by H. B. Nisbet in the Reiss edition of Kant's *Political Writings*. Kant did not write that the federation he espouses "would not be" the same thing as an international state, but that it "need not be" such. Nor did he write "the idea of a *Völkerstaat* is contradictory." The German phrase "*darin aber wäre ein Widerspruch*" could refer to the idea of a civil condition among independent nation states, which he is discussing in this paragraph. In any case, this is one of the very few passages in which there is any ambiguity on the point. As I shall now argue, his principled opposition is to a universal monarchy that ignores the ethnocultural differences among peoples and not to a state of nations that builds them into its institutional arrangements.

22. This is rendered by Nisbet as "welded together" and "amalgamation" at PP, 102 and PP, 113, respectively.

23. See the Second Definitive Article, PP. 102.

24. See, for instance, "Theory and Practice," 74–79.

25. See, for instance, TP, 75: "This uniform equality of human beings as subjects of a state is however perfectly consistent with the utmost inequality of the mass in the degree of its possessions," where "possessions" is meant in the broadest sense.

26. See, for instance, TP, 77: "In the question of actual legislation, all who are free and equal under existing public laws may be considered equal, but not as regards the right to make these laws," which is, roughly speaking, reserved to male property owners. Accordingly, on 100 ff. of "Perpetual Peace," as elsewhere, he warns against confusing the republican constitution with the democratic one.

27. PP, 105, Third Definitive Article. For the three types of law involved, see the note at PP, 98f.

28. PP, 106. Pauline Kleingeld, "Kant's Cosmopolitan Law. World Citizenship for a Global Order," unpublished ms, gives a good account of this aspect of Kant's theory of right.

29. MM, 121. The Gregor translation renders *Verkehr* as "commerce," adding a note on its broad range of meanings from social interaction to economic exchange. In this passage, it is clear that Kant intends the broadest sense of *commercium*; thus to foreclose misleading identifications with our previous use of "commerce" to render *Handel*, I have here rendered *Verkehr* as interaction.

30. PP, 106f. See also MM, 53 and MM, 121f.

31. MM, 89. The Gregor translation does not capture the idea of the third resulting from the combination of the first and second which is conveyed by the German *"beides zusammen."*

32. In "On Perpetual Peace, and On Hope as a Duty," in the volume of *Proceedings* cited in n.20, Jules Vuillemin surmises that Kant was influenced by contemporary discussions of federalism in the United States and France: 19–32, at 22 and 31, n.24.

33. MM, 119. Kant variously designates such arrangements as congresses, leagues, federations, associations, and coalitions, among other things. But the essential point remains the same: the more feasible kind of arrangement is "a coalition of different states that can be dissolved at any time, and not a union like that of the American states which is based on a constitution and therefore cannot be dissolved" (MM, 120). The latter, stronger kind of federal union among nations would call for just the sort of constitutional *Völkerstaat* that he has conceded to be unachievable.

34. Kant appears to have had some doubts of his own about the naturalness of nationhood—nurtured, perhaps, by observing the formation of the first modern nation state. Thus, writing of the state in *The Metaphysics of Morals*, he notes: "Because the union of the members is (presumed to be) *[anmasslich]* one they inherited, a state is also called a nation *[Stammvolk] (gens)*" (MM, 89). That this parenthetical reservation was no mere slip of the pen is suggested by a remark later in the same work: "As natives of a country, those who constitute a nation *[Volk]* can be represented analogously to descendents of the same ancestors *(congeniti)* even though they are not" (MM, 114).

35. PP, 113. See also AP, 182: "This much we can judge with probability: that a mixture of races (by extensive conquests), which gradually extinguishes their characters, is not beneficial to the human race . . ."

36. These efforts culminated in *Between Facts and Norms. Contributions to a Discourse Theory of Law and Democracy*, trans. W. Rehg (Cambridge: The MIT Press, 1996); cited in brackets in the text as [FN]. See also his 1986 Tanner Lecture, "Law and Morality," in *The Tanner Lectures on Human Values, VIII* (University of Utah Press, 1988), 217–279, and *The Inclusion of the Other* (Cambridge: The MIT Press, 1998).

37. See especially the papers collected in *The Inclusion of the Other*. I shall be citing "Struggles for Recognition in the Democratic Constitutional State," in that volume. Cited in brackets in the text as [SR].

38. "Aus Katastrophen Lernen? Ein zeitdiagnostischer Rückblick auf das kurze 20. Jahrhundert," unpublished ms, 18.

39. J. Habermas, *The Structural Transformation of the Public Sphere*, trans. T. Burger and F. Lawrence (Cambridge: The MIT Press, 1989); idem, *The Theory of Communicative Action*, vols. I and II, trans. T. McCarthy (Boston: Beacon Press, 1984, 1987).

40. J. Rawls, "The Law of Peoples." See my discussion of his approach in "On the Idea of a Reasonable Law of Peoples," in *Perpetual Peace. Essays on Kant's Cosmopolitan Ideal*, 201–217.

41. PP, 114. Like Kant, Habermas sees cultural convergence as extending beyond the legal and political spheres to include science and technology as well as aspects of morality and even of art. The resulting disagreement with Rawls on the "reasonability" of "comprehensive doctrines" generally, and on the relation of law to morality particularly, comes through clearly in Habermas's discussion of human rights in "Kant's Idea of Perpetual Peace," 134–140, where he argues that though they are properly legal and not moral rights, part of their distinctness derives from the fact that the principal arguments for them are themselves moral in nature. See also Habermas's exchange with Rawls in *The Journal of Philosophy*, XCII (1995): 109–180.

42. J. Habermas, *Communication and the Evolution of Society*, trans. T. McCarthy (Boston: Beacon Press, 1979).

43. J. Habermas, "On Legitimation through Human Rights," this volume, p. 203; hereafter cited in the text as HR.

44. See *Between Facts and Norms*, especially sections 1.3, 2.3, and 3.2, and *The Inclusion of the Other*, passim.

45. C. Taylor, "A World Consensus on Human Rights?" in *Dissent* (Summer, 1996): 15–21; hereafter cited in the text as UC. This is an abbreviated version of an unpublished ms on the "Conditions of an Unforced Consensus on Human Rights." I will also be drawing upon his discussion of "Nationalism and Modernity" (NM), in *The Morality of Nationalism*, 66–73, and his paper "Two Theories of Modernity" delivered in December of 1997 at a conference on "Alternative Modernities" at the India International Center in Delhi.

46. See "Two Theories of Modernity." This is a highly tendentious rendering of both the claim and the culture.

47. See the interesting discussion between Susan Moller Okin and her critics, "Is Multiculturalism Bad for Women?" in *Boston Review*, vol. XXII, no. 5 (October/November, 1997): 25–40.

9

Constitutional Patriotism and the Public Sphere: Interests, Identity, and Solidarity in the Integration of Europe

Craig Calhoun

Europe has occupied a special place in imaginings of postnational and transnational politics, just as it did and still does in imaginings of national and international politics. Europe has been imagined as civilization, as the state system of the post-Westphalian balance of power, and as a theater of war. It was the continent most thoroughly remade by the nationalist social imaginary. It has been imagined as the defender of Christianity and as Christendom's West. It was a frontier to the Roman Empire and later claimed ancient Rome and Greece as definitive ancestors, imagining itself as the birthplace of democracy, republican virtues, and the rule of law. At the same time, it was reimagined as the cluster of imperial centers from which such virtues—along with simple exploitation—might be extended to the rest of the world. It was the nexus of an astounding new "dynamic density" of trade relations in the early modern era and of revolutionary transformations in industrial production—both harnessed to the capitalist imagination of self-interested individuals competing, investing, accumulating, and producing the public good out of private greed.

The capitalist imaginary, however European its roots, transcended the continent. Along with colonialism, missionary religion, and projects of secular salvation—not least socialism—it propelled Europeans out into the rest of the world, making them crucial agents in the production of a new global web of relationships. The outward flow of Europeans and European institutions was of course

complemented by flows in other directions, including some transforming Europe itself. The nationalist imaginary flourished as one
way of trying to grasp and organize—as well as sometimes resist—
the growing global flows of people, goods, and ideas. It shaped the
idea of a domestic realm within which outsiders were not allowed to
intervene and of an international realm within which nations were
conceived as unitary actors in relation to each other.[1] Although
nationalism and capitalism grew hand-in-hand, they were also in
tension. Capitalist accounting might use nations as categories with
which to constitute statistics on international trade, but from Adam
Smith's critique of mercantalism forward, the project of constituting
trade on the model of (political) international relations was limited
at best. Capitalist relations were organized transnationally, cutting
across the ostensibly autonomous spheres of nations and often
linking parts of each without involving any as wholes or actors. The
latest phase of capitalist globalization has dramatically intensified this
process, not least by allowing more of production as well as exchange
to be organized in transnational fashion and on an increasingly
worldwide scale.[2]

The reality of the transnational organization of capitalism—and
migrations, media, religion, and even sometimes war—gives impetus
to attempts to forge transnational politics. So does the troubled
nature of contemporary international relations—not their impo-
tence or disappearance so much as their recurrent insufficiency to
the challenges placed before them. Yet what does transnational politics mean? On what bases might it rest? How democratic might it
be? I shall consider this in three steps.

First, I shall argue that the project of cosmopolitanism (or constitutional patriotism) requires a stronger approach to social solidarity
than has been offered in existing theory. This is partly a matter of
the construction of identity but also of mutually interdependent
social relations. In both regards, the notion of "constitution" may
be developed beyond narrowly legal-political senses to include a
broader idea of "world making" in Hannah Arendt's sense. This is
shaped by various forms of "social imaginary" that underpin the
creation and reproduction of institutions and the organization of
solidarity. These ways of understanding life together make possible
specific forms of social relations. If nationalism is to give way to some

postnational organization of social life, it will not be simply a matter of new formal organization, but of new ways of imaginatively constituting identity, interests, and solidarity. A key theme will be the importance of notions of mutual commitment—solidarity—that are more than similarities of preestablished interests or identities. Can shared participation in the public sphere anchor a form of social solidarity in which the nature of life together is chosen as it is constructed?

Second, such constitutional processes both shape and are shaped by public discourse. This is not only a matter of (ideally) rational-critical debate over formal propositions, however; the public sphere is important also as a realm of sociability and solidarity. That is, public discourse figures in two ways in the constitution of new forms of social solidarity. First, shared participation in public life enables broad populations to chose—at least to some extent—the institutional forms and character of their lives together. Second, the mutual commitments forged in public action are themselves a dimension of solidarity. The moment of choice can never be separated fully from that of creativity or construction.

In the third section, I shall return to the case of Europe more explicitly. One form of transnational politics involves the attempt to create new institutional organizations above the level of existing nation states. The European Union offers the most developed example of such regional integration. Because of the relatively high level of democracy within European states, the relative freedom of the press and flourishing not only of political parties but of the public sphere, Europe is also a test case for considering how democracy fares as a regional polity develops. I shall suggest that democracy faces a number of challenges and focus especially on the question of what sort of public sphere would allow for the effective organization of a democratic Europe.[3]

Cosmopolitanism and Constitutional Patriotism

Contemplating simultaneously the questions of German integration and European integration, Jürgen Habermas has called for grounding political identity in "constitutional patriotism."[4] This is an important concretization of a more general and increasingly widespread but not uncontested cosmopolitanism. The concept suggests both constitutional limits to political loyalty and loyalty to the constitution as such. In the latter dimension, which Habermas emphasizes, the constitution provides both a referent for public discussion and a set of procedural norms to organize it and orient it to justifiable ends. The specific contents of any conception of the good life may vary, then, and modern societies will always admit of multiple such conceptions. Constitutional patriotism underwrites no one of these but rather a commitment to the justification of collective decisions and the exercise of power in terms of fairness. It is thus compatible with a wide range of specific constitutional arrangements and to a varying balance between direct reference to universal rights and procedural norms and more specific political culture.

Similarly, ideas of rights and justice underpin a new movement of calls for cosmopolitan democracy, democracy not limited by nation-states.[5] Though this is not uniquely European, the cosmopolitan message is most linked to a sense of movement in European intellectual life. It hearkens back directly to the Enlightenment (complete with residual echoes of eighteenth century aristocratic culture). It also commonly expresses a sense of what Europeans have learned about living together in a multinational region and of how Europeans may take on a civilized (if not precisely civilizing) mission in a conflict-ridden larger world. Cosmopolitanism is potentially consonant with a vision of a Europe of the nations—preserving not only cultural difference but political autonomy—as long as nationalism is not ethnically communitarian and is subordinated to human and civil rights. It has a stronger affinity with visions of confederation or even greater integration, though it emphasizes the outward obligations of Europeans. What it eschews most is application of the nationalist vision of cultural community to supranational polities. What it claims most, in the spirit of Kant, is that people should see themselves as citizens of the world not just of their countries.

Central to both cosmopolitanism and constitutional patriotism is an image of "bad nationalism." Nazi Germany is paradigmatic, but more recent examples like Milosevic's Serbian nationalism also inform the theories. At the core of each instance, as generally understood, is an ethnic solidarity triumphant over civility and liberal values and ultimately turning to horrific violence. Indeed, the negative force of the nationalist imaginary is so strong that each of these theoretical positions is defined more than its advocates admit by its opposition to nationalism, by the other it would avoid.

Advocates of a postnational Europe—or world—do themselves and theory no favors by equating nationalism with ethnonationalism and understanding this primarily through its most distasteful examples. Nations have often had ethnic pedigrees and employed ethnic rhetorics, but they are modern products of shared political, culture, and social participation not mere inheritances. To treat nationalism as a relic of an earlier order, a sort of irrational expression, or a kind of moral mistake is to fail to see both the continuing power of nationalism as a discursive formation and the work—sometimes positive— that nationalist solidarities continue to do in the world. As a result, nationalism is not easily abandoned even if its myths, contents, and excesses are easily debunked.[6] Not only this, the attempt to equate nationalism with problematic ethnonationalism sometimes ends up placing all "thick" understandings of culture and the cultural constitution of political practices, forms, and identities on the nationalist side of the classification. Only quite thin notions of political culture are retained on the attractive postnationalist side.[7] The problem here is that republicanism and democracy depend on more than narrowly political culture; they depend on richer ways of constituting life together.

Recognizing this, Habermas suggests that "the question arises of whether there exists a functional equivalent for the fusion of the nation of citizens with the ethnic nation."[8] He is right that democracy has depended on national identities more than many critics of nationalism recognize. His formulation, however, tends to equate all nationalism with ethnic nationalism. "The nation-state owes its historical success to the fact that it substituted relations of solidarity between the citizens for the disintegrating corporative ties of early modern society. But this republican achievement is endangered when, conversely, the integrative force of the nation of citizens is traced back to the prepolitical fact of a quasi-natural people, that is, to something independent of and prior to the political opinion- and will-formation of the citizens themselves."[9] It is true that nationalist rhetoric often invokes the notion of a prepolitical people as the basis for all legitimate politics. Relying only on the negative image, though, leads Habermas to neglect the importance of other nationalist imaginaries to the nurturance of democratic politics. The American founding and subsequent constitutionalism offers one useful example. It is true that the colonists turned nationalists largely thought of themselves as bearers of "the rights of freeborn Englishmen" but theirs was not an appeal mainly to an ethnic identity. Crucially, it was an appeal to an identity forged by public discourse itself.[10] This is part of what Hannah Arendt celebrated, seeing the American Revolution as a prime example of the capacity of public life for world-founding.[11] In this sense, the nation appears more as a common project, mediated by public discourse and the collective formation of culture, not simply as inheritance.

The American example could inform a different, stronger sense of constitutional patriotism. While the emphasis on norms underwriting a justifiable life together would remain, this would not appear so much as a matter of getting the abstractly "right" procedures in place. The idea of a basic law (especially a written document) would be complemented first by the Arendtian notion of founding. This idea of constitution as world making would clarify the role of the social imaginary. This is not simply about the imagining of counterfactual possibilities—for example, utopias—however instructive. It is about the ways of imagining social life that actually make it possible. In this sense, it is a way of approaching culture that emphasizes agency and history in the constitution of the language and understandings by which we give shape to social life. To speak of the social imaginary is to assert that there are no fixed categories of external observation adequate to all history, that ways of thinking and structures of feeling make possible certain social forms, and that the thinking, feeling, and forms are thus products of action and historically variable.[12] In this way, cultural creativity is basic even to such seemingly "material" forms as the corporation or the nation. These exist because they are imagined; they are real because they are treated as real; new particular cases are produced through recurrent exercise of the underlying social imaginary.

Second, the notion of constitution as legal framework therefore needs to be complemented by the notion of constitution as the creation of concrete social relationships—the solidarity of social networks and bonds of mutual commitment forged in shared action—and institutions—shared modalities of practical action. This expanded sense of constitution would, I think, be much richer. It would also imply an understanding of "peoplehood" much stronger than that acknowledged in Habermas's account of constitutional patriotism (or in the common variants of cosmopolitanism). This is important, as Charles Taylor has argued forcefully, because of "the need, in self-governing societies, of a high degree of cohesion."[13]

Democratic states, in other words, require a kind and level of "peopleness" that is not required in other forms of government. They offer a level of inclusion that is unprecedented—the government of *all* the people—but they place a new pressure on the constitution of this people in sociocultural and political practice. This makes it clear, I think, that although all the aspects of constructing peoplehood cannot be brought into explicit political contention, nonetheless the process of constructing the relevant people should not be treated as prepolitical, simply the taken-as-given basis for politics. This is what much nationalist discourse does, and it is also what much political philosophy does—even in classic forms like Rawls's theory of justice. It says, in effect, "given a people, how should it be governed or socially organized?" It is important to see the constitution of "the people" as much more theoretically, and practically, problematic. One of the consequences of doing so, however, is that this entails rejection of any purely external or objective approach to resolving questions of political identity.

Neo-Kantian and more generally liberal models of collective life run into difficulties in grappling with the reliance of democracy on a strong notion of the people. Yet, as Habermas's question about the functional equivalent of the ethnic nation implies, it is crucial to understand not simply that constitutional arrangements are in some abstract sense good, but how they may have force for specific people.

Attempts to resolve this question without a strong account of how a population conceived as many individuals constitutes itself as a people are deeply problematic and perhaps fatally flawed. This is because it is crucial to account not only for closure (as long as the polity is not a single world polity—as indeed Europe is not) but also for mutual commitments among the members of the polity, including commitments to the constitution. Citizens need to be motivated by solidarity not merely included by law.

In particular, external approaches to identifying "the people" fail to provide an understanding of why and when the definition of the whole becomes a political problem, and which issues become the key signifiers in debate. Why, for example, are there contexts where race matters less than language and others in which that ordering is hard to imagine? This is closely related to the fact that belonging to (or being excluded from) "the people" is not simply a matter of large-scale political participation in modern society. It is precisely the kind of question of personal identity that produces passions that escape the conventional categories of the political. This is so, we can see following Taylor, because of the extent to which ideas and feelings about "the people" are woven into the moral frameworks of "strong evaluation" in relation to which we establish our senses of self.[14]

There is an important Hegelian moment, thus, a dialectic of the whole and its parts. Without grasping this dialectic, we can understand neither of its polar dimensions—nation and individual. We are also especially apt to be misled into seeing them as opposites rather than complicit with each other. But in fact, the ideas of nation and individual grew up together in Western history and continue to inform each other. Far from being an objective distinction of collective from singular, the opposition of nation and individual reflects a tension-laden relationship. Nations are themselves treated as individuals—by ideologues, of course, but also by diplomats, lawyers and comparative sociologists. Moreover, the relationship between human persons and nations is commonly constructed as immediate, so that intermediate associations and subsidiary identities are displaced by it. In this way, nations commonly appear in rhetorical practice as categories of similar individuals as well as organic wholes.[15]

An external account of peoplehood is apt to rely on identity (cultural similarity) and/or interests (and implicitly or explicitly a social contract). Identity and/or interests can then be invoked to explain why people accept shared institutions and indeed accept each other. The dominant discourses about membership in a European polity work on these bases. Either people are Europeans because they are culturally similar to each other or they are Europeans because this is in their interests (usually described in economic terms). In either case, the emphasis is on passive preconditions not projects, adaptation to external necessity not creative pursuit of an attractive solidarity. The implication is that the people in question are already formed as either similar or different in cultural terms, as either having or lacking common interests. Such accounts rely on a notion of the public sphere as a setting in which such already constituted people exercise reason to debate what institutions and policies they should have. It is understood crucially as the setting in which people transcend differences in identity and particularities of interests. What is missing from such accounts is the role of public life in actually constituting social solidarity and creating culture.

Taking ethnic nationalism as his model, Habermas treats the attempt to ground European unity in some sense of peoplehood as tantamount to ethnic exclusion. He sees peoplehood, in other words, as necessarily a matter of some preestablished, passive cultural similarity rather than as potentially an active creation of public engagement. Habermas hopes the public sphere will produce a rational agreement that can take the place of preestablished culture as the basis for political identity. He works, however, with an overly sharp dichotomy between inherited identity and rational discourse. He identifies voluntary public life entirely with the latter, and thus he obscures the extent to which it is necessarily also a process of cultural creativity and modes of communication not less valuable for being incompletely rational.

This leaves only a thin form of identity to be produced by the rational discourse of the cosmopolitan public sphere. It is then hard to see how the cosmopolitan public can overcome the disjuncture between the (ideally rational) sources of legitimation and the (too commonly irrational) sources of integration. "Whereas the voluntary nation of citizens is the source of democratic legitimation, it is the inherited or ascribed nation founded on ethnic membership that secures social integration."[16] In Habermas's dichotomous view, the alternative to such ascription is conscious, rational agreement. This neglects the extent to which agreement and common culture alike are neither rationally chosen nor simply inherited but produced and reproduced in social action. When this is appreciated, we can see also that there is not simply an alternative between "thick" but irrationally inherited identities and "thin" but rationally achieved ones. First, neither of these ideal types fits well with how identities are actually produced and reproduced. Second, the opposition obscures the possibilities for producing new and different but still relatively thick common identities. Third, we should take care not to reduce social solidarity to common identity and especially not to assume that this is somehow settled before political action or its legitimation.

The problem with which Habermas is grappling is real, for there is indeed a widespread tendency to treat common culture as always inherited and to separate normative analysis of legitimacy from the givenness or facticity of existing collectivities. But his solution to the problem is inadequate. In the first place, however common in political argument it may be to treat cultural similarity as the basis of solidarity, this is not a sociologically adequate account. Common membership of such a category may be one source of solidarity but hardly the only one. Functional integration, concrete social networks, and mutual engagement in the public sphere are also sources or dimensions of solidarity. Moreover, there is no reason to accept the rhetoric of ethnic nationalists who treat tradition as "the hard cake of culture," simply to be affirmed on the basis of its prepolitical ancientness. Culture is subject to continual reformation or it dies; reproduction involves an element of creative practice.

European identity is growing, thus, but although this process involves creativity the extent to which it involves widespread choice is questionable (and no doubt will be widely debated). Marketing, product design, food, and leisure activities all convey images of a European identity. Although news media are not effectively organized on a European scale, entertainment is a bit more so. And both news and entertainment media carry more and more content about an integrated Europe—and implicitly a European culture. Participation in democratic public life is not, however, separate from the processes through which culture is produced and reproduced in modern societies, and part of the process by which individual and collective identities are made and remade. The problem with which Habermas rightly wrestles remains insoluble as long as culture is treated as inheritance and sharply opposed to reason conceived as voluntary activity. I have invoked the notion of the social imaginary partly to suggest an approach to culture as activity not only inheritance. It suggests also the impossibility of fully disembedding reason from culture. The choice of social institutions is not simply an exercise of abstract reason about phenomena outside itself, but at the same time the imaginative constitution of institutions in the formation and reformation of culture.

Habermas's call for constitutional patriotism—like most appeals to cosmopolitanism—tries to establish political community on the basis of thin identities and normative universalism. The key questions to ask include not simply whether such a community would be ordered by good principles, though, but whether it would achieve a sufficient solidarity to be really motivating for its members.[17] There is no intrinsic reason why "constitutional patriotism" could not work on the scale of Europe, but there are questions about whether it can stand alone as an adequate source of belonging and mutual commitment. It is therefore important to address legitimacy and solidarity together not separately. This need not involve a reduction of the normative content of arguments about legitimacy to mere recognition of the facticity of existing solidarities. On the contrary, it could involve the development of stronger normative analysis of the legitimacy of different forms and concrete organizations of solidarity. Attending to the dynamic processes by which culture is produced and reproduced also makes it easier to conceptualize the introduction into public space of other kinds of identities besides those that unify the polity as a whole. This does not mean that multiculturalism is not challenging, but it suggests that it does not introduce a radically new element into previously unproblematic uniformity and fixity of collective identity. The key is to reject the notion—which nationalist ideology indeed commonly asserts—that the cultural conditions of public life, including both individual and collective identity, are established prior to properly public discourse itself.

The Public Sphere and Solidarity

Can we conceive of public discourse as (among other things) a form of social solidarity? This flies to some extent in the face of common usage. Solidarity or integration is treated as a question distinct from and generally prior to that of collective decision-making or legitimate action. The implication is that the collective subject is formed first, and activity in the public sphere is about steering it, not constituting it.

One reason for this is the extent to which the collective subject was conceived in the most influential early modern accounts not as the people but as the state. Or more precisely, the people was arguably the subject of *legitimacy* (in a modern, "ascending" approach to legitimacy as distinct from a medieval "descending" approach emphasizing divine right or heredity). But the state was the subject of collective *action* that was either legitimate or not. So in a sense, states were actors and public discourse (where it was influential) steered states. Legitimacy came in some combination from serving the interests of "the people" or from the process by which the people contributed to the steering of the state. But in approaches deriving from this sort of account (notably, for example, Habermas's classic exposition), a clear distinction was made between the public sphere and the state.[18]

The public sphere appeared, then, as a dimension of civil society, but one which could orient itself toward and potentially steer the state. In this sense, the public sphere did not appear as itself a self-organizing form of social solidarity, though another crucial part of civil society—the market (or economic system)—did. Rather than a form of solidarity, the public sphere was a mechanism for influencing the state. Civil society provided a basis for the public sphere through nurturing individual autonomy. But the public sphere did not steer civil society directly; it influenced the state. The implication, then, was that social integration was accomplished either by power (the state) or by self-regulating systems (the economy). If citizens were to have the possibility of collective choice, they had to act on the state (which could in turn act on the economy—though too much of this would constitute a problematic dedifferentiation of spheres according to many analysts, including the later Habermas). What was not developed in this account is the possibility that the public sphere is effective not only through informing state policy but through forming culture; that through exercise of social imagination and forging of social relationships the public sphere could constitute a form of social solidarity.

The public sphere is important as a basic condition of democracy. But it signals more than simply the capacity to weigh specific issues in the court of public opinion. The public sphere is also a form of social solidarity. It is one of the institutional forms in which the members of a society may be joined together with each other. In this sense, its counterparts are families, communities, bureaucracies, markets, and nations. All of these are arenas of social participation. Exclusion from them is among the most basic definitions of alienation from contemporary societies. Among the various forms of social solidarity, though, the public sphere is distinctive because it is created and reproduced through discourse. It is not primarily a matter of unconscious inheritance, of power relations, or of the usually invisible relationships forged as a byproduct of industrial production and market exchanges. People talk in families, communities, and workplaces, of course, but the public sphere exists uniquely in, through, and for talk. It also consists specifically of talk about other social arrangements, including but not limited to actions the state might take. The stakes of theories and analyses of the public sphere, therefore, concern the extent to which communication can be influential in producing or reshaping social solidarity.

What are some of the other choices? Let me borrow Durkheim's famous distinction of mechanical from organic solidarity to illustrate two main ones.[19] Mechanical solidarity, Durkheim suggested, obtains in societies where people and social units are basically similar to each other; it is produced above all by a shared *conscience collective*. Organic solidarity is characteristic of differentiated societies with a complex division of labor, considerable variation among individuals, and constituent groups formed on different principles. Durkheim used the distinction largely to analyze the contrast between traditional and modern societies.[20] It may be more helpful, however, to think of these as suggesting two dimensions of solidarity-formation at work in modern societies. Rename organic solidarity "functional interdependence" and recognize that this includes market relations as well as the other ways in which different social institutions and groups depend on each other. Less familiarly, rename mechanical solidarity "categorical identity" (with nationalism as a prime example). Think of it as describing the ideology of equal membership in a whole defined by the similarity of its members, complete in the nationalist case with the strong sense of the primacy of the whole over its members such that they will die for it and kill for it. Both forms of solidarity are at work in every country today—material relations of interdependence, more or less managed by states and markets, and collective identities, reflecting various combinations of inheritance and energetic reproduction and shaping by intellectuals and cultural producers. Neither of these types of solidarity, however, is the product of a process of autonomous choice for both are largely externally determined.

Let us round out the list by identifying four forms of social solidarity:[21]

1. *Functional integration.* This is loosely analogous to "system" in the sense in which Habermas employs the term, informed by Luhmann and Parsons. Interdependence based on various kinds of flows (e.g., of goods) joins people in mutuality that is not based primarily on their common recognition of it but instead can operate behind their backs. Much of modern life depends on such quasi-autonomous systems. While in principle it may be possible to unmask systems of functional integration as products of human choices, they are not chosen as such.

2. *Categorical identities.* If the primary example is nationality, race, class, and a range of other identities work the same way. They posit a set of individuals equivalent to each other insofar as they share a crucial category of similarity. This is not the same as sharing culture (despite some attempts to treat it so, including by nationalist ideo-

logues) because it refers to sharing a specific dimension of culturally significant similarity; how well that stands for participation in a common way of life is an empirical question. While those who try to mobilize others on the basis of categorical identities commonly claim that one identity is a kind of trump against other possible identities or interests, there is in fact always some element of choice as to which identity one accepts as salient.[22]

3. *Direct social relations.* Here the referent is concrete networks of actual connections among people who are identifiable to each other as concrete persons. Much reference to community privileges such worlds of direct relations (but when the term is used to refer to solidarity in nation-states, scale dictates that this cannot be the primary meaning and that some other sense of solidarity is at least implicitly being invoked). Referring to direct relations also avoids the implication of harmony or affection common to some usages of community.[23] While social structure and other largely external conditions shape patterns of direct relations substantially, there is also room for choice. This occurs both directly, as people choose relationships, and indirectly, as they choose forms of social participation (say social movements or jobs) that introduce them to particular populations of potential network partners.

4. *Publics.* Publics are self-organizing fields of discourse in which participation is not based primarily on personal connections and is at least in principle open to strangers.[24] A public sphere comprises an indefinite number of more or less overlapping publics, some ephemeral, some enduring, and some shaped by struggle against the dominant organization of others. Engagement in public life establishes social solidarity partly through enhancing the significance of particular categorical identities and partly through facilitating the creation of direct social relations. Beyond this, however, the engagement of people with each other in public is itself a form of social solidarity. This engagement includes but is not limited to rational-critical discourse about affairs of common concern. Communication in public also informs the sharing of social imaginaries, ways of understanding social life that are themselves constitutive of it. Both culture and identity are created partly in public action and

interaction. An element of reasoned reflection, however, is crucial to the idea of choice as a dimension of this form of solidarity, to the distinction of public culture from simple expression of preexisting identity.

Emphasizing the public sphere is a challenge, thus, to speaking of institutions as though they were produced simply by adaptation to material necessity (as some market ideology would suggest). It is equally a challenge to the ways in which nationalists present membership in France, say, or Serbia as being an undifferentiated and immediate relationship between individuals and a collective whole which is always already there and about which there are few legitimate variations in opinion. The public sphere is an arena simultaneously of solidarity and choice.

Hannah Arendt's account of public action and public spaces bring this out more than Habermas's.[25] The term "public," she wrote, "signifies two closely interrelated but not altogether identical phenomena: It means, first, that everything that appears in public can be seen and heard by everybody and has the widest possible publicity. . . . Second, the term "public" signifies the world itself, in so far as it is common to all of us and distinguished from our privately owned place in it."[26] Public action, moreover, is the crucial terrain of the humanly created as distinct from natural world, of appearance and memory, and of talk and recognition. We hold in common a world we create in common in part by the processes through which we imagine it. It is these processes that the "social imaginary" shapes. Arendt emphasized creativity, including the creation of the forms of common political life through founding actions—as in revolution and constitution making. Imagination is not involved only in founding moments but also in all social action, and the notion of a social imaginary draws attention to broad patterns of stability in imagination as well as to occasional more or less radical changes. Equally important, Arendt's account of public space approached people as radically plural, not necessarily similar, but bound to each other by promises that are explicit or implicit in their lives together.[27]

In both Arendt's and Habermas's accounts, the emphasis was on political publics, but in Arendt's case the notion of politics was extended to include all public action. In his classic early account of the public sphere, Habermas worked with a narrower, state-centered notion of politics, though he recognized the ways in which a literary public sphere foreshadowed, shaped, and overlapped with the political one—making the distinction at best an analytic rather than a purely empirical one.[28] In any case, the public sphere is a crucial site for the production and transformation of politically salient identities and solidarities, including the category and practical manifestation of the people that is basic to democracy.[29]

Recognizing politics beyond or outside the state is especially important to seeing how transnational public spheres might be effective. The questions of how a European public sphere might be organized and what influence it might have are as basic to Europe's future as the rise of democratic institutions within nation-states was to its past. Indeed, Habermas himself has returned to this theoretical framework in considering relations among nation, rule of law, and democracy in a changing Europe:

> The initial impetus to integration in the direction of a postnational society is not provided by the substrate of a supposed "European people" but by the communicative network of a European-wide political public sphere embedded in a shared political culture. The latter is founded on a civil society composed of interest groups, nongovernmental organizations, and citizen initiatives and movements, and will be occupied by arenas in which the political parties can directly address the decisions of European institutions and go beyond mere tactical alliance to form a European party system.[30]

This is clearly a statement of hopes and conditions for a desirable future as much as description of trends. Such a European public sphere is a question more than a reality, as is an integrated European party system, but the conceptual point is clear. The creation of such a public sphere is the condition of a democratic, republican integration of Europe and the safeguard against a problematically nationalist one.[31]

The production of a flourishing public sphere, thus, along with a normatively sound constitution, allows for a good answer to Habermas's orienting question: "When does a collection of persons constitute an entity—'a people'—entitled to govern itself democratically?"[32] The common answer is much less good:

In the real world, who in each instance acquires the power to define the disputed borders of a state is settled by historical contingencies, usually by the quasi-natural outcome of violent conflicts, wars, and civil wars. Whereas republicanism reinforces our awareness of the contingency of these borders, this contingency can be dispelled by appeal to the idea of a grown nation that imbues the borders with the aura of imitated substantiality and legitimates them through fictitious links with the past. Nationalism bridges the normative gap by appealing to a so-called right of national self-determination.[33]

At the heart of the notion of a democratic public sphere lie differences, both among participants and possible opinions. If a public sphere is not able to encompass people of different personal and group identities, it can hardly be the basis for democracy. If people have the same views, no public sphere is needed—or at least none beyond ritual affirmation of unity or plebiscites. Differences among opinions challenge not only nationalist pressures to conform, but insistence on the application of technical expertise, as though it (or the science that might lie behind it) embodied perfect, unchanging, perspectiveless, and disinterested solutions to problems. Differences among participants also pose a challenge. If a public sphere needs to include people of different classes, genders, even nations, it also requires participants to be able—at least some of the time—to adopt perspectives distanced from their immediate circumstances and thus to carry on conversations that are not determined strictly by private interest or identity. The point is not that any escape influences from their personal lives, but that none are strictly determined by those influences, unable to see the merits in good arguments presented by those who represent competing interests or worldviews. If there are no meaningful differences within the public sphere, it may reaffirm solidarity and *conscience collective*, but it cannot address choices about how solidarity and institutional arrangements could be other than they are.

The differences within a public sphere may be bases for the development of multiple publics (specific fields of discourse) and public spaces (settings for discourse which is always open-ended). We speak of a public sphere to the extent that these both overlap and address some common concerns—for example, about how people should live together or what a state should do. Some of the multiple publics may claim to represent the whole, while others oppose dominant discursive patterns and still others are neutral. Nancy Fraser has influentially emphasized the importance of "subaltern counterpublics" such as those framed by race or gender.[34] In thinking about the multiplicity of publics forming a public sphere, though, it is important to be critical about the distinction of some as marked while others remain unmarked; unmarked does not automatically equal either universal or univocally dominant. If the attempt to establish closure to outsiders is sometimes a strategy of counterpublics, as Michael Warner has suggested, the deployment of claims on an unmarked public as *the* public sphere is also a strategy, generally a strategy of the powerful.[35]

In speaking of counterpublics, it is important to keep in mind both that their existence as such presupposes a mutual engagement in some larger public sphere and that individuals may participate in multiple publics. A newspaper opinion essay by a gay rights activist, thus, may address simultaneously members of a specifically gay public (and even a queer counterpublic within that) and participants in the unmarked broader public.[36] Moreover, the segmentation of a distinct public from the unmarked larger public may be a result of exclusion not choice. During the classic heyday of the eighteenth- and early nineteenth-century British public sphere, thus, many artisans and workers were denied participation in the public sphere. They were not simply and unambivalently members of a proletarian public sphere, though they did develop their own media and organizations and to some extent constituted a counterpublic. They claimed the right to participate in the dominant, unmarked public sphere and challenged those who introduced restrictive measures to make it a specifically "bourgeois" (or more generally, propertied) public sphere.[37] The same people who excluded those with less wealth from the public sphere nonetheless claimed it in unmarked form as simply *the* British public.

The issue of democratic inclusiveness is not just a quantitative matter of the scale of a public sphere or the proportion of the members of a political community who may speak within it. While it is clearly a matter of stratification and boundaries (e.g., openness to the propertyless, the uneducated, women or immigrants), it is also a matter of how the public sphere incorporates and recognizes the diversity of identities that people bring to it from their manifold involvements in civil society. It is a matter of whether, to participate in such a public sphere, for example, women must act in ways previously characteristic of men and avoid addressing certain topics defined as appropriate to the private realm (the putatively more female sphere). Marx criticized the discourse of bourgeois citizenship for implying that it fit everyone equally when it in fact tacitly presumed an understanding of citizens as property owners. The same sort of false universalism has presented citizens in gender neutral or gender symmetrical terms without in fact acknowledging highly gendered underlying conceptions. Moreover, the boundaries between public and private are part of the stakes of debate in the public sphere, not something neatly settled in advance.[38]

All attempts to render authoritative a single public discourse privilege certain topics, certain forms of speech, certain ways of constructing and presenting identities, and certain speakers. This is partly a matter of emphasis on the single, unitary whole—the discourse of all the citizens rather than of subsets, multiple publics—and partly a matter of the specific demarcations of public from private. If sexual harassment, for example, is seen as a matter of concern to women, but not men, it becomes a sectional matter rather than a matter for the public in general; if it is seen as a private matter, then by definition it is not a public concern. The same goes for a host of other topics of attention that are inhibited from reaching full recognition in a public sphere conceptualized as a single discourse about matters consensually determined to be of public significance.

The classical liberal model of the public sphere, on Habermas's account, pursues discursive equality by disqualifying discourse about the differences among actors. These differences are treated as matters of private, but not public, interest.[39] The best version of the public sphere was based on "a kind of social intercourse that, far from presupposing the equality of status, disregarded status altogether."[40] It worked by a "mutual willingness to accept the given roles and simultaneously to suspend their reality."[41] This "bracketing" of difference as merely private and irrelevant to the public sphere was undertaken, Habermas argues, to defend the genuinely rational-critical notion that arguments must be decided on their merits rather than the identities of the arguers. This was, by the way, as important as fear of censors for the prominence of anonymous or pseudonymous authorship in the eighteenth-century public sphere.[42] Yet it has the effect of excluding some of the most important concerns of many members of any polity—both those whose existing identities are suppressed or devalued and those whose exploration of possible identities is truncated. If the public sphere exists in part to relate individual life histories to public policies (as Habermas suggests), then bracketing issues of identity is seriously impoverishing.[43] In addition, this bracketing of differences also undermines the self-reflexive capacity of public discourse. If it is impossible to communicate seriously about basic differences among members of a public sphere, then it will be impossible also to address the difficulties of communication across such lines of basic difference.

Democratic Public Life and European Integration

The postwar institutional ancestors of the European Union were created as economic organizations with a political purpose. They sought to limit the potential for continental (and world) wars by tying members into new webs of shared institutions and markets. In some cases these were specifically linked to military agendas, as the coal and steel community sought to limit the autonomy of national industries in strategic lines of production. In a growing proportion of the fields of cooperation, however, the principle was simply to increase the bonds of solidarity that kept Europeans committed to cooperation with each other. This was not done without idealism, but it was a matter of strategic action, not simply reflection of popular will or common identity. And of course, the political purpose was increasingly backed up with directly economic ones, notably to compete more effectively in global markets. As in the making of the European nation-states, the internal peace was sought partly to facilitate external gain.

Economic motivations have remained important (albeit in fluctuating extent) throughout the history of European integration.

Among the messages of the discourse that paved the way for the Maastricht treaty, for example, was the notion that a mere "Europe of the nations" could not compete effectively against Asia or the United States. More generally, an economistic imaginary has been basic to arguments for European integration. The notion that "we must compete" has been recurrent, framing the interests of Europeans as producers and marketers of goods. At the same time, consumers have been encouraged to think of European integration as a program for the improvement of restaurants and supermarkets.

Other reasons also exist for European integration. Nonetheless, economism has been a dominant feature of the social imaginary mobilized in pursuit of this integration. A result is that integration appears as strategic accommodation to necessity, a response— perhaps even a clever, winning response—to the requirements of a global economic system rather than a democratic project. Collective agency is focused on system maintenance while individual agency is focused on consumption or entrepreneurship (both portrayed typically as dimensions of private life). This is cognate with a culture of public decision-making based on expertise—finding the "right" technical-strategic solutions to problems defined as the pursuit of common interests. The quality of expertise is judged by outcomes and ratified through plebiscitarian processes. Diffuse democratic participation is not presented as good in itself. This in turn reduces the extent to which processes of public life provide citizens with occasions for the exercise (and through practice the development) of good public judgment; it undermines the self-educative capacity of democracy.[44] Alternatives to economism could offer stronger bases for legitimacy.

The institutions of the European Union have gradually come more and more to resemble a kind of state. This process is resisted by advocates of a Europe of the nations, and it is seldom recognized in common speech or even academic analysis. It is true that governance of the EU is still largely effected by the collective decisions of the constituent states (e.g., by the heads of state meeting together) rather than by an autonomous process. Nonetheless, the power of the EU is growing. It will be furthered by the completion of monetary union; it is advanced by the replacement of internal border controls with a single external border; it is augmented by the development of a common foreign policy and aid structure.[45] EU governmental power may lag behind the integration of capitalist activity on a continental scale. The prospect of expansion of the EU membership may slow further integration (though it may also produce differentiated tiers of membership). Nonetheless, even if the EU "state" is weak, it is a kind of state and it is growing stronger. On what basis is the EU legitimate?

Discussion of EU legitimacy has been pursued largely through questions of national sovereignty. That is, the question posed has been less about the legitimacy (or normative value) of the EU as such than about the relative strength or autonomy of EU and nation-state institutions. Two major arguments have legitimated the transfer of power from constituent states to the EU: peace and economic interests. Over time, the balance has shifted from the former to the latter. Increasingly, it has been complemented by a third: the assertion of a common European identity. In effect, though seldom openly in discourse, Europe is being described in ways common to much nationalist discourse. Advancing the whole will serve the interests of all members (or at least the greatest good of the greatest number); fundamental to the identity of each member, moreover, is participation in the identity of the whole.[46]

Nationalism and economic interest are only two of the powerful discourses of legitimacy in modern Europe, however; democracy and republicanism are also important. The EU is described as able to deliver economic goods and arguably peace, at least internally; does it deliver political liberty and civic virtue?

Republican traditions raise not only questions about the form of political institutions but also the ideals of virtuous citizenship that shaped republican understandings of membership in a polity. These ideals required a level of individual liberty of political subjects (in a sense, transforming the very meaning of the word subject from that of obedient underling to the more grammatical sense of autonomous actor) and emphasized that with such liberty came obligations. Republican political institutions depend, however, not only on political commitments, strictly understood, but on social solidarity and collective identity.

Likewise, democracy is more than a formal matter of elections and other mechanisms of selection for office and distribution of power. In the European context, these formal questions have been intimately bound to a shift in understandings of political legitimacy. Instead of judging governments by their conformity to top-down structures of authority—those of God or tradition—modern Europeans came to place ever-greater stress on having governments serve the interests of the ordinary people under them. This claim to have one's interests served has become basic to citizenship. Even regimes that were not in any sense formally democratic—from Victor Emmanuel's Italy and Bismarck's Germany to Jaruzelski's Poland—presented themselves as serving the interests of their "peoples."

Here democracy was intimately bound to nationalism. The development of national identities and nationalist projects gave a sense of internal coherence, boundaries, and even moral righteousness to the "peoples" whose interests states were obliged increasingly to serve. Indeed, the replacement of medieval "descending" claims to political legitimacy with modern "ascending" ones depended crucially on establishing the identity of the people from which such claims ascended, and this was accomplished largely through the production of national identities. This poses a challenge to those who would conceptualize political identities today in "postnational" terms, raising the question posed by Habermas as to what can be the "functional equivalent" of the ethnic nation.

But here it is important to emphasize that ethnicity is not the whole of the nationalist imaginary. Nations are also imagined through representations of collective action, for example, the taking of the Bastille. They are constituted through images of collective participation in processes of nation building. Nationalism does not just provide democracy with a vocabulary for establishing what counts as the people on a priori grounds (e.g., ethnicity). It also provides an account of the subjectivity of ordinary people, the collective action of the people, processes of self-making, and popular guidance of government. In this sense, the honor of membership in the nation is not simply ascribed but achieved, ethnic members can fail when called upon to live up to nationalism, and nonethnic members can be assimilated by active choice.

Renan's famous description of the nation as a "daily plebiscite" is indicative of the merger of nationalism and democracy.[47] But it describes this in interestingly ambiguous terms, placing individuals in the position of responding (or choosing not to respond) to the calls of the nation. It does not clearly describe individuals as authoring the nation through participation in collective action, including sometimes public discourse. The idea of democracy as genuine self-rule and self-making thus demands political participation as a good in itself. It is not met simply by government purporting expertly to serve the interests of the people (let alone determining in non-democratic ways what the people's interests ought to be). Varying degrees of "constitutional patriotism" may also be incorporated into nationalist self-imagining as normative ideals or substantive features of collective life.

Attempts to match states to coherent and self-recognized peoples in order to make an ascending principle of legitimacy operate have kept nationalism a live issue in Europe. In the early 1990s, many were quick to label this just a transitional concern in the East, but it quickly became a central feature of Western European politics as well, with new populisms and antagonism toward immigrants. The project of a democratically integrated Europe—as distinct from a top down or primarily functional union—inherently raises questions about the collective identity and social solidarity of the citizens who form its base.

This context is crucial for considering the development of a European public sphere, because it suggests something of what is at stake in discussion of this seemingly abstract concept. It belongs alongside nationalism and civil society in discussion of the sociocultural foundations for democracy and republicanism. On the one hand, it is important to see how each purports to offer answers to questions about the constitution of the "people" basic to a particular polity: those who share identity, those who share interests, those who self-organize through discourse. On the other hand, it is also important to see that while these answers compete, they are not opposites. To place nationalism on the side of "mere history," and thus implicitly of power without justification, is to encourage too thin a view of culture. To see civil society as simply a realm of voluntary action is

to neglect the centrality of systemic economic organization to it—
and of the public sphere to the self-constituting capacity of civil
society. To see the public sphere entirely as a realm of rational-
critical discourse is to lose sight of the importance of forming
culture in public life, and of the production and reworking of a
common social imaginary. Not least of all, both collective identity
and collective discourse depend on social organization and capacities for action—whether provided by states or civil society.

Given a recent wave of celebration of civil society as the potential
cure to all ills of democracy, it is important to recall that the dominant forces in transnational civil society remain businesses and organizations tied to business and capital. Businesses are important in
ways distinct from markets—they operate as institutions that organize much of the lives of employees and coordinate production as
well as exchange on several continents. The business dimension of
global civil society is not limited to multinational corporations; it
includes nongovernmental organizations (NGOs) that set accoun-
tancy standards and provide for arbitration and conflict resolution,
a business press, lawyers, and a range of consultants. The point is not
whether this is good or bad, but that this is civil society on a global
scale but not totally unlike what Adam Smith and Adam Ferguson
saw on a local and national scale in the late eighteenth century. Civil
society meant then and still means the extension of more or less self-
organizing relationships on a scale beyond the intentional control of
individual actors and outside of the strict dictates of states. It offers
many freedoms—but so do states. Neither is automatically liberal or
democratic.

There is no doubt that a transnational civil society is emerging in
Europe. What needs to be questioned is the extent to which this provides for a democratic public sphere. The question bears not only on
the value of democracy in itself but on the legitimacy of the EU and
support for Europe generally. The "democratic deficit" of the EU has
been remarked frequently, but Europe also faces a potential and
linked legitimacy deficit that could under some circumstances turn
into a crisis. As we have seen, discourses of legitimacy are linked to
forms of solidarity.

European integration so far has produced solidarity mainly in systemic terms—above all, the integration of the European economy. As long as commitment to Europe is based largely on promises of economic gains, however, a downturn poses a threat. More paradoxically, so does relative satiation as the European welfare states learned in the 1960s.[48] A more or less utilitarian attempt to serve public interests by technocratic-bureaucratic management makes the EU especially vulnerable. Whether or not there is ever a crisis, however, an economistic social imaginary is unlikely to advance democracy or citizenship. As Siedentrop puts it, "If the language in which the European Union identifies and creates itself becomes overwhelmingly economic, then the prospects for self-government in Europe are grim indeed."[49]

To some extent, Europe has drawn on and furthered solidarity in terms of common identity. Basing legitimacy on shared identity, however, raises the prospect of a Europe imagined on nationalist lines—that is, as a sort of supernation matching a superstate. Legitimation on the basis of shared identity faces a long path before it outstrips identifications with and within the constituent nations. This is one of the messages of the populist-nationalist responses to monetary union, immigration, and other issues in the last few years. Nonetheless, the nationalist approach to European legitimacy is entirely plausible, just as diverse provinces were integrated into what is now France, obliterating regional differences of language and political institutions.[50] A federal Europe could take this form, and it could achieve legitimacy on nationalist grounds, but in itself this need not be democratic.

The limits of both nationalist and economistic approaches to legitimating European integration suggest the importance of developing an active European public sphere. This indeed could underwrite more cosmopolitan visions such as Habermas's idea of constitutional patriotism. It seems important, however, that the public sphere be adequate to more than the production of a thin layer of political or legal agreement—however useful this might be and however much it remains a challenge. Through public life, solidarity and mutual commitment could be forged on a European scale and legitimacy of the larger polity strengthened. A vigorous European public sphere could be culturally transformative and a challenge to purely market-oriented production of shared identity. Activity in such a public sphere could not only give the constitution (and thus the law) greater than merely technical-bureaucratic significance—engaging issues through that constitution—it could also extend the meaning of constitution beyond the specific written document to the more general making of common life.

Such a public sphere is basic to hopes that Europe might be ordered—and achieve legitimacy—in democratic and/or republican fashions. It is the most important alternative at the scale of Europe to reliance on interests and identity alone. But though such a public sphere is fully imaginable, its development faces important challenges. Perhaps the most telling of these is the extent to which media are organized on national or global bases but not specifically European.

As European communications media become less national, they do not clearly become "European." They become in different degrees and ways part of a global information and entertainment production and marketing system in which a handful of firms dominate and in which the United States is the largest market. English publishers—even academic ones like Polity—choose what books to publish in Britain partly on the basis of what they can sell in America. Other publishing houses—like Bertelsmann—consolidate like car companies, even across once insuperable national and linguistic boundaries. Whatever its shifting evaluation by critics, Hollywood still sells films, as does Bombay—Indian cinema is big business in parts of Europe and as big a competitor as the United States is globally. Pop music tastes differ among European countries and between Europe and elsewhere, but the trend in taste cultures is toward multiple differentiations that do not follow either national or continental lines: is hip-hop European, or Caribbean, or American?[51]

It is not yet clear whether this will be the pattern for the political public sphere. Some of Europe's great newspapers and magazines remain largely national. This is especially the case for Germany, partly because German does not sell well abroad. French periodicals that are at least as nationalist in content have a slightly larger—but generally not growing—international market. Spanish publications sell in Latin America and vice versa. In Portugal's case the trade is even more imbalanced, with Brazil increasingly the intellectual center rather than periphery (though Brazil in turn shows deference to France and America). Major English magazines and newspapers—notably the *Economist*, somewhat less successfully the *Guardian*, and more recently, the *Financial Times*—have all become international publications. A current *Economist* slogan is "Business knows no boundaries. Neither do we." In short, there is no single trend (except for the growing status of English as the ironic *lingua franca* of the age). Rather, several different patterns of European integration into global public spheres emerge. If this is true for print publications, consider how much more so it is for TV and is likely to be for the Internet.

Conclusion

"From a normative perspective there can be no European federal state worthy of the title of a European democracy unless a European-wide, integrated public sphere develops in the ambit of a common political culture. . . ."[52]

Constitutional patriotism depends on a vital public sphere. It is entirely possible, however, that European collective identity might be achieved without an effective and democratic European public sphere.[53] This might grow out of economic relations and marketing. There might be a sort of European-wide nationalism without the institutional basis to make it democratic. But if Europe is to be democratic, it needs a specifically European public sphere. It needs this as a realm of social solidarity and culture formation as well as critical discourse. It needs it for the nurturance of a democratic social imaginary as much as for informing any specific policy decisions. The development of a European public sphere, however, lags behind functional integration and powerful organizations.

At the same time, it is equally important to remember the extent to which life together is made possible not simply by systemic integration, the construction of formal organizations, and rational-critical discourse. It is made possible, as Arendt argued, by promises that bind people to each other. This is a crucial dimension of con-stitution making. It is made possible also by acts of imagination, communicated and incorporated into common culture. Think of the ways in which such acts of promising and imagination are implicated in the creation of the very institutions of this shared world. Not just the nation, but the business corporation exists as the product of such imagining (and is none the less real and powerful for that). How is the corporate whole called into being, granted legitimacy in law and the capacity to act in contracts, suits, or property holding? It is a product of the social imaginary. Like the way in which ideas of indi-vidual and nation are embedded in much modern culture, however, this acceptance of corporations is deeply rooted. It is reproduced in a host of quotidian practices as well as more elaborate legal proce-dures. This is indeed part of what turns a mere formal organization into an institution. This is something that can be grasped only from within the very culture that makes it possible, not externally to it. It can never, therefore, be rendered altogether objective.

The most helpful conception of the public sphere, therefore, is one that includes within it *both* a dimension of rational-critical dis-course and a dimension of social imagination and promising. Among the many virtues of the former is the capacity to challenge and poten-tially improve existing culture, products of social imagination, and relationships. But among its limits is the fact that in itself it cannot create them.

Alternative imaginaries are operative in the constitution of global culture and social relations. From Islamism to deep ecology, there are multiple ways of imagining the possible institutions of a new and different social order. A common humanity is imagined most promi-nently in discourses of human rights. And in fact the most powerful postnational or cosmopolitan social imaginary is that of the market.[54] Affirmation of global society comes less from expression of some positive value than from the notion that the market demands it. "The market" in such discourse is always represented in external and deterministic terms, as a force of necessity rather than an object of choice. And this raises the basic issue.

The speed with which global civil society is gaining capacity to self-organize autonomously from states may be debated. But there is little doubt that the global public sphere lags dramatically behind the less democratic, less choice-oriented dimensions of global society. Among the many questions to ask about global society is what kinds of identity and solidarity will orient participation within it. Are there attractive forms for collective identity that offer nationalism's potential to integrate large populations and produce mutual commitment without its tendency to external exclusion and internal rejection of difference? Fear of bad nationalism leads many to hope that relatively thin identities will predominate. Cosmopolitans and constitutional patriots may presumably orient themselves to many spheres of action from the very local to the global. But are these forms of identity that can create the new social imaginary that will commit people to each other on a global scale? Are they by their nature restricted to elites and meaningful only in relationship to the nationalism of others? Or are they attractive possibilities that follow from rather than lay the basis for more democratic public institutions?

Through this inquiry into Europe, I have tried to explore more general issues. One is the extent to which discussion of civil society fails to provide an adequate underpinning for analyzing democracy unless it includes substantial attention to the specific conditions of the public sphere. Civil society is indeed advancing globally, but most of the connections being forged appear as adaptations to necessity or power rather than choices, or as byproducts of choices made by a few rather than the collective achievements of a public process.

Second, I have argued that the idea of constitution is deepened by attending to the question of what kind of "social imaginary" underpins the creation of institutions and the organization of solidarity, that is, what ways of understanding life together actually make possible specific forms of social relations. Not least, it is important to conceive of solidarity not only in terms of common economic interests but in terms of a range of mutual interdependence, including engagement in shared projects of constituting a better future.

Third, I have suggested that the importance of the public sphere lies not only in achieving agreement on legal forms and political identity but in achieving social solidarity as such. For this to happen it needs to be a realm of cultural creativity as well as rational discourse and a realm of mutual engagement. If nationalism is to give way to some postnational organization of social life it will not be simply a matter of new formal organization, but of new ways of imaginatively constituting identity, interests, and solidarity. A key theme will be the importance of notions of mutual commitment—solidarity—that are more than similarities of preestablished interests or identities. Can shared participation in the public sphere anchor a form of social solidarity in which the nature of life together is chosen as it is constructed?

Acknowledgments

Earlier versions of parts of this essay were presented to the EUI conference on "The Future of the European Public Sphere," Florence, June 17–19, 1999; to the Department of Sociology, University of Michigan, January 2000; as a Benjamin Meaker Lecture at the University of Bristol in June 2000; and to the Center for Transcultural Studies, July 2000. I am grateful for discussions from each audience, also to the editors of this book, and especially to colleagues in the Center for sustained challenge to and shaping of my ideas over many years.

Notes

1. It is worth remarking the extent to which this vision of internal and external is informed by the ancient Greek opposition of the domestic realm of the household to the public realm of relations among autonomous individuals. Economic production was imagined as part of the domestic *oikos* and the public life outside was understood to stand on this foundation. How different (male, property-owning) individuals managed their households was not a proper topic for attention in the public realm.

2. See discussion in Saskia Sassen, *Losing Control?* (New York: Columbia University Press, 1996).

3. I make no pretense to presenting a detailed empirical study of the European public sphere and still less European civil society in general or the politics of integration. Rather, I hope that by keeping a concrete case in mind one can better understand abstract issues. It is, moreover, the concrete case behind much of the abstract theoretical discussion of postnational identity and citizenship.

4. Habermas's abstract theoretical formulations are not altogether separate from his contributions to German public debate—in this case notably in relation to the incorporation of the East into a united but Western-dominated Germany, to the "histori-

ans' debate" over the legacy of the Third Reich, and to the contention over change in the citizenship law, enacted in watered down form to allow the children of immigrants rights to "naturalization."

5. For thoughtful examples, see essays in Daniele Archibugi and David Held, eds., *Cosmopolitan Democracy* (Cambridge: Polity Press, 1995) and Daniele Archibugi, David Held, and Martin Köhler, eds., *Re-Imagining Political Community* (Cambridge: Polity Press, 1998) and the more sustained exposition in David Held, *Democracy and the Global Order: From the Modern State to Cosmopolitan Governance* (Cambridge: Polity, 1995). Habermas offers a similar call in *The Inclusion of the Other* (eds. C. Cronin and P. De Greiff; Cambridge, MA: MIT Press, 1998). See the essays connecting the present to Kant's cosmopolitan project in James Bohman and Matthias Lutz-Bachmann, eds., *Perpetual Peace: Essays on Kant's Cosmopolitan Ideal* (Cambridge, MA: MIT Press, 1997).

6. I have discussed nationalism as a discursive formation in *Nationalism* (Buckingham: Open University Press, 1997).

7. See, for example, "Struggles for Recognition in the Democratic Constitutional State," Habermas's surprisingly fierce response to Charles Taylor's "The Politics of Recognition" (both in Amy Gutmann, ed., *Multiculturalism: Examining the Politics of Recognition*. Princeton: Princeton University Press, rev. ed., 1994). On the cosmopolitan side, see Janna Thompson's distorting examination of "communitarian" arguments, "Community Identity and World Citizenship," 179–197 in Daniele Archibugi, David Held, and Martin Köhler, eds., *Re-imagining Political Community: Studies in Cosmopolitan Democracy* (Cambridge: Polity Press, 1998).

8. *The Inclusion of the Other*, 117.

9. *The Inclusion of the Other*, 115.

10. Michael Warner's *Republic of Letters* (Cambridge, MA: Harvard University Press, 1988) is especially informative on the ways in which debate in print informed the constitutive American public. Larry Siedentrop has noted the surprising asymmetry between the intensive and intellectually vital public discussion that informed America's founding and the relative absence of such debate in contemporary Europe; *Democracy in Europe* (London: Penguin, 2000). It is in this sense, I am suggesting here, that Europe is being given shape and solidarity from economic integration, political institutions, and even some growing cultural commonalties far more than any founding public sphere.

11. Arendt, *On Revolution* (New York: Penguin, 1977; orig. 1963); see also *The Human Condition* (Chicago: University of Chicago Press, 1958).

12. The idea of a social imaginary derives from Cornelius Castoriadis, though my own usage is different. For Castordiadis it addresses the dimensions of society not graspable as a functional system nor as a network of symbols, but crucial to the idea that there can be a social choice about the functional and symbolic order or social life. The imaginary includes "significations that are not there *in order to* represent something else, that are like the final articulations the society in question has imposed on the world, on itself, and on its needs, the organizing patterns that are the conditions for the representability of everything that the society can give to itself," *The Imaginary Institution of Society* (Cambridge, MA: MIT Press, 1987, orig. 1975), 143. Compare Taylor: "The social imaginary is not a set of 'ideas'; rather it is what enables,

through making sense of, the practices of a society." "Modern Social Imaginaries," draft ms., 1.

13. "Modern Social Imaginaries," draft ms., 1.

14. Charles Taylor, *Sources of the Self* (Cambridge: Harvard University Press, 1989).

15. I have explored these issues in *Nationalism* (Minnesota, 1997).

16. *The Inclusion of the Other*, 115.

17. Emphasis on the public sphere also suggests a greater freedom in the important sense that it treats culture-forming activity as an open-ended process. As Arendt suggested, it is never entirely possible to know where activity in public will lead or what will be created. Just as culture is produced and reproduced, not simply inherited, so creativity not simply tolerance mediates cross-cultural relations.

18. Jürgen Habermas, *The Structural Transformation of the Public Sphere* (Cambridge, MA: MIT Press, 1989; orig. 1962). It is worth noting that the classical vision of the public sphere that Habermas articulates does stress that citizens forge a public sphere through their interactions with each other; it is not simply called into being top-down by subjection to a common power. Indeed, in line with a long tradition of political theory, including Locke, subjects of a state become citizens by virtue of their capacity for lateral communication.

19. Emile Durkheim, *The Division of Labor in Society* (New York: Free Press, 1975; orig. 1893).

20. Durkheim has puzzled a century of commentators by insisting that in principle organic solidarity knit people together more tightly and all the failures of modern social integration were merely exceptions to the rule. What is clear is that organic solidarity can knit together larger populations.

21. Note that power is not in itself the basis for a conception of social solidarity; subjection as such is not solidarity, though it may create a polity. This is why the ideal cases of pure despotism place a premium on the absence of active unity among the subjects.

22. By the same token, interests are therefore not fixed or objectively ascertainable. They vary with the salience of different identities to individuals. Not all individual identities reflect categories of similarity to others, and while there may be an element of choice, much identification happens outside conscious recognition or choice.

23. On the effort to distinguish networks of relations from shared sentiments, see Calhoun, "Community: Toward a Variable Conceptualization for Comparative Research," *Social History*, vol. 5 (1980) no. 1, 105–129. On the problematic extension of the concept of community from networks of concrete, interpersonal relationships to broad cultural or political categories, see Calhoun, "Nationalism, Political Community, and the Representation of Society: Or, Why Feeling at Home Is Not a Substitute for Public Space," *European Journal of Social Theory*, vol. 2 (1999) no. 2, 217–231. Such networks are sharply limited in capacity to constitute the social order of a complex, large-scale society. The overall order of such a society is necessarily shaped much more by the mediation of markets, formal organizations, and impersonal com-

munications. See Calhoun, "Imagined Communities and Indirect Relationships: Large Scale Social Integration and the Transformation of Everyday Life," in P. Bourdieu and J. S. Coleman, eds.: *Social Theory for a Changing Society* (Boulder, CO: Westview Press, 1991), 95–120 and "The Infrastructure of Modernity: Indirect Relationships, Information Technology, and Social Integration," in H. Haferkamp and N. J. Smelser, eds.: *Social Change and Modernity* (Berkeley: University of California Press, 1992) 205–236. The conception of categories and networks is indebted to Siegfried Nadel, *Theory of Social Structure* (London: Cohen and West, 1957). It has also been employed creatively by Harrison White in dispersed work partially summarized in *Identity and Control* (Princeton: Princeton University Press, 1992). White sees networks as basic, categories as more typically epiphenomenal, and he believes a structural network theory can dispense with the need for separate reference to functional integration. He does not consider publics.

24. In an unpublished manuscript (forthcoming in revised form in his *Publics and Counterpublics* (Cambridge, MA: Zone Books)), Michael Warner helpfully lists five dimensions to the meaning of public:

1. A public is self-organizing.

2. A public is a relation among strangers.

3. The address of public speech is both personal and impersonal.

4. A public is the social space created by the circulation of discourse.

5. Publics exist historically according to the temporality of their circulation.

25. Arendt, *The Human Condition* (Chicago: University of Chicago Press, 1958).

26. *The Human Condition* (Chicago: University of Chicago Press, 1958), 50, 52.

27. The plurality Arendt emphasized extended not only to subjects but to public spaces that in modern large-scale societies she thought would inevitably need to be many and imperfectly integrated. See *Crises of the Republic* (New York: Harcourt, Brace, Jovanovich, 1972), 232; also Calhoun, "Plurality, Promises, and Public Spaces," 232–259 in C. Calhoun and J. McGowan, eds.: *Hannah Arendt and The Meaning of Politics* (Minneapolis: University of Minnesota Press, 1997).

28. Habermas reaffirms this emphasis in more recent work: "the 'literary' public sphere in the broader sense, which is specialized for the articulation of values and world disclosure, is intertwined with the political public sphere," *Between Facts and Norms*, 365. His recent work, however, is less state centered.

29. This sheds some light on disputes over whether Habermas's theory implies a unitary public sphere or multiple publics (Nancy Fraser, "Rethinking the Public Sphere: A Contribution to the Critique of Actually Existing Democracy," 109–142 in C. Calhoun, ed., *Habermas and the Public Sphere* (Cambridge, MA: MIT Press, 1992); Michael Warner, "Public and Private" in Gil Herdet and Catherine Stimpson, eds., *Critical Terms for the Study of Gender and Sexuality* (Chicago: University of Chicago Press, forthcoming). Clearly publics may be multiple in several senses, but where public discourse addresses and/or is occasioned by a state, there is a pressure for reaching integration at the level of that state. The plural publics need relation to each other in a public sphere if they are to be able to facilitate democracy within that state by informing its actions.

30. Habermas, *The Inclusion of the Other* (Cambridge, MA: MIT Press, 1998), 153.

31. In *Structural Transformation*, Habermas's attention was focused not just on the ideals of public life, but on the question of why apparently democratic expansions in the scale of public participation had brought a decline in the rational-critical character of public discourse, a vulnerability to demagogic and mass-media manipulation, and sometimes a loss of democracy itself. The distorted publicity of American-style advertising, public relations, and political campaigns was a manifest focus, but an underlying concern was also the way in which public life lost its links to both democracy and rational-critical understanding in the Third Reich.

32. *Inclusion of the Other*, 141.

33. Ibid.

34. "Rethinking the Public Sphere: A Contribution to the Critique of Actually Existing Democracy," in Craig Calhoun, ed., *Habermas and the Public Sphere* (Cambridge, MA: MIT Press, 1992), 109–142.

35. Warner, *Publics and Counterpublics*. Warner rightly questions Fraser's identification of counterpublics with "subalterns," noting that many groups not clearly in subaltern positions identify themselves by contraposition to the dominant culture or institutions of a society, and that they may constitute counterpublics opposed to the dominant patterns of the public sphere. His chief example is the Christian right in the United States. The new populist right wing in Europe appears largely similar in this respect. Electoral victors take pride in describing themselves as outsiders to dominant institutions, even while claiming to be the ultimate insiders to, and defenders of, national traditions.

36. I distinguish the idea of a "gay public" from a "queer counterpublic" to make two points. One, following Warner (in *The Trouble with Normal*, Durham: Duke University Press, 1999), there is a tension among gay men and lesbians over both practical politics and discursive practices focused specifically on the question of whether to demand reduction of the demarcation of gay from straight or to assert queer identities in a potentially disruptive (and/or liberating) fashion. Second, distinction of a gay public from a queer counterpublic is a reminder that not all demarcation of publics is necessarily the production of counterpublics.

37. Habermas famously focused only on the bourgeois public sphere, contrasting it to an earlier aristocrat-dominated public, thus sparking complaints that he neglected the proletarian public sphere. See crucially Oscar Negt and Alexander Kluge, *The Public Sphere and Experience* (Minneapolis: University of Minnesota Press, 1993; orig. 1964); see also Geoff Eley, "Nations, Publics and Political Cultures: Placing Habermas in the Nineteenth Century," in Calhoun, ed. *Habermas and the Public Sphere*. Cambridge, Mass: MIT Press, 1992, 289–339. But Habermas and Negt and Kluge both accept the separation between bourgeois and proletarian as already established based on objective economic conditions rather than as something forged in large part in the contestation within and over the public sphere. Habermas thus posits inclusion as an issue about the later broadening of the public sphere rather than a formative theme from the start. Tactics like raising taxes on newspapers to discourage the popular press (or disparaging workers as insufficiently rational) were, in a sense, counterpublic mobilization from above.

38. See, among many in this large literature, Nancy Fraser, *Unruly Practices* (Minneapolis, MN: University of Minnesota Press, 1992) and *Justice Interruptus* (New York: Routledge, 1997); Jean Bethke Elshtain, *Public Man, Private Woman* (Princeton: Princeton University Press, 1993); Michael Warner, "Public and Private," in Catherine Stimpson, ed.: *Blackwell Companion to Gender Studies* (Cambridge, MA: Blackwell, forthcoming). See also the early response to Habermas and very different development of the idea of public sphere in Oscar Negt and Alexander Kluge, *The Public Sphere and Experience* (Minneapolis: University of Minnesota Press, 1993; orig., 1964).

39. In a similar sense, many approaches to multiculturalism treat ethnicity and community as terrains of privacy—protected precisely because they are not public. The discourse of rights encourages both communitarian advocates and liberal critics to ask what kind of private right—of individuals or groups—might protect differences rather than what kind of public good it is, or what kind of public claim supports it.

40. *Structural Transformation of the Public Sphere* (Cambridge, MA: MIT Press, 1989; orig. 1962), 36.

41. Ibid., 131.

42. See Michael Warner: *Letters of the Republic* (Cambridge, MA: Harvard University Press, 1992).

43. *Between Facts and Norms*, chapter 8.

44. This dimension is one of the important reasons not to see the public sphere as simply a setting for rational-critical debate among citizens already formed in private life. It is largely through participation in public life that people can become good citizens; this educative dimension of democratic public life is one of its modes of self-organization.

45. The issue is not just one of the power of the center, but of the mutual implication of the political processes in different parts of the EU. This came out sharply with the rise of Jörg Haider in Austria. Other members of the EU leadership believed they had no choice but to respond precisely because the matter was internal—Austrian claims to sovereignty notwithstanding. One meaning of "internal" was that the electoral fortunes of political parties throughout the continent were interdependent; another was that each leader could potentially be held responsible for his or her response to events perceived as a danger to the collective body politic.

46. Crucial to the shift is a growing description of individuals as Europeans, and increasingly as directly European not simply European by virtue of their membership in a European nation. This is advanced by development of a common framework of citizenship (pressed forward partly by attempts to provide similar structures of benefits as part of economic integration, partly by attempts to deal similarly with immigrants, partly by legal integration). Even though European "citizens" elect representatives to the European Parliament only through the mediation of national parties and delegations, there is a growing reference to such direct citizenship (e.g., in reference to border controls). Technically, the EU is composed of nation-states and exists as an agreement among them. In everyday practice, however, it is growing more common for individuals to understand themselves directly as members (and to make claims on the EU that are not mediated by nation-states but by regional or

other groupings if they are mediated at all). This does not mean that individuals or localities wield effective countervailing power. In many regards, the EU has furthered a process shaped also by other currents that gives more power to central governments and their individual leaders. Thus the heads of state could decide to pursue war in Kosovo without substantial recourse to national parliaments or other ostensibly countervailing powers.

47. Ernst Renan, "What Is a Nation?" in Homi Bhabha, ed., *Nation and Narration* (London: Routledge, 1990; orig. 1871).

48. Habermas's *Legitimation Crisis* (Boston: Beacon, 1975) explored this in terms of both the limits of economistic legitimation faced with 'postmaterial' values and the problems of a culture of bureaucratic expertise managing public policy as technical problem-solving without democratic participation.

49. *Democracy in Europe*, 32. Siedentrop explores the prospects for self-government with a stronger opposition of democratic and republican visions (that is, of egalitarian but privacy-oriented civil society and often inegalitarian but public-oriented civic virtue) than appears necessary. His book deserves fuller attention but appeared only as the present article was going to press.

50. Lest this appear far-fetched, recall that the process is not entirely ancient in the French case, but extends well into the nineteenth century (with echoes afterward). Eugen Weber's often-quoted point is telling: there was no point before the middle of the nineteenth century when the majority of Frenchmen spoke French. *Peasants into Frenchmen* (Stanford: Stanford University Press, 1976).

51. As Paul Gilroy suggests, the answer must be "all of the above," but it is an answer obscured by the organization of even racialized resistance on nationalist lines; see *The Black Atlantic: Modernity and Double Consciousness* (Cambridge, MA: Harvard University Press, 1993).

52. *Inclusion of the Other*, 160.

53. See also my own "Identity and Plurality in the Conceptualization of Europe" and other discussions of this question in Lars-Eric Cederman, ed.: *Constructing Europe's Identity: Issues and Trade-offs* (Boulder, CO: Lynne Reiner, 2000).

54. Robbins notes that the first cited usage under "cosmopolitan" in the Oxford English Dictionary comes from John Stuart Mill's *Political Economy* in 1848: "Capital is becoming more and more cosmopolitan." *Intellectuals, Professionalism, Culture*, 182.

Contributors

Craig Calhoun is President of the Social Science Research Council and Professor of Sociology and History at New York University. Among Calhoun's most recent books are *Critical Social Theory: Culture, History and the Challenge of Difference* (Blackwell, 1995); *Neither Gods nor Emperors: Students and the Struggle or Democracy in China* (California); and *Nationalism* (Minnesota, 1997). He is also editor-in-chief of the *Oxford Dictionary of the Social Sciences.*

Ciaran Cronin is an Assistant Professor in the Departments of Philosophy and German at the University of Illinois at Chicago. His has published papers on social and political theory and is currently working on a book on *Nationalism, Democracy, and the Crisis of Global Governance.* His recent work has been supported by grants from the DAAD and the Institute for the Humanities at UIC.

Pablo De Greiff is an Assistant Professor of Philosophy at the State University of New York at Buffalo. He is editor of *Drugs and the Limits of Liberalism* (Cornell), and the coeditor (with Ciaran Cronin) of Jürgen Habermas's *The Inclusion of the Other; Deliberative Democracy and Transnational Politics* (MIT, 1998), and (with J. Gracia) of *Hispanics/Latinos in the United States: Ethnicity, Race, and Rights* (Routledge). He has published essays on international justice, deliberative democracy, and transitions to democracy. He is currently the recipient of a Laurance S. Rockefeller Fellowship from the Center for Human Values at Princeton University and of a fellowship from the National Endowment for the Humanities.

Jürgen Habermas is Professor Emeritus of Philosophy and Sociology at the University of Frankfurt and former Director of the Max Planck Institute for Social Research at Starnberg. His is the author of numerous books on social and political theory, including *Between Facts and Norms* (MIT, 1996), *The Inclusion of the Other* (MIT, 1998), and *The Postnational Constellation* (MIT, 2001).

David Luban is Frederick Haas Professor of Law and Philosophy at Georgetown University Law Center. His books include *Lawyers and Justice: An Ethical Study* (Princeton, 1988) and *Legal Modernism* (Michigan, 1994). He has written articles on just war theory, nationalism, and transitional justice.

Thomas McCarthy is Professor of Philosophy and John Shaffer Professor in the Humanities at Northwestern University. He is the author of *The Critical Theory of Jürgen Habermas* (MIT, 1978) and *Ideals and Illusions* (MIT, 1991), the coauthor, with David Hoy, of *Critical Theory* (Blackwell, 1994), and the series editor of Studies in Contemporary German Social Thought (MIT Press). His current work concerns theories of race and development.

Martha Nussbaum is the Ernst Freund Distinguished Service Professor of Law and Ethics at the University of Chicago, with appointments in the Philosophy Department, Law School, and Divinity School. On the topic of cosmopolitanism and international justice alone, she is the author of numerous essays and of *For Love of Country* (Beacon, 1996) and *Sex and Social Justice* (Oxford, 1999). Beginning in 2001 she will direct a new Center for Comparative Constitutionalism and Social Justice.

Thomas Pogge teaches moral and political philosophy at Columbia University. He is a member of the Norwegian Academy of Science and a director of the Columbia University Center for the Study of Human Rights. He is the author of *Realizing Rawls* (Cornell, 1989) and of numerous essays on Kant, Rawls, and global justice. His recent work has been supported by the Princeton Institute for Advanced Study and the Global Security and Sustainability Program of the John D. and Catherine T. MacArthur Foundation.

Amartya Sen is Master of Trinity College, University of Cambridge, and former Lamont University Professor at Harvard University and Drummond Professor of Political Economy at Oxford University. He was the recipient of the Nobel Prize in Economics in 1998 and has authored numerous papers and books on economics and political theory, including *Inequality Reexamined* (Harvard, 1992) and *Development as Freedom* (Knopf, 1999).

Leif Wenar teaches philosophy at the University of Sheffield. His work on liberal political theory, property rights, constitutional interpretation, and global justice has appeared in *Ethics, Mind, The Columbia Law Review*, and *Metaphilosophy*. He is currently writing a book on the nature and justification of rights.

Index